THE MODERN SLA'

Policy, politics ;
in the UK

Edited by
Gary Craig, Alex Balch, Hannah Lewis
and Louise Waite

First published in Great Britain in 2019 by

Policy Press
University of Bristol
1-9 Old Park Hill
Bristol
BS2 8BB
UK
t: +44 (0)117 954 5940
pp-info@bristol.ac.uk
www.policypress.co.uk

North America office:
Policy Press
c/o The University of Chicago Press
1427 East 60th Street
Chicago, IL 60637, USA
t: +1 773 702 7700
f: +1 773-702-9756
sales@press.uchicago.edu
www.press.uchicago.edu

British Library Cataloguing in Publication Data
A catalogue record for this book is available from the British Library

Library of Congress Cataloging-in-Publication Data
A catalog record for this book has been requested

978-1-4473-4679-1 hardback
978-1-4473-4680-7 paperback
978-1-4473-4681-4 ePdf
978-1-4473-4682-1 ePub
978-1-4473-4683-8 Mobi

Cover design by Qube Design Associates, Bristol
Front cover image: istock

Dedication

The book is dedicated to all those struggling against exploitation. Shortly before we finished it, the untimely death was announced of Paul Broadbent, Chief Executive of the Gangmasters Licensing Authority (GLA) and then the Gangmasters and Labour Abuse Authority (GLAA). We found him to be a committed, hard-working and engaging person, typical of the hundreds of activists and officials who have given their lives to combating the exploitation of human beings. We honour his work.

Contents

List of tables, figures and boxes

Tables

Figures

Boxes

Notes on contributors

Alex Balch (A.R.Balch@liverpool.ac.uk) is Professor in the Department of Politics at the University of Liverpool, UK. He is also Associate Head of the School for Research and Impact and Co-Director of the Centre for the Study of International Slavery. He has researched widely on issues of modern slavery but particularly on forced labour, migration, support for survivors and the organisational systems working around the issue of modern slavery in the UK, such as the Gangmasters and Labour Abuse Authority (GLAA) and Border Agency. His latest book is *Immigration and the state: Fear, greed and hospitality* (Palgrave Macmillan, 2016), and recent journal articles include 'A deadly cocktail? The fusion of Europe and immigration in the UK press' (with E. Balabanova), *Critical Discourse Studies*, 2017, 1–20. He co-convenes the Modern Slavery Research Consortium.

Vicky Brotherton (Vicky.brotherton@antislaverycommissioner.gsi.gov.uk) currently works as Protection and Partnerships Lead in the Office of the UK's Independent Anti-Slavery Commissioner. Previously, Vicky worked at Anti-Slavery International for five years, the majority of which was spent coordinating the Anti-Trafficking Monitoring Group – a UK-wide coalition of anti-trafficking non-governmental organisations. In this role, she led on the group's research and advocacy work, monitoring the UK's anti-slavery response and lobbying for improvements. She has a background in health research and holds an MA in Human Rights from the Institute of Commonwealth Studies at the University of London.

Patrick Burland (patrickburland@hotmail.com) is a Senior Project Officer on Human Trafficking and Modern Slavery at the International Organisation for Migration (IOM) in the UK. (The author's contribution is written entirely in a personal capacity and does not represent the views of the IOM.) He was awarded his PhD from the University of the West of England in 2015 for his thesis 'The responses to trafficked adults in the UK: rights, rhetoric and reality'. He received a 2017 Anti-Slavery Day Media Award for best opinion piece on human trafficking. He has previously volunteered with domestic workers and immigration detainees in the UK.

Gary Craig (Gary.craig@garyc.demon.co.uk) is Visiting Professor at the Law School, University of Newcastle upon Tyne and at three other universities. He worked for half his career as a community development activist. He has researched and published widely in the fields of poverty, 'race' and ethnicity, and modern slavery; recent books include *Community organising against racism* and *Understanding 'race' and ethnicity*. His *Global handbook on social justice* is now available.

Dr Hannah Lewis (H.J.Lewis@Sheffield.ac.uk) is a Vice-Chancellor's Fellow at the University of Sheffield, UK. She is interested in understanding how policies shape the daily lives of people who migrate. Her research interests include: community and social relationships; migration and refugee studies; immigration and asylum policy; forced labour and 'modern slavery'; faith and anti-trafficking; and the ethics and methodologies of research with migrant populations. Her work on these themes has been published in various journals. She is co-author of *Precarious lives: Forced labour, exploitation and asylum* (Policy Press, 2014) and co-editor of *Vulnerability, exploitation and migrants* (Palgrave Macmillan, 2015). She has a recent chapter in *Entrapping asylum seekers: Social, legal and economic precariousness* (edited by A. Gerard and F. Vecchio) (Palgrave Macmillan, 2017).

Aidan McQuade (Aidanmcquade2017@gmail.com) is an independent consultant. From 2006 to 2017, he was Director of Anti-Slavery International. Before that, he worked for 13 years in development and humanitarian response in different parts of the world, including five years in Angola during the civil war leading an emergency relief programme for over a quarter of a million people in the besieged cities of the interior. He comes from South Armagh in Ireland.

Kate Roberts (Kate@humantraffickingfoundation.org), who currently heads the Human Trafficking Foundation, has over 10 years' experience in anti-trafficking work. Kate has a particular understanding of forced labour and particularly domestic servitude and has always taken a workers' rights approach to reducing trafficking and slavery. Kate worked at Kalayaan with migrant domestic workers for more than a decade, where she delivered direct support and casework, as well as led on policy. Kate has been a first responder to the UK's National Referral Mechanism since the system was developed in 2009 until early 2016. Kate has given evidence to several parliamentary inquiries relating to modern slavery, including at all stages of the Modern Slavery Act.

Chloe Setter (Cj_Setter@yahoo.co.uk) was, until recently, Head of Advocacy, Policy & Campaigns at the leading children's rights charity ECPAT (End Child Prostitution and Trafficking) UK, which campaigns against child exploitation and trafficking, trains front-line professionals, and runs a Youth Programme for young people affected by modern slavery. In her role, she authored research and briefings, contributed to the drafting of national policy, and managed campaigns and European projects on human trafficking. She chaired the Home Office Child Trafficking Group, sat on various advisory groups across the UK, wrote expert reports concerning child victims of exploitation and was the organisational lead for the Anti-Trafficking Monitoring Group, a coalition monitoring the UK's response to trafficking and modern slavery. She has just become a senior adviser on trafficking and modern slavery for Lumos.

Klara Skrivankova (k.skrivankova@antislavery.org) is a recognised expert on modern slavery in the UK and internationally. She has been working in the field since 2000. Since 2005, she has been working in Anti-Slavery International where she now leads its UK & Europe Programme and business advisory services to numerous commercial organisations, including ASOS, The White Company, White Stuff, Daimler and Herbert Smith Freehills. She frequently provides expert witness statements in courts in the UK, Ireland and Hong Kong in modern slavery cases, and in 2007, co-founded the UK Trafficking Law and Policy Forum, an educational think tank on human trafficking and related issues. For several years, she was also Programme Adviser to the Joseph Rowntree Foundation and a specialist advisor with the Ethical Trading Initiative.

Colleen Theron (Colleen.theron@ardeainternational.com) is a tri-qualified solicitor and founder of CLT envirolaw, a niche sustainability, business and human rights consultancy with expertise in modern slavery issues enabling companies to meet both their legal obligations and develop voluntary best practice standards. Prior to establishing Ardea International, she worked as an environmental lawyer in the City of London and was recognised by The Legal 500 and Chambers as a leading environmental law practitioner. Colleen has an LLM (with distinction) in Environmental Law from the University of Aberdeen. She founded the non-governmental organisation Finance against Trafficking and was a member of the Slavery Garden team, which won gold at the Chelsea Flower Show.

Ruth Van Dyke (Ruth.VanDyke@stmarys.ac.uk) is a Visiting Fellow at the Centre for the Study of Modern Slavery at St Mary's University. She has been researching human trafficking and modern slavery since 2009, initially on behalf of Capital Humano y Social Alternativo, a non-governmental organisation working on human trafficking in Peru. This research entailed investigating the trafficking of people from the Andean community to Europe. Since 2013, Ruth's research has focused on investigating the competences necessary for police to tackle human trafficking, the police response to modern slavery and partnership working. She has also produced reports on the work of a London partnership, and devised a toolkit for monitoring and evaluating anti-slavery initiatives.

Louise Waite (L.Waite@leeds.ac.uk) is Professor of Human Geography at the University of Leeds, UK. Her research interests span migration and slavery, with a particular focus on discourses of 'modern slavery', unfree/forced labour and exploitative work among asylum seekers and refugees. She has published on these themes in a range of peer-reviewed journals and in recent collaborative books: *Vulnerability, exploitation and migrants: Insecure work in a globalised economy* (Palgrave, 2015), *Precarious lives: Forced labour, exploitation and asylum* (Policy Press, 2014) and *Citizenship, belonging and intergenerational relations in African migration* (Palgrave, 2012).

Editorial introduction: the modern slavery agenda: policy, politics and practice

Gary Craig, Alex Balch, Hannah Lewis and Louise Waite

If slavery is not wrong, then nothing is wrong.
ABRAHAM LINCOLN

Introduction

Until very recently – the last 15 years or so – common understandings of slavery related to its historical manifestations. Every major empire in the world – Egypt, Greece, Rome, Britain, Ottoman, Muscovy and China – was literally built on the back of slaves, usually associated with military and religious conquest. It is only in this last short period that the renaming of severe forms of exploitation, found almost everywhere in the world, as slavery has begun to happen. Even now, many people do not believe that such practices are something that may happen in their own country and often, more or less, 'In plain sight'.[1] For example, a poll undertaken by the University of Hull of local East Yorkshire (UK) residents in late 2017 discovered that although 75% of those interviewed understood that slavery was something that might happen in their own country now, only 8% had any idea of its scale.[2] In a recent ITV 'serious' politics programme, one contributor suggested that 'modern slavery' was a myth generated by migrants. Yet, mounting evidence, media coverage and policy and political debate appear to confirm that slavery is, indeed, an alarming, contemporary global phenomenon. To take examples emerging from the chaos of refugees fleeing from conflicts in the Middle East and North Africa; it is clear now that thousands of young people, many unaccompanied, making the hazardous journey to seek asylum in Western Europe have disappeared, often linked to human trafficking, and some parts of the media are reporting on what they are terming 'slave auctions' in Libya (CNN 2017). In both cases, the language of slavery is being used to describe consequences derived from Europe's system of borders and immigration controls (O'Connell Davidson 2017a). The metaphor of 'Fortress Europe', once dismissed by scholars as exaggerating the capacity of states to exclude (Geddes 2003: 175), has become tragically real, demonstrating the hypocrisy of liberal-democratic structures when it comes to the treatment of vulnerable newcomers (Balch 2016; see also *The Observer*, 2018).

In this context, this introductory chapter notes the recent heightened profile of the term 'modern slavery' in the UK. Various phenomena, practices and policies have been bundled together under this term. This requires careful analytical and critical attention. We argue here that it is vitally important to understand how the discourse of modern slavery has recently emerged – and the histories that continue to shape present-day discourses – as the terms of engagement shape what are considered appropriate and adequate policy responses. The main goal of the rest of the book is to develop a robust critique of the development of law, policy and practice relating to modern slavery in the UK, in particular, for the benefit of those engaged in some way in anti-slavery work. This critique has significant relevance to parallel developments elsewhere in the world. Some countries are modelling new legislation and policy on the UK model (acclaimed by its sponsors as 'world-leading') and we are anxious that those doing so learn from the limitations of the UK approach.[3]

This introduction thus sets the scene for the chapters to follow. We do not propose to provide a detailed summary of the content of individual chapters, which can speak for themselves and are well signposted in the chapter headings and with links in this introduction. The chapters are written by academic researchers in some cases and by those working in non-governmental organisations (NGOs) in others. While this may lead to inconsistencies in style, we do not apologise for this as this mix faithfully reflects the interplay – particularly between research, policy and practice – that has been very significant in moving forward both the critique of government policy in this area and demonstrating good practice as far as is possible within the limits of that policy framework.

The outlines of the emerging critique of the UK Modern Slavery Act 2015 (MSA) (and parallel legislation in Scotland and Northern Ireland) are already fairly well developed (see later and Chapter Two in particular). We have taken what we regard as the major elements of this critique and allowed authors from their own expert personal and organisational knowledge and perspectives of one or more of the key aspects of the legislation, policy and practice to develop the critique further. Fundamentally, we would argue that the growing interest in the notion of modern slavery at present fails to acknowledge properly the role of the state in creating the conditions for modern slavery to thrive. There is thus a fundamental paradox at the heart of present policy and practice, as well as in political responses to the phenomenon. The government's fixation on uttering the words 'world-leading' every time the Act is mentioned in Parliament completely fails to recognise this paradox.

Following a first draft of a Bill that disappointed many of those contributing to previous consultative processes, the Act was still significantly deficient in many respects from the moment it entered the statute book, and serious further failings have become apparent, as testified to by a growing weight of evidence from many official quarters (and not just from disaffected academics and NGOs). As it stands, it would probably not be appropriate to conclude that the Act is not fit for purpose – although that term has been applied to elements of it by senior officials charged with making it work – but it is appropriate to suggest that it already requires major revision. Whether that implies fundamentally returning it to the statute book is a question of legal and political judgement but the longer the government delays in making major changes to the current framework for addressing modern slavery, the more likely it is that that might have to happen.

This introduction: starts by questioning definitions and linking historical and contemporary slavery; describes the growing move towards international action; summarises the emergence of discussion within the UK in particular; and, finally, highlights a range of key outstanding issues to be addressed, which are analysed within the individual chapters that follow.

Is modern slavery either 'modern' or 'slavery'?

The term 'modern slavery' has become widespread in debates in the UK around most forms of severe exploitation, not least because of the MSA, which uses the term as an umbrella concept to cover those forms. There have been a growing number of concerns about the term from activists, historians and social scientists, who claim that the kinds of exploitation that it covers are neither 'modern' nor 'slavery'. They have argued, among other things: that the transatlantic slave trade was itself a 'modern' form of slavery; that equating contemporary forms and using imagery from this period appropriates the suffering of black people, obscuring our understanding of ongoing legacies of racial chattel slavery (Beutin 2017); and that it is supportive of the conservative moral agendas and narrow security interests of police and immigration forces (O'Connell Davidson 2010, 2017b). Indeed,

Dottridge (2017a), ex-director of Anti-Slavery International, advances at least eight reasons why we should not use the term 'modern slavery'. These include the damage that human rights activists believe the term has done to their work to eradicate severe exploitation, or in fostering development cooperation. Others have pointed out that incremental adoption of the term 'slavery' to cover different types of exploitative practices has the effect of a kind of 'exploitation creep', with the side effect that states can use this terminology to reduce their efforts to only the most severe and 'exceptional' forms of exploitation, packaged as 'modern slavery' (Chuang 2014). Bearing these debates in mind, we move to an examination of some of the continuities and disjunctures between historical and contemporary slavery.

The condemnation of forced labour, human trafficking and other contemporary forms of exploitation as modern slavery self-consciously evokes the history of Britain's involvement with the transatlantic slave trade. It is worth remembering how that trade was ended, and what happened next. In 1807, after a long parliamentary campaign involving several failed attempts to introduce legislation, William Wilberforce and his supporters finally managed to get a law banning Britain's involvement with the transatlantic slave trade onto the British statute book. The parliamentary campaign operated alongside widespread extra-parliamentary action, including boycotts of Caribbean sugar, the striking of a commemorative medallion depicting a kneeling slave ('Am I not a man and a brother?') by the Wedgwood family (used particularly by female activists), the thousands of miles travelled by Thomas Clarkson and other agitators to speak at public meetings, and occasional strikes by sailors, increasingly appalled by images of the conditions under which slaves were transported. There was also increasing understanding that, in the end, slavery, as then constituted, might not be such a profitable enterprise as had been thought, particularly in the face of competition from other slaving nations such as Portugal, France and Spain, as well as concern that increasing militancy from black slaves themselves (leading to full-scale rebellion in Haiti) might put the whole enterprise at risk. These contextual factors are important to register since – and we shall provide a similar contextualisation when coming to discuss the phenomenon of modern slavery – it is important to understand that while the highly moral motives of Wilberforce and his supporters cannot wholly be dismissed, we should simultaneously acknowledge that morality was only one of several factors driving the process of abolition.

British politicians and some historians have long claimed that this process of abolition led a worldwide movement towards ending slavery.

This claim is not historically accurate since the Danish government had ended slavery in its Caribbean territory 20 years earlier. Interestingly, this claim has contemporary echoes since the MSA in England and Wales in 2015 (and parallel legislation in Scotland and Northern Ireland) has, as noted earlier, consistently been presented as 'world-leading' by the government and its supporters. This has apparently been substantiated by the fact that other governments such as Australia may mimic its provisions in introducing legislation in 2018.[4] Again, however, this claim is somewhat economical with the truth. It may be the case that the precise form of the UK legislation is unique and that some of its provisions are novel; however, in terms of adhering fully to the provisions of international legislation such as the Palermo Protocol,[5] and some of the International Labour Organisation (ILO) Conventions, the benchmarks against which such policy and practice is measured, the UK has been both slower in signing up to this legislation and less than wholehearted in its commitment to key aspects than, say, the Netherlands and Finland. These countries introduced fully independent national rapporteurs in 2000 and 2009, respectively, a role required by the terms of the Palermo Protocol, only ratified by the UK in 2006. Not only was the creation of a 'national rapporteur' in the UK in 2015 preceded by appointments in other jurisdictions, but the complete independence of the UK role continues to be questioned. The Independent Anti-Slavery Commissioner (IASC) (Kevin Hyland), as the post is named in the UK, reports to the government (and not to Parliament, as is the case in other countries), and the government retains the power to redact elements of any report produced by the IASC. While it is not known whether there have been tussles between the government and the IASC over the precise content of his reports, and the performance of the IASC himself has largely been welcomed by many involved in the struggles against modern slavery, the fact remains that the post is not entirely open to parliamentary and public scrutiny. We return to this issue later.

Returning briefly to history again, following the 1807 Act, the campaign continued not simply to abolish the transatlantic slave trade, but to abolish slavery itself. Consistent with the moral framing of Britain's 'leading' role, the Royal Navy, which had hitherto been protecting British slaving ships, now had the task of intercepting slaving vessels from other nations, freeing the slaves, seizing the cargoes and destroying the boats. There is, of course, and this also has contemporary resonance, an alternative perspective on the activity of British warships. These were now engaged not in facilitating slavery, but in preventing it, protecting Britain's imperial trading position by undermining the trade of those who might, through the continued use of slaves, be able to undercut Britain's market position. The strength of Britain's growing industrial and commercial class was to be revealed in 1834, just before Wilberforce's death, with the Act abolishing slavery itself. This was only achieved by the provision of a massive level of compensation to slave-owners, the sum being paid (£20 million) to those giving up the ownership of slaves being equivalent to half of Britain's then gross domestic product (GDP).[6] Slaves themselves were not compensated. Compensated slave-owners included both large-scale enterprises, often associated with and defended in Parliament by peers of the realm, as well as obscure individuals, such as the wife of a vicar of a parish just outside York, who was paid £20 for her share of a single Caribbean slave.[7]

As we now know, slavery never really went away. In some countries, the struggle to introduce primary legislation took some time (eg in Brazil, slavery was only abolished in 1888), and in others, ruling elites were effectively above the law. Slavery continued in the-then Belgian Congo until well into the 20th century, a country that was effectively the personal private fiefdom of the Belgian King, Leopold (Hochschild 2012). Once Belgium had fallen into line (a process that required divesting the King of his personal control of the Congo), the slave trades were legally abolished by all European powers by early into the 20th century. Slavery, however, persisted, increasingly being driven underground as an illegal activity, and morphing into new forms of enslavement. It took the dissolution of other major imperial powers, such as the Muscovy and Ottoman empires, to address the issue of slavery (serfdom) in these territories, although, again, as in the Russian gulags (and later in Nazi Germany's labour camps, China, Burma and North Korea), private slaveholding was replaced by state-sponsored 'political' slavery. In Australia, many indigenous people were kept in forms of slavery well into the 20th century and slavery was known to exist in the Southern US until the 1930s.

In the 200 years since the 1807 British abolition, slavery has taken many forms, each of which having had an impact on present-day demographic and political realities: Africans were transported to the present-day Gulf area; within Central and West Africa, enslavement of Africans by Africans or Arabs continued, with 30% of this African population remaining enslaved at the beginning of the 20th century; and in the 1960s, more than 200,000 adult slaves remained in former French colonies, their descendants still present as the Sahel's familial slaves (see Quirk 2009[8]). Although the 1834 Act abolished slavery, it remained present in British imperial possessions for many years thereafter. At the beginning of the 20th century, there were still up to 2.5 million slaves in British-controlled Northern Nigeria (Quirk 2009). Slaves remained in their hundreds of thousands within the Arabian peninsula until the 1960s but have now been replaced by migrants from countries such as India, the Philippines and Malaysia, many of them working effectively as slaves – in construction (most notoriously on the stadia for the football World Cup in Qatar) – and as nannies, nurses, drivers and cleaners.[9]

Similarly, although slavery was formally abolished in India in 1843, most slaves were transformed overnight into debt bondsmen. Here, there remains the largest single concentration, with tens of millions of adults and children enslaved in debt bondage, particularly in agricultural work, further illustrating the links between historical and contemporary worlds of slavery. Forced labour (including prostitution) remained a familiar part of the colonial landscape throughout the early 20th century.

Although most countries have now formally made slavery illegal, slavery-like conditions – including many millions of children – continue to be found in many Asian and Latin American countries in a variety of modern economic sectors. These include brick-making, fish processing, mining, carpet production, charcoal burning, gem-making and the production of fireworks, alongside girls trafficked from neighbouring countries into sexual slavery. Although slavery is usually hidden, difficulties in abolishing it in many countries, despite laws, are also accentuated by complicity between slave-masters and the state in maintaining it. It is well known, for example, that police raids on brothels in India are often preceded by bribes to the police, who ensure that the raids are flagged up well in advance.

This brief historical review suggests that it is wrong to see modern slavery as isolated from its previous manifestations, and many of the commodities historically associated with slavery continue to be so. While pressure to end slavery has grown with the emergence of international legislation from the early 20th century (Craig et al 2007; see also later), legal instruments and international political pressure have failed to abolish it. Slavery has changed its forms to reflect an industrialised and increasingly globalised world where the migration of people – almost half female[10] – to new contexts enhances vulnerability to enslavement. Ironically, comprehensive data that were widely available during the period when slavery was legal and diligently recorded are now far less accessible in a context of illegality. Estimates of numbers and types of slaves in any country thus come with a health warning as to their understated nature. We return to the issue of numbers later.

Modern slavery worldwide takes many forms, some of them very modern phenomena, others historically familiar, and includes chattel slavery, forced labour, debt bondage, serfdom, forced marriage, the trafficking of adults and children, child soldiers, domestic servitude, the severe economic exploitation of children and organ harvesting[11]; many of them exist now within the UK or in other countries linked to it through the supply of goods and services, an issue that came unexpectedly to the fore during debates leading to the MSA. More recent manifestations in the UK include large-scale farming of cannabis plants by young Vietnamese boys imprisoned in domestic properties, and the use of children and adults by, predominantly, Eastern European criminal gangs to beg, pickpocket or shoplift.[12]

International action against slavery

Although the United Nations (UN) passed an anti-trafficking Convention in 1949, interest in trafficking in the UK did not really begin to emerge until the middle of the 1990s (Farrior 1997). McQuade's and Skrivankova's chapters in this book (Chapters One and Ten, respectively) touch on the current international policy and legal frameworks against slavery. Skrivankova also reflects on some aspects of the difficulties likely to arise should the UK leave the European Union (EU) and become isolated from the range of Europe-wide criminal justice agencies with which it is currently working. It is nevertheless useful in this introduction to summarise the historical development of legislation against slavery on an international scale in order to place the UK's policy and legal initiatives in a wider context, a context that also illuminates some of the UK's current shortcomings.

Growing awareness of the continued existence of slavery worldwide finally led to international action to combat it, facilitated by the growth of international organisations created after the First World War. One very early example, in 1925, was the League of Nations' Temporary Slavery Commission condemning the transfer of children for domestic service under the pretext of adoption as slave-dealing. The Commission's findings underpinned the League of Nations' 1926 Slavery Convention, which considered slavery to encompass 'any or all of the powers of ownership' (Article 1(1)) and called for the 'abolition of slavery in all its forms' (Article 2(b)). This international standard broadened the definition of slavery beyond that of chattel slavery, encompassing practices similar in nature and effect – subsequently taken to include forced labour, servitude and trafficking.

From the 1930s, several more international Conventions, often associated with the growing influence of the ILO, addressed differing aspects of slavery, focusing on the position of children as well as adults (Craig 2017b). The wide-ranging 1956 UN Supplementary Convention on the Abolition of Slavery, the Slave Trade, and Institutions and Practices Similar to Slavery included a number of definitions that remained in place for many years, including that of 'child servitude' as, among other things:

> any institution or practice whereby a child or young person under the age of 18 years is delivered by either or both his natural parents or by his guardian to another person, whether for reward or not, with a view to the exploitation of the child or young person or of his labour. (Article 1(d))

However, testament to the difficulties of identifying people – in this case, children – held in slavery or slavery-like conditions, more than 17 million children worldwide, mostly girls, are now estimated to be in paid or unpaid domestic work in households other than their own, many located in the world's poorest countries (ILO 2013). Of these children, over two thirds are considered to be in unacceptable conditions, either being below the country's legal minimum working age or working in hazardous circumstances. Domestic work remains a uniquely gendered, hidden and burdensome form of work; children involved, often as a result of family poverty, a lack of education, migration and, ironically, fleeing violence, are particularly vulnerable to exploitation. The culture of child domestic labour is often exported, illicitly, into other countries. Many of the factors pushing and pulling children into domestic work are common to other forms of child labour.

The definition of what is and is not slavery has appeared increasingly important as a rhetorical device that serves in separating out which kinds of exploitation require political priority (Quirk 2011, 2018). How different forms of exploitation should be addressed is an issue remaining to this day (Skrivankova 2014). The ILO has, for example, attempted to define the worst forms of child labour in Convention No 182 (1999). These include:

(a) all forms of slavery or practices similar to slavery such as the sale and trafficking of children, debt bondage and serfdom and forced or compulsory labour, including forced or compulsory recruitment of children for use in armed conflict;

(b) the use, procurement or offering of a child for prostitution, for the production of pornography or for pornographic performances;

(c) the use, procuring or offering of a child for illicit activities, in particular for the production and trafficking of drugs;

(d) work which, by its nature or the circumstances in which it is carried out, is likely to harm the health, safety or morals of a child.

The ILO (2012) also developed six indicators of forced labour in 2005, and later expanded these to 11 indicators (as outlined in Table I.1).

Fundamentally, slavery can be said to exist where a situation involves these three characteristics: severe economic exploitation; an absence of human rights; and control through the threat or reality of violence or coercion. However, it remains the case that there is no internationally agreed definition of slavery. The definition used in the 1926 Convention (Article 1), on which later international definitions have been built, talks of 'the condition of a person over whom any or all of the powers attaching to the right of ownership are exercised', a definition now somewhat dated. The notion of 'control' rather than 'ownership' now seems more apposite.

Subsequent international Conventions have addressed other issues, such as domestic servitude, which has provided a legal basis for

Table I.1: ILO forced labour indicators

ILO (2005) six indicators	ILO (2012) 11 indicators
• Threats of actual physical or sexual violence	• Physical and sexual violence
• Restriction of movement of the worker or confinement to a very limited area	• Restriction of movement
• Debt bondage, where the worker works to pay off debt	• Debt bondage
• Withholding wages or refusing to pay the worker	• Withholding of wages
• Retention of passports and identity documents	• Retention of identity documents
• Threat of denunciation to the authorities	• Intimidation and threats
	• Isolation
	• Abuse of vulnerability, when an employer takes advantage of a worker's vulnerable position
	• Abusive working and living conditions
	• Excessive overtime, obligation to work hours beyond national legal limits
	• Deception, failure to deliver what has been promised to the worker

many women to take action across the world. One key international legislative instrument has been the setting of international standards for the minimum age for admission to employment and work (enshrined in the ILO Convention No 138 of 1975), although, like other Conventions, it has been found to be important to acknowledge the differing circumstances of adults and children in so-called 'developing' countries. More recently (ie in the last 20 years), child domestic work has been identified also as a trafficking issue in the 'Protocol to Prevent, Suppress and Punish Trafficking in Persons, Especially Women and Children' (supplementing the UN Convention against Transnational Organized Crime 2000; see note 4).

This Palermo Protocol is an example of the growing influence on human trafficking policy exercised for European countries by the EU (formed in 1993) and the Council of Europe (a geographically wider body concerned with the protection and development of human rights and democracy, formed in 1947). One important instrument has been the Group of Experts on Action against Trafficking in Human Beings (GRETA), established by the Council of Europe, which monitors and assesses progress by individual states to give effect to the provisions of the Convention through an inspection regime. (Some of GRETA's work is described in Chapter Two.) In general, where concern about human trafficking has emerged in government policy, it has usually been framed in terms of criminal justice responses, most recently, towards organised crime.

Although the UK has now incorporated most of the UN, ILO and European Conventions, as well as EU regulations and directives, into domestic law and policy, it often did so hesitantly and, in some cases, only partially (Balch and Geddes 2011). The UK government has often conveyed the feeling that its own national framework is adequate for addressing trafficking and modern slavery – a feeling not supported by the outcomes of governmental practice – and that it does not need the additional impetus provided by international frameworks. Frequently, it has needed pressure both from within the UK (particularly from NGOs: see Chapters Four, Five and Six, for instance) and from outside it to ensure that UK policy and legal frameworks are as up to date as they might be. One good example of this is the issue of forced labour, which is now becoming one of the most numerically significant forms of modern slavery offence in the UK. Until 2009, it was not possible to prosecute the offence of forced labour as a free-standing offence; this was only allowed by the UK legislative system where forced labour was associated with trafficking, and cases of forced labour therefore had to be referred to the European Court of Human Rights, resulting in considerable delays to those few cases that ever made it to Strasbourg. Lobbying by prominent UK anti-slavery NGOs – Antislavery International and Liberty – resulted in forced labour being included as a free-standing offence in section 71 of the Coroners and Justice Act 2009 (see Craig et al 2014). Relatively few cases have yet been successfully prosecuted through the UK courts but the number is slowly growing and sentences are generally becoming heavier.

'Modern slavery' in the UK: developing understandings

If, 20 years ago, you stopped someone in the street and asked them what came to mind when the word 'slavery' was mentioned, the chances are that one of four responses would be given: something 'to do with William Wilberforce'; with the transatlantic slave trade; to the effect that it involved people working in appalling conditions elsewhere in the world (generally associated with the growth of the Fairtrade movement); or, possibly, with child sexual exploitation in South-east Asia (as the issue of sex tourism was becoming a publicly discussed phenomenon). What is almost certain is that nobody would have observed that it was a phenomenon commonly to be found on the streets of the UK.

This lack of knowledge and understanding was, as noted, reflected in political discourse some 20 years ago, and political discussion of the issue of modern slavery was, to say the least, muted – and, further, focused almost entirely on trafficking without appreciating non-trafficked forms of modern slavery. While the UK generally responded fairly rapidly to most ILO Conventions – with the implicit assumption that these were intended primarily for so-called poor or 'developing' countries – it was far less ready to sign up to international legislation or Conventions premised on the assumption that slavery was a domestic political issue. The 2000 Palermo Protocol is a case in point. Parliamentary debates reflected this general lack of knowledge or, indeed, political urgency about the issue. Evidence provided by individual academics and NGOs (eg on domestic servitude, see Anderson 1993; on the trafficking of women for sexual exploitation, see Kelly and Regan 2000; on forced labour and migration to the UK, see Anderson and Rogaly 2005; on the trafficking of children, see NSPCC 2006; ECPAT 2007; see also Van der Anker 2004; Pai 2008), as well as from other 'developed' countries such as the US (UNICEF 2005), provided an environment that prompted the UK to introduce both the Sexual Offences Act 2004 and the Immigration and Asylum Act 2004 (both addressing trafficking). However, a lack of effective protection for those escaping from trafficking often compounded the abuse that they had already suffered, preventing victims from bringing their plight to the attention of the authorities. As with rape, this led to undercounting. Many victims were removed as 'illegal' immigrants, with little assessment of the risks that they might return to and without their traffickers being held to account.

The extent of trafficking for sexual exploitation to the UK was unknown, although the government suggested in 2005 that 10,000 women and perhaps 3,000–4,000 children had been trafficked to the UK for the purpose of sexual exploitation over a 10-year period (UNICEF 2006). At any one time, about 5,000 sex workers were thought to be in the UK, most of them trafficked here, with 75% of them female and 30% children (ie aged under 18) (UNICEF 2006). The inadequacy of data and lack of concern about the scale of the issue was reflected in Parliament, where one parliamentary statement from Harriet Harman, the-then Solicitor General (in 2006), suggested that the number of trafficked women in the UK was anywhere between 71 and 1,420, an estimate that managed to be simultaneously precise and laughably vague. Public attitudes were reflected in media comment. In 2006, the London *Evening Standard*, reporting on the discovery of several trafficked women, recorded the incident as 'a bunch of Eastern European hookers wanting to make money off our men' (personal communication to author, Senior Police Officer, 30 November 2017),[13] while the normally liberal *Guardian* (20 October 2009) claimed that the numbers of those trafficked had been exaggerated both by evangelistic faith-based groups and by the police in pursuance of their own self-interests.

Difficulties of accurate counting within marginal populations were, and remain, only one of the issues to note here. Of persistent relevance as a framer for many debates and responses to trafficking is the frequent association of trafficking with prostitution (with the assumption that the majority of sex workers are trafficked), and also of the moral landscape that presents acute differences between those who view all prostitution as potential trafficking (often from so-called 'prostitution abolitionists'), and those who see sex work as a choice, with coercion playing a relatively minor role. It is thus nigh on impossible to accurately count 'victims' – in part, due to contestation over what forms of sex work and/or exploitation are viewed as trafficking or slavery. Concern abounds that while, of course, trafficking into sexual exploitation remains an issue for a relatively small number of people, the tackling of this has been undermined by moral panics induced by inflated claims about numbers. This has had the associated effect of shaping the construction of *certain* types of people as victims and the pushing of 'crackdown' responses (such as the criminalisation of prostitution), which, in the view of many, are highly damaging to those working in the sex industry (O'Connell Davidson 2010; Mai 2013; Andrijasevic and Mai 2016).

In recognition that trafficking can be for exploitation in sectors aside from sex work, and that forced labour can emerge with no trafficking element, pressure had meanwhile been growing in parallel for better regulation of the labour market. Trades unions, coordinated through the Trades Union Congress (TUC) and eventually armed with the findings of an investigation by the Commission on Vulnerable Employment (TUC 2008) – identifying 2 million workers in 'vulnerable' employment, most in unorganised sectors often characterised by subcontracting, agency supply (Markova and McKay 2008) and complex supply chains – led campaigns to establish what became the Gangmasters Licensing Authority (GLA) (Scott et al 2007). This was initially charged with regulating labour supply in agriculture/horticulture, food processing/packaging and shellfish collecting/processing. The TUC had found itself eventually pushing at an open parliamentary door after the tragedy of Morecambe Bay, in which 23 young trafficked Chinese people had drowned while picking cockles (HoC 2004). Interestingly, the revelation that more than 50 Chinese people had suffocated in the back of a lorry entering a channel port a few years earlier led not to growing concern about the occurrence of forced labour within the UK, but rather criticism of the slackness of immigration procedures (a recurrent and confusing theme) and the possibility of people smuggling (see the point later, and in Chapters Three and Nine, on recent anti-immigration policies perversely providing landscapes in which severe exploitation will flourish). Nevertheless, research covering both the UK and elsewhere has now firmly established the growing incidence of forced labour in so-called mature economies (Geddes et al 2014; Skrivankova 2014; Payne and Phillips 2015; Crane et al 2017).

Community organisations had also been concerned about highly exploitative conditions in certain industrial sectors (for cleaners, see Artemis 2004; for domestic workers, see Kalayaan 2008; for hotels, see TELCO 2009). Although forced labour clearly existed in the UK prior to 2004, migrant workers arriving from 'A8' accession countries found themselves entering increasingly unregulated, casualised and competitive low-paid labour market sectors, often in isolation and with little effective support, some experiencing high levels of exploitation in workplaces and housing alike (Adamson et al

2008; Scott et al 2013). The GLA-led Operation Ruby identified Eastern Europeans trafficked for probably forced labour but the GLA was unable to police most exploited workers' conditions effectively given its very limited resources and remit (Rogaly 2006; Wilkinson et al 2009) and the rapidly increasing numbers of workers operating at the margins of the labour market. The greatest driver for labour exploitation was arguably the increasing deregulation of the UK economy, making it, the Organisation for Economic Co-operation and Development (OECD) argued, the second least protected of all 'developed' economies after the US, as reflected in high proportions of agency workers in the labour market. The two New Labour former Prime Ministers Blair and Brown frequently celebrated the fact that the UK has an increasingly 'flexible' labour market, one now regarded as the most flexible in Western Europe. However, flexibility appears to be a code for high levels of exploitation, including low wages, long hours, insecure contracts, poor working conditions and little trades union organisation. The 2010 UK Coalition and 2015 Conservative governments both continued this trend. Migrant workers, with their various immigration statuses and entitlements to work (including some workers without permission to work and regular migrants working in conditions that breach labour laws), are often at risk of becoming subjected to severe exploitation (Waite et al 2015). This has been overlooked in recent media-driven moral panics about the impact of migrant workers on the UK economy (which had been shown, in any case, to be either neutral or slightly benign [Craig 2007]).

The process and events generating increased demand for legislation over the period 2007–14, the announcement of the government's intention to legislate, and the complex process of consultation, lobbying and revision that eventually led to the emergence of the MSA legislation in March 2015, immediately prior to a general election, have, as noted, been described elsewhere in some detail and will not be repeated here (see, eg, Craig 2009, 2017a, 2018; Craig et al 2014; see also Chapter Two). The development of the discourse and policy from human trafficking to modern slavery in the UK is also dealt with at some length in O'Connell Davidson (2015) and Broad and Turnbull (2018).

Key milestones included:

• The publication of the Joseph Rowntree Foundation report (Craig et al 2007), the first comprehensive scoping study of the situation in the UK. Two years later, this led to a major research programme on the extent and nature of forced labour in the UK and many influential reports (eg Skrivankova 2010; Dwyer et al 2011; Balch 2012; Scott et al 2013; Allain et al 2013; Geddes et al 2014; Skrivankova 2014). These helped analyse a number of key issues, including supply chains and business complicity with slavery, the links with immigration status, the occurrence of forced labour in many industrial sectors, and the fact that victims of forced labour could include white UK nationals.

- The establishment by government in 2007 of the Human Trafficking Centre, rapidly subsumed into the less accessible National Crime Agency.[14]
- The creation of an All-Party Parliamentary Group on Human Trafficking, later (in 2015) to be renamed the All-Party Parliamentary Group on Human Trafficking and Modern Slavery in recognition of the awareness of the many forms in which modern slavery was now manifested.
- The agreement of Parliament in 2010 to establish an Anti-Slavery Day (18 October), acknowledged by a growing number of events across the UK on or around that day, as well as in Parliament.
- The establishment, also in 2010, of the Human Trafficking Foundation, a charitable body that has since become an effective coordinating mouthpiece for many NGOs working in the field.
- The announcement by Home Secretary Theresa May, following the publication of a report on trafficking by the Centre for Social Justice (2013), that the government planned to bring forward a Modern Slavery Act.
- The publication of a Bill, followed by scrutiny by a committee of both Houses of Parliament, as well as through the normal parliamentary process, leading to the publication of a revised Bill and the enactment of legislation early in 2015. Some proposed provisions of the Act were, in fact, introduced before the Bill had become law.
- Passage of the Immigration Act 2016, which included in its provisions arrangements for the enlargement of the remit of the GLA, now to be renamed the Gangmasters and Labour Abuse Authority (GLAA), and for the appointment of a Director of Labour Market Enforcement with a role bringing together the work of the GLAA, the Employment Agencies Advisory Inspectorate (EASI) and the low-wage function of Her Majesty's Revenue and Customs (HMRC) service.
- The inclusion in 2016 of the goal of eradicating slavery by 2030 in UN sustainable development goal (SDG) 8.7.

The critical issues that have emerged from research and debate following the enactment of legislation include: contradictions and tensions between the legislative forms in the three UK jurisdictions (England and Wales, Scotland, and Northern Island); the effectiveness of the National Referral Mechanism (NRM)[15]; the provision of Child Advocates; the inadequate protection of overseas domestic workers; the remit and resources available to the GLAA and the growth in scale and depth of labour exploitation (see Waite et al 2015; Scott 2017); the weakness of the transparency in supply chains provision; and the support available to victims of slavery. These are all addressed in subsequent chapters. Major concerns remain about the extent and quality of training available to all those tasked with addressing modern slavery, from High Court judges through to hotel receptionists, as well as about the effectiveness of current arrangements for collecting and analysing data.

The last-named issue has been reflected, in part, in continuing debates about the numerical extent of modern slavery in the UK. Although the Home Office (Bales et al 2015) published what it regarded as a definitive figure (of 10,000–13,000), this was challenged at the time by many commentators, not least because of the increasing numbers (5,140 in 2017) of those entering the NRM (despite the many barriers to entry), and since by the National Crime Agency, which suggested that the real number is in the 'tens of thousands'.[16] To those in slavery or working to combat it, the precise numbers may be of little interest, and there are fulsome debates about the veracity, usefulness and political expediency of counting efforts (see, eg, Dottridge 2017b; Gallagher 2017b; Yea 2017), but there is clearly a political drive for robust evidence to inform 'evidence-based policymaking' that is hard to ignore. It was only in 2016 that police were required to introduce a separate recording category for modern slavery offences and thus effectively to double-count modern slavery offences in terms of both the specific offence and the associated crime, such as rape or grievous bodily harm. This probably accounts, at least in part, for the Home Office's earlier serious underestimate.

There can be no doubt that having legislation – whatever the present Prime Minister's *political* motivation for introducing it (and it would probably be churlish to doubt her moral conviction) – presents an opportunity to influence policy and practice for those involved in anti-slavery activity due to this era of increased political attention. However, there can also be no doubt that it can be strengthened and improved very significantly. Critical voices raised have come not just from NGOs and researchers, but from those closer to the parliamentary process: these include Her Majesty's Inspectorate of Constabulary and Fire and Rescue Services (HMICFRS 2017), which has been strongly critical of the response of police forces; the Select Committee on Work and Pensions (DWP 2017), which has strongly challenged the current arrangements for victim support; the National Audit Office (NAO 2017), which has also described the government's modern slavery strategy as inadequate and inconsistent; and the IASC in his 2017 annual report (IASC 2017b), who has described the NRM for suspected victims of trafficking as 'not fit for purpose'. In May 2018, the IASC announced his impending resignation, citing, among other things, the continued interference of government in his work, an announcement that validated the criticisms made by many at the time of his first appointment that the role was limited by government oversight.

It is crucial to note that this apparently progressive piece of social policy legislation not only sits uncomfortably with the Prime Minister's general political stance on related matters, such as the 'hostile environment' for certain migrants that she intends to create, but also totally contradicts elements of current government economic policy, which, as noted, are pursuing a determined strategy of deregulation and hence creating the conditions for greater exploitation (Quirk 2018). There is great concern that these policies and the creation of 'discomfort' for some categories of migrants have played, and will continue to play, important roles as *facilitators* of exploitative labouring conditions and widespread discrimination (FLEX 2016; Lewis et al 2017; Lewis and Waite, 2018). Certainly, the government's stance on migrants has managed to confuse many as to the differences between trafficking and immigration, and continues to suggest that trafficking is the result of migration (Dando et al 2016; Broad and Turnbull 2018).

Before moving on to the individual chapters, we conclude by considering the wider political context of the debates about modern slavery, which has echoes of the debates 200 years ago. We noted that the behaviour of the Royal Navy, intercepting non-British slaving ships, after the passage of the 1807 legislation could be interpreted in two ways: first, as a mission underpinning the moral campaign of Wilberforce and his supporters, inside and outside Parliament; and, second, to protect the financial interests of an industrialising class in the UK and the economic exploitation of the growing empire. Much of the developing campaign over the past 10 years surrounding the emergence of modern slavery in the UK has been vigorously associated with a highly moral stance, with the frequent use of words such as 'rescuing', 'missing' and 'saving'. While no one should, again, doubt the integrity and morality of most of those active in this field, it is still possible to observe some fundamental contradictions inherent in the work. As Kempadoo (2015: 18) observes, modern anti-slavery campaigns are often reflective of:

> a neoliberal white chivalrous crusade across the world, born of a moral sense of goodness that shores up the power and subjectivity of the North, with the 'developing' Global South and East as the dumping grounds for helping imperatives involving rescue and charity.

We have already noted Theresa May's strong advocacy for anti-slavery campaigns while, at the same time, leading a government that, in many ways, generates the conditions creating severe labour exploitation (Lewis et al 2017). However, perhaps most fundamentally of all, the question of the supply of goods and services from other countries, which has now been condensed into discussion about the requirement for large companies to observe the terms of Clause 54 (producing modern slavery statements that report action taken to investigate supply chains[17]), raises some important questions about motivations.

At the time of the 1807 Act, and during Lincoln's campaign to end slavery in America, it was relatively easy to identify who benefitted from the slave trade and from slavery: slavery was in full public view, slave-owners were a matter of public record and the commodities that slavery generated were obvious, particularly cotton, cocoa and sugar. Things are not so clear-cut now: slave-owners are acting illegally, their involvement is hidden from view and the commodities produced from slaving are much more numerous and sourced from across the world. Supply chains are complex and companies can easily obscure their involvement with slavery. If we ask who benefits from slavery now, while those running criminal gangs and private slaving enterprises clearly do so for the substantial profits they generate,[18] it is difficult to conclude other than that we all do, however unknowingly, in the goods we buy that come from unknown destinations. When those lobbying for what became Clause 54 in the Act pressed the government to take action, it was reluctant to do so (an earlier attempt in 2012 to introduce a supply chain provision had failed). It was only when a coalition of larger companies also pressed it to do so that it included the Clause. Leaving aside the weakness of the Clause (discussed by Theron in Chapter Nine),[19] this can also be understood in a completely amoral way, with larger companies wishing to protect themselves from being undercut by smaller ones that might take market share and thus profit from them.

More widely still, we might characterise the campaign against modern slavery, and certainly this aspect of it, as highly hypocritical (Faulkner 2017). In Faulkner's (2017) view, the 'moral stance of the contemporary abolitionist movement' hides a deeply – and perhaps unconscious – racist and imperialist bias: the numbers of those claimed to be in modern slavery by organisations such as the Walk Free Foundation 'hide an implicit racist bias. The "best" states fighting modern slavery are all Euro-American, the worst African and Asian'. This, Faulkner (2017) argues, is an incomplete and selective view that praises the UK legislation, on the one hand, while overlooking the 'lethal consequences of UK immigration policies or the effects of neo-liberalism on the non-West', a form of cultural imperialism, on the other. Thus, the contemporary abolitionist movement as a whole is 'being wielded as a hypocritical weapon of morality ... [which does not] acknowledge the West's role in perpetuating inequality, injustice and exploitation overseas', of which much slavery, a legacy of colonialism and imperialism, is a part. From this point of view, it could be argued that those companies that declined to compensate the victims of the Rana Plaza disaster, in which more than a thousand Bangladeshi garment workers died while working in slavery conditions supplying garments to UK companies, are behaving more consistently in a historical sense than their competitor companies, which have paid up.

To put it another way:

> human exploitation is not an aberration, rather it's built our world and continues to power economic growth. It's sobering to reflect that global wealth and productivity [which refers to the wealth of the richest countries, built in many cases on the proceeds of the slave trade] ... would be under serious threat if exploitation were suddenly and completely removed from the equation. These painful realities shouldn't stop us but they should make us very wary of quick fixes. (Gallagher 2017a)

Or, as Quirk (2018, forthcoming) puts it:

> much of the popular appeal ... of anti-slavery and anti-trafficking can be largely traced to the degree to which slavery has been constructed as a singular and exceptional problem that rarely threatens major political and economic interests, particularly in the Global North.

We hope that this book will add strength to our understandings of, and the activities and campaigns to improve the UK's response to, modern slavery, but place those understandings in a wider political economy context rather than one of a narrow 'civilising mission', redolent of the religious missions of the 19th century.

Notes

1   This is the title of an Australian government inquiry into modern slavery published late in 2017 (see Gallagher 2017a).

2   See: www.hull.ac.uk/WISE

3   Australia, for example, in currently constructing similar legislation, will apparently ensure that the provisions for transparency in supply chains apply equally to public bodies as they will do to private sector businesses.

4   The inquiry into establishing a Modern Slavery Act in Australia actually argued that the only provisions that might be new to Australia were the creation of the role of the commissioner and the requirements regarding supply chains since slavery has formally been outlawed in Australia since 1901.

5   See: https://ec.europa.eu/anti-trafficking/legislation-and-case-law-international-legislation-united-nations/united-nations-protocol-prevent_ en

6   The UK Treasury, in one of its FridayFact tweets (since hurriedly deleted), made much of the fact that this sum of money – with interest – was not finally paid off until 2015, congratulating the current UK public on helping to abolish slavery! See: www.theguardian.com/commentisfree/2018/ feb/12/treasury-tweet-slavery-compensate-slave-owners

7   The scope of compensation has been mapped in the Legacies of Slave-Ownership Project at University College London, see: www.ucl.ac.uk/ lbs/

8   We are indebted to Joel Quirk for some of the data in this section.

9   The 'kafala' sponsorship system emerged in this region in the 1950s – ostensibly to regulate the relationship between employers and migrant workers – yet, it has led to the latter being completely dependent on their employer for livelihood/residency and is therefore likened to slavery.

10   The 2018 World Migration Report states that 52% of international migrants are male and 48% are female, see: https://publications.iom.int/ system/files/pdf/wmr_2018_en_chapter2.pdf

[11] Organs such as livers and kidneys are removed under compulsion or duress of some kind (eg to settle cases of debt bondage), often in dangerous contexts, for sale to wealthy people requiring transplants. The Group of Experts on Action against Trafficking in Human Beings' (GRETA's) (2017) monitoring report on the UK suggested that there were eight cases in the UK in the past year, see: https://rm.coe.int/ CoERMPublicCommonSearchServices/DisplayDCTMContent?docum entId=09000016806abcdc

[12] See, for example, the various publications produced by Anti-Slavery International, available at: www.antislavery.org/?gclid=CNTE4_ D60tICFYYcGwoduPELwA. For a recent Home Office Modern Slavery Unit typology of 17 types of modern slavery offence grouped around the four meta-types of labour exploitation, domestic servitude, sexual exploitation and criminal exploitation, see also Cooper et al (2017).

[13] Ironically, and both demonstrating the considerably heightened recent awareness of the issue and speaking to considerable public sympathy for *some* victims of slavery, the same newspaper started a major campaign in September 2017 'Slaves on our Streets', allegedly with the blessing of the Pope, with the intention of drawing the attention of the general public to the growing scale of modern slavery in the UK.

[14] As it is not covered by Freedom of Information provisions.

[15] The NRM is a framework for identifying victims of human trafficking or modern slavery and ensuring that they receive the appropriate support. The NRM was introduced in 2009 to meet the UK's obligations under the Council of Europe Convention on Action against Trafficking in Human Beings. The government's 'independent' IASC joined the growing criticism of the NRM in 2017, arguing that its reliance on 'a coherent, consistent and undelayed victim disclosure' was flawed (IASC 2017b; see also IASC, 2017a).

[16] See, for example, www.theguardian.com/world/2017/aug/10/modern-slavery-uk-nca-human-trafficking-prostitution

[17] A clause that continues to be observed by its breach with, by mid-2018, barely 20% of those companies covered by the Act's provisions complying with the legislation.

[18] Slavery is reckoned to produce the third largest profits – at around £80 billion – of all global trades, after drugs and arms, see: www.rt.com/ news/160460-un-slavery-billions-profits/

[19] One weakness is that the Clause only applies at present to private businesses whereas many public companies have annual turnovers well above the defined threshold for reporting of £36 million. This issue is being addressed both by some parliamentarians and in the research literature (see Martin-Ortega 2017).

References

Adamson, S., Craig, G. and Wilkinson, M. (2008) *Migrant workers in the Humber*, Hull: Humber Improvement Programme.

Allain, J., Crane, A., LeBaron, G. and Behbahani, L. (2013) *Forced labour's business models and supply chains*, York: Joseph Rowntree Foundation.

Anderson, B. (1993) *Britain's secret slaves: An investigation into the plight of overseas domestic workers*, London: Anti-Slavery International.

Anderson, B. and Rogaly, B. (2005) *Forced labour and migration to the UK*, London: Trades Union Congress.

Andrijasevic, R. and Mai, N. (2016) 'Editorial: trafficking (in) representations: understanding the recurring appeal of victimhood and slavery in neoliberal times', *Anti-Trafficking Review*, 7: 1–10.

Artemis (2004) *Underground Londoners*, DVD. Available at: http://creativecommons.org/policy

Balch, A. (2012) *Regulation and enforcement to tackle forced labour in the UK: A systematic response?*, York: Joseph Rowntree Foundation.

Balch, A. (2016) *Immigration and the state*, Basingstoke: Palgrave.

Balch, A. and Geddes, A. (2011) 'Opportunity from crisis? Organisational responses to human trafficking in the UK', *British Journal of Politics and International Relations*, 13(1): 26–41.

Bales, K., Hesketh, O. and Silverman, B. (2015) 'Modern slavery in the UK: how many victims?', *Significance*, 12(3): 16–21.

Beutin, L.P. (2017) 'Black suffering for/from anti-trafficking advocacy', *Anti-Trafficking Review*, 9: 14–30. Available at: www.antitraffickingreview.org

Broad, R. and Turnbull, N. (2018) 'From human trafficking to modern slavery', *European Journal on Criminal Policy and Research*, pp 1–15. Available at: https://link.Springer.com/article/10.1007/s10610-018-9375-4

Centre for Social Justice (2013) *It happens here*, London: Centre for Social Justice.

Chuang, J. (2014) 'Exploitation creep and the unmaking of human trafficking law', *The American Journal of International Law*, 108(4): 609–49.

CNN (2017) 'People for sale. Where lives are auctioned for $400', October. Available at: https://edition.cnn.com/2017/11/14/africa/libya-migrant-auctions/index.html

Cooper, C., Hesketh, O., Ellis, N., Fair, A. and Home Office Analysis and Insight (2017) *A typology of modern slavery offences*, Research Report 93, October, London: The Home Office. Available at: www.gov.uk/government/publications/a-typology-of-modern-slavery-offences-in-the-uk

Craig, G. (2007) 'They come over here …. And boost our economy', *Regional Review*, Summer: 23–5.

Craig, G. (2009) '"Flexibility", xenophobia and exploitation: modern slavery in the UK', in C. Holden, I. Greener and M. Kilkey (eds) *Social policy review*, Bristol: The Policy Press.

Craig, G. (2017a) 'The UK's modern slavery legislation, an early assessment of progress', *Social Inclusion*, 5(2): 16–27.

Craig, G. (2017b) 'Child labour exploitation: a historical and global view', in P. Dolan and N. Frost (eds) *The Routledge handbook of global child welfare*, London: Routledge, pp 165–75.

Craig, G. (2018) 'The UK Modern Slavery Act: an incoherent response', in C. Needham, E. Heins and J. Rees (eds) *Social policy review 2018*, Bristol: Policy Press.

Craig, G., Gaus, A., Wilkinson, M., Skrivankova, K. and McQuade, A. (2007) *Contemporary slavery in the UK: Overview and key issues*, York: Joseph Rowntree Foundation.

Craig, G., Balch, A., Geddes, A., Scott, S. and Strauss, K. (2014) *What next for forced labour?*, Durham: Forced Labour Monitoring Group.

Crane, A., LeBaron, G., Allain, J. and Behbahani, L. (2017) 'Governance gaps in eradicating forced labour: from global to domestic supply chains', *Regulation and governance*, September. Available at https://onlinelibrary.wiley.com/doi/abs/10.1111/rego.12162.

Dando, C., Walsh, D. and Brierley, R. (2016) 'Perceptions of psychological coercion and human trafficking in the West Midlands of England', *PLOS One*, 5 May.

Dottridge, M. (2017a) 'Eight reasons why we shouldn't use the term "modern slavery"'. Available at: www.opendemocracy.net/beyondslavery/michael-dottridge/eight-reasons-why-we-shouldn-t-use-term-modern-slavery

Dottridge, M. (2017b) 'Global trafficking prevalence data distorts efforts to stop patterns of human trafficking', *Anti-Trafficking Review*, 8: 161–4.

DWP (Department for Work and Pensions) (2017) *Victims of modern slavery*. Report of Select Committee on Work and Pensions. Available at: https://publications.parliament.uk/pa/cm201617/cmselect/cmworpen/803/80303.htm#_idTextAnchor003

Dwyer, P., Lewis, H., Scullion, L. and Waite, L. (2011) *Forced labour and the UK immigration policy: Status matters*, York: Joseph Rowntree Foundation.

ECPAT (End Child Prostitution and Trafficking) (2007) *Missing out*, London: ECPAT.

Farrior, S. (1997) 'The international law on trafficking in women and children for prostitution: making it live up to its potential', *Harvard Human Rights Journal*, 10: 213–56.

Faulkner, E. (2017) '40.3 million slaves: challenging the hypocrisy of modern slavery statistics'. Available at: www.opendemocracy.net/elizabeth-faulkner/403-million-slaves-challenging-hypocrisy-of-modern-slavery-statistics (accessed 7 December 2017).

FLEX (Focus on Labour Exploitation) (2016) 'FLEX briefing: Immigration Bill part one – January 2016'. Available at: www.labourexploitation.org/sites/default/files/publications/FLEXImmBillBriefFINAL.pdf

Gallagher, A. (2017a) 'Evidence to the Australian government's inquiry into establishing a Modern Slavery Act in Australia', para 1.9. Available at: https://www.aph.gov.au/Parliamentary_Business/Committees/Joint/Foreign_Affairs_Defence_and_Trade/ModernSlavery/Final_report

Gallagher, A. (2017b) 'What's wrong with the Global Slavery Index?', *Anti-Trafficking Review*, 8: 90–112.

Geddes, A. (2003) *The politics of migration and immigration in Europe*, London: Sage.

Geddes, A., Craig, G. and Scott, S. (2014) *Forced labour in the UK*, York: Joseph Rowntree Foundation.

HMICFRS (Her Majesty's Inspectorate of Constabulary and Fire and Rescue Services) (2017) *Stolen freedom*, London: HMICFRS.

HoC (House of Commons) (2004) *Gangmasters (follow up) eighth report of session 2003–4*, HC 455, Environment Food and Rural Affairs Committee, London: House of Commons.

Hochschild, A. (2012) *King Leopold's ghost*, London: Pan Macmillan.

IASC (Independent Anti-Slavery Commissioner) (2017a) 'Letter to Minister of State, Sarah Newton'. Available at: www.antislavery commissioner.co.uk/media/1114/letter-to-sarah-newton-mp-on-the-national-referral-mechanism.pdf

IASC (2017b) *The annual report of the Independent Anti-Slavery Commissioner, 2017*, London: TSO.

ILO (International Labour Organization) (2012) *Giving globalization a human face – general survey on the fundamental conventions concerning rights at work in light of the ILO Declaration on Social Justice for a Fair Globalization, 2008*. Report of the Committee of Experts on the Application of Conventions and Recommendations. Report II (Part 1B), ILC, 101st Session, Geneva: ILO.

ILO (2013) *Child domestic work: Global estimates 2012* (factsheet), Geneva: ILO.

Kalayaan (2008) *The new bonded labour?*, London: Kalayaan and Oxfam.

Kelly, L. and Regan, L. (2000) *Stopping traffic*, Police Research Series Paper No 125, London: Home Office.

Kempadoo, K. (2015) 'The modern-day white (wo)man's burden: trends in anti-trafficking and anti-slavery campaigns', *Journal of Human Trafficking*, 1(1): 8–20.

Lewis, H. and Waite, L. (2018) 'Manipulating welfare, rights and agency: UK asylum policy and susceptibility to forced labour', in F. Vecchio and A. Gerard (eds) *Tracing responsibility: Entrapping asylum seekers in precarious livelihoods*, Basingstoke: Palgrave Macmillan.

Lewis, H., Waite, L. and Hodkinson, S. (2017) '"Hostile" UK immigration policy and asylum seekers' susceptibility to forced labour', in F. Vecchio and A. Gerard (eds) *Entrapping asylum seekers: Social, legal and economic precariousness*, Basingstoke: Palgrave Macmillan.

Mai, N. (2013) 'Only a minority of UK sex workers have been trafficked', *The Conversation*, 19 December. Available at: https://theconversation.com/only-a-minority-of-uk-sex-workers-have-been-trafficked-21550

Markova, E. and McKay, S. (2008) *Agency and migrant workers*, London: TUC.

Martin-Ortega, O. (2017) 'Human rights risks in global supply chains: applying the UK Modern Slavery Act to the public sector', *Global Policy*, 8(4): 512–21.

NAO (National Audit Office) (2017) *Reducing modern slavery*, HC 630, London: National Audit Office.

NSPCC (National Society for the Prevention of Cruelty to Children) (2006) *Tackling human trafficking – consultation on proposals for a UK action plan*, London: NSPCC.

O'Connell Davidson, J. (2010) 'New slavery, old binaries: human trafficking and the borders of "freedom"', *Global Networks* 10(2): 244–61.

O'Connell Davidson, J. (2015) *Modern slavery: The margins of freedom*, Basingstoke: Palgrave Macmillan.

O'Connell Davidson, J. (2017a) 'Libyan outrage: slavery or borders?', *Open Democracy*, 12 December. Available at: www.opendemocracy. net/beyondslavery/julia-oconnell-davidson/libyan-outrage-slavery-or-borders

O'Connell Davidson, J. (2017b) 'Editorial: the presence of the past: lessons of history for anti-trafficking work', *Anti-Trafficking Review*, 9: 1–12. Available at: www.antitraffickingreview.org/index.php/atrjournal/article/view/260 (accessed 30 January 2018).

Pai, H-H. (2008) *Chinese whispers*, London: Penguin Books.

Payne, A. and Phillips, N. (eds) (2015) *Handbook of the international political economy of governance*, Cheltenham: Edward Elgar.

Quirk, J. (2009) *Unfinished business*, Paris: UNESCO.

Quirk, J. (2011) *The anti-slavery project: From the slave trade to human trafficking*, Pennsylvania: University of Pennsylvania Press.

Quirk, J. (2018, forthcoming) 'Evaluating the political effects of anti-slavery and anti-trafficking activism', in G. LeBaron (ed) *Researching forced labour in the global economy*, Oxford: Oxford University Press.

Rogaly, B. (2006) 'Intensification of work-place regimes in British agriculture', University of Sussex Migration Working Paper No. 36.

Scott, S. (2017) *Labour exploitation and work-based harm*, Bristol: The Policy Press.

Scott, S., Geddes, A., Nielson, K. and Brindley, P. (2007) *Gangmasters Licensing Authority annual review*, Nottingham: GLA.

Scott, S., Craig, G. and Geddes, A. (2013) *The experience of forced labour*, York: Joseph Rowntree Foundation.

Skrivankova, K. (2010) *Between decent work and forced labour: Examining the continuum of exploitation*, York: Joseph Rowntree Foundation.

Skrivankova, K. (2014) *Forced labour in the United Kingdom*, York: Joseph Rowntree Foundation.

TELCO (The East London Community Organisation) (2009) *Rooms for change*, London: London Citizens.

The Observer (2018) 'How we all colluded in Fortress Europe', 10 June.

TUC (Trades Union Congress) (2008) *Hard work, hidden lives*, London: Commission on Vulnerable Employment.

UNICEF (United Nations Children's Fund) (2005) *The true extent of child trafficking*, London: UNICEF.

UNICEF (2006) *Commercial sexual exploitation*, London: UNICEFUK.

Van der Anker, C. (2004) *The political economy of slavery*, Basingstoke: Palgrave.

Waite, L., Craig, G., Lewis, H. and Skrivankova, K. (eds) (2015) *Vulnerability, exploitation and migration*, Basingstoke: Palgrave.

Wilkinson, M., Craig, G. and Gaus, A. (2009) *Turning the tide*, Oxford: Oxfam.

Yea, S. (2017) 'Editorial: the politics of evidence, data and research in anti-trafficking work', *Anti-Trafficking Review*, 8: 1–13.

ONE

Modern slavery in global context: ending the political economy of forced labour and slavery

Aidan McQuade

Introduction

In 2017, the International Labour Organization (ILO), together with the Walk Free Foundation and the International Organization for Migration (IOM), estimated that there were 40.3 million people in slavery worldwide, doubling its 2012 estimate of 20.9 million (Kelly 2017b). By any reckoning, the scale of 21st-century slavery is daunting. It is also perplexing given the efforts of 19th-century figures, such as Lincoln, Wilberforce, Buxton and countless others, to bring this human rights abuse to an end. However, there is a simple reason why slavery is still such a considerable feature of the contemporary world. It is that we, as a human society, still permit it to exist. Such an assertion may seem at odds with the considerable body of international anti-slavery law, such as the 1926 Slavery Convention and the 1956 Supplementary Convention on Slavery, and the substantial body of national law, such as the UK Modern Slavery Act (MSA) and Articles 23 and 24 of the Indian Constitution, which prohibit trafficking in human beings and child labour.

However, what the black letter of the law says is one thing. How that law is interpreted, or whether it is enforced, can be something else entirely. So, when considering the question of how there can still be so much slavery in the world when there are so many laws banning it, it is perhaps useful to consider the idea of political economy. For the purposes of this chapter, the term 'political economy' is taken to mean the laws, policies and customs that we, as human societies, use to govern business, trade, employment, income and wealth. In many parts of the world, the principles of human rights are not foundational to the conduct of these issues. So, when viewed from this perspective, it can be argued that slavery has become not so much banned, but rebranded, that is, slavery persists across the world but is simply called by other names, facilitated by different laws (by omission or commission) or simply ignored by those with the power to end the diverse practices of contemporary slavery.

The chapter will begin by setting out the root causes of slavery, and demonstrating the fundamental role of the failure of the rule of law in enabling slavery to persist. It will then set out how particular failures in the rule of law give rise to four 'peacetime' political economies of slavery. Where international mechanisms exist to uphold human rights standards, these political economies may be reformed somewhat. However, in addition, what is needed is a more fundamental reform of the nature of all political economies to establish processes to empower vulnerable individuals and groups and to uphold human rights standards. This chapter then sets out what forms these reforms must take to establish political economies with the potential to reduce slavery, if not eliminate it completely.

The constituent elements of slavery

Contemporary slavery reflects a diversity of human experience: a life lived in bonded labour in Indian brick kilns is different in important respects from that of a Nepalese domestic worker in Lebanon, someone born into chattel slavery in West Africa, a 'restavek' child slave in Haiti or a forced labourer in American agriculture. However, in spite of the spectrum of experiences catalogued in contemporary and historical slavery, empirical studies conducted by Anti-Slavery International (see, eg, Upadhyaya 2008; Anti-Slavery International et al 2006) indicate that slavery emerges at the conjunction of three common factors: individual vulnerability (usually, but not exclusively, emerging from poverty); social exclusion; and failure of the rule of law. When demands for cheap labour and reduced costs are introduced into these situations by unscrupulous employers, they act as a catalyst to create slavery and exploitation. This analysis is similar to that offered by LeBaron et al (2018) (see Figure 1.1).

The issue of social exclusion and discrimination is a fundamental one in slavery; when we look at historical slavery in the Americas, we see that racism was both a cause and a consequence of that slavery (Kaye 2005). In Latin America, many in forced labour are indigenous people (Kaye 2008). In Western Europe and South-east Asia, many of those in slavery are migrant workers (Anti-Slavery International et al 2006; Dominguez 2015). In South Asia, most people in slavery are Dalits ('untouchables') or from other scheduled castes or minority

Figure 1.1: The underlying causes of slavery

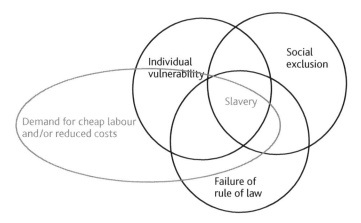

groups (Anti-Slavery International and Volunteers for Social Justice 2017). The depth of prejudice against the rights of women and girls is so profound that it was only in 2017 that forced marriage, including that of children, was included in the global slavery and forced labour estimates (see Kelly 2017b). Of the 40.3 million currently estimated to be in slavery, it is also estimated that there are 15.4 million in forced marriages, and the vast majority of these are girls and women. Over a third of those who were forced to marry were children (ie under 18), of whom 40% were below 15 at the time when marriage took place. The toleration of forced marriage, particularly that of children, represents such a fundamental denial of the rights of millions of girls that it provides a fertile ground for the evolution of yet more egregious abuses, such as the misogynistic depredations of Boko Haram and Islamic State.

The occurrence of prejudice is important for a variety of reasons, not least because it inhibits the issue from becoming a political one: if slavery is being inflicted upon groups and individuals who are voiceless, or whom the wider society disdains, then that wider community is more likely to tolerate the abuses (see also McQuade 2017b) and not exert the political pressure required to obtain the sort of law and policy reform necessary to eliminate the abuse and exploitation that the oppressed endure.

The political economies of slavery

Hence, the persistence of slavery is a political problem. It is a failure of governments' most fundamental responsibility: establishing rule of law. Bingham (2010) argued that human rights, including, of course, an absolute prohibition on slavery, must be at the heart of any credible system of rule of law. Unfortunately, too often, this is not the case and different political economies emerge depending on the nature of these failings.

Setting aside consideration of war and the human rights abuses and slavery that emerge from the chaos that war provides, the political economies of slavery may be categorised in four distinct ways, each directly dependent on the manners in which governments fail to protect human rights. The first category is *state-sponsored* slavery. In 2017, this is exemplified by nations such as North Korea, which trafficks its citizens across the world for hard currency to maintain the dictatorship (McQuade 2016b), and Uzbekistan and Turkmenistan, in which the governments utilise forced labour – including many children – for their cotton harvests (Kelly 2017a), cotton that finds its way into manufactured products worldwide.

The second category may be termed *state-tolerated* slavery. For example, in one study (Anti-Slavery International 2012) of children enslaved in the garment workshops of Delhi, children told how, despite protections promised by Indian law, including the Constitution itself, when workshop owners fail to bribe the police, the latter came, arrested the children and held them hostage, stopping work until the bribes were paid. In other parts of India, Dalits enslaved in brick kilns or agricultural labour find it next to impossible to obtain legal remedy for the situations in which they find themselves. These are not aberrant examples. South Asia has the largest numbers of slaves in the world because for almost one third of the population, over 300 million Dalits, Adavasi and others from 'lower' and 'scheduled' castes, the most basic ideals of the rule of law are completely meaningless. There is simply too much corruption, and too few police, labour inspectors and judges to administer the law.

The refusal to apply basic protections of the rule of law to some within a society is sometimes deliberate in order to obtain some aristocratic privilege over a group of people, as was the case with the 19th-century US system of slavery, even when free labour and emancipation were more attractive economically. This remains the case with India's caste-based apartheid today (see McQuade 2016a).

In some parts of the world, the rule of law is much more explicitly undermined. These form the third category: *state-facilitated slavery*. For example, in Qatar, the United Arab Emirates and Saudi Arabia, there is the 'kafalah' system. This is a so-called sponsorship system that ties workers to their employers even to such an extent that in the most abusive employment relationships, up to and including forced labour, the workers cannot change jobs or even go home. It is this system that has underpinned the trafficking for forced labour of thousands of South Asian labourers for work on the infrastructure and venues for the 2022 World Cup in Qatar (Pattisson 2013), something that has risked making that the bloodiest sporting event since, perhaps, the Caesars organised the spectacle of enslaved gladiators fighting to the death for the entertainment of the masses.

Kafalah is a cynical system that, across the Gulf states, facilitates exploitation up to and including slavery. It is also essentially the same system that the UK government has in place for migrant domestic workers (see, eg, Sloan 2013; see also Chapter Six). In spite of recent superficial reforms, the UK system for domestic workers' visas still de facto legalises trafficking for forced domestic servitude. It does this by placing in the hands of unscrupulous employers the power to impoverish workers who make any effort to escape abusive conditions under the threat of deportation or loss of income, which is critical to remittances supporting family members back home.

This brings us to the fourth category of slavery political economy, perhaps the largest category, of which the UK is a classic example but by no means the only one: *state-muddled*. The UK has criminalised forced labour and enacted victim protection measures and supply chain transparency in the 2015 MSA. However, there remain problematic areas of policy and practice that betray an over-simplistic level of thinking relating to the issue of slavery, and that allow sectors of the economy in which slavery, as a result of mistake or oversight, is able to thrive. For example, insufficient police numbers and training as a result of austerity policies reduces police capacity to address all that the MSA implicitly expects of them. The consequences of this are to be seen in the report of Her Majesty's Inspectorate of Police and Fire and Rescue Service (HMICFRS 2017), demonstrating the failure of the police to respond adequately to the demands placed on them in relation to modern slavery. In early 2018, three years after the MSA passed into law, it was reported (*The Guardian*, 2018) that seven police forces in England and Wales had yet to press charges against any perpetrator of modern slavery.

However, sometimes, the state muddle relating to slavery can have more sinister roots than simply a lack of resources. Lack of robust and principled leadership on the issue can allow not only ignorance of responsibilities to flourish, but also ideology and xenophobia. In the UK, for example, the Anti-Trafficking Monitoring Group, a coalition of non-governmental organisations including Anti-Slavery

International, found in 2013 that if a person from the European Union presents themselves to the authorities as a potential survivor of trafficking, then there is a greater than 80% chance that they will be recognised as such and offered protection and support. However, if they come from outside the European Union, there is less than a 20% chance that they will be recognised as such (Anti-Trafficking Monitoring Group, 2013). That sort of imbalance in decision-making can only be, in the opinion of the authors, the result of institutionalised discrimination and racism.

This finding is in keeping with an obdurate tendency in the UK government to comprehensively and consistently refuse to address the trafficking risks that aspects of their immigration policy pose. In addition to those issues noted earlier, with the introduction of the offence of 'illegal working' in the Immigration Act 2016, the UK government has potentially given additional powers to human traffickers by enabling them to threaten workers with prosecution and deportation by making their migration status irregular (Grant 2015).

States in this fourth category may often mean well. However, they have not marshalled sufficient resources in terms of learning and training, the coordination of law and policy, and the implementation of strategy to systematically reduce the opportunities for the unscrupulous to exploit and enslave the vulnerable.

Slavery and the rule of international law

The question of the rule of law is not merely a national, but an international, issue. With globalisation, the capacity of states to regulate business, as envisioned by classical economics, is increasingly limited because too few states recognise that this responsibility now requires extraterritorial legislation to ensure the legal accountability of transnational corporations, and of the individual business executives who are running those corporations. In the absence of such legislation, the opportunities for slavery and exploitation multiply, particularly as businesses extend their operations into countries with limited rule of law and high levels of corruption.

There are, of course, some transnational legal mechanisms that offer leadership on slavery. Article 4 of the European Convention on Human Rights, administered by the European Court of Human Rights, recognises slavery as a human rights abuse (European Court of Human Rights 2017). This is vital because while there is much heartfelt rhetoric from international political leaders against slavery, these statements can sometimes belie the fact that slavery frequently occurs, as described earlier, because of acts or omissions by governments that provide the opportunities for unscrupulous individuals to exploit the vulnerable. For example, the cases *Siliadin v France* in 2005,[1] and *CN and V v France* in 2012[2] found that France had failed to make sufficient legislative and law enforcement provisions in domestic law to protect the applicants from servitude. Also, the 2010 case of *Rantsev v Cyprus and Russia*[3] found those countries in breach of their positive obligations to protect people from human trafficking.

CN v the United Kingdom in 2012[4] concerned allegations of domestic servitude by a Ugandan woman who complained that she had been forced into working as a live-in carer. The Court held that there had been a violation of the Convention, finding that the legislative provisions in force in the UK at the relevant time had been 'inadequate to afford practical and effective protection against treatment contrary to Article 4 [prohibiting slavery and forced labour]'.

In 2017, the European Court of Human Rights held that Greece violated Article 4 of the European Convention of Human Rights prohibiting forced labour in that it failed to protect a group of Bangladeshi migrant workers from trafficking, and ordered compensation of over €500,000 to be paid. The judgment underlined signatory states' obligations to prevent and investigate trafficking, protect victims, and punish traffickers.

Such international judicial leadership is not limited to Europe. The Court of the Economic Community of West African States demonstrated this in 2008, when a case that Anti-Slavery International helped to bring on behalf of a young woman called Hajiatou Mani resulted in a judgment of that court that found against the state of Niger for failing to protect its citizens from slavery (BBC 2008). The effect of that judgment was not just compensation for Hajiatou, but also the self-liberation of thousands more enslaved people across West Africa who were made aware by the judgment of their right to be free from slavery.

Each of these judgments advanced the protections of people at risk of slavery by deepening our collective understanding of the manifestations of modern slavery and how it should be combated, and by compelling unaware or unwilling governments to act to uphold their responsibilities. As such, these judgments have helped to protect the human rights of all. It could be said that they forced states to become less muddled in how they address slavery and less tolerant of it where it exists.

Where adequate and enforceable human rights protections do not exist in national law to hold governments to account on these protections, then the perpetration of slavery against vulnerable individuals is all the easier. The absence of key mechanisms of international rule of law allows state-sponsored, state-tolerated and state-facilitated slavery more readily to persist; were North Korea, Saudi Arabia and India liable to the censure of international courts, then their political economies of slavery would have much greater difficulty surviving, and the standards of the rule of law in each country would be improved as a result.

The state we are in

In any given age, there is no shortage of people who feel that slavery is wrong. However, as Batman teaches us, it is not what we feel, but what we do, that defines us. Global action against slavery and forced labour is currently inadequate to the challenge. This is evidenced by the consistency of the estimate of child slavery since 2005, when it was estimated at 5.5 million, the same as the estimate in 2012. By 2017, the estimate of children in slavery has risen to 10 million, a figure that has been, in part, augmented by a belated recognition that forced child marriage is also slavery. Le Baron et al (2018) sets out a range of political-economic actions that are necessary in order to obtain meaningful action against slavery. This work echoes that of Anti-Slavery International, which published an 'Anti-Slavery Charter' in 2017 that also recognised the political-economic nature of slavery and hence set out a broad policy agenda necessary to obtain sustainable change (Anti-Slavery International 2017). Both these perspectives on slavery eschew the simplified notion of slavery as principally a criminal justice matter requiring the rescue of those enslaved. Instead, they argue that slavery is a matter that requires the empowerment of those at risk of slavery to uphold their own rights.

Unlike previous struggles against aspects of slavery or more recent struggles to end, for example, apartheid in South Africa or to advance the peace process in Northern Ireland, the contemporary efforts of indigenous campaigners against slavery are very poorly supported by international efforts. While the 'Call to Action to End Forced Labour, Modern Slavery, and Human Trafficking', promulgated by the British government and endorsed by 37 other countries at the United Nations General Assembly in September 2017 (McQuade 2017c), promises increased international efforts, the focus reflected in that document remains predominantly a criminal justice one. A narrow focus on the law enforcement aspects of anti-slavery work may be more ideologically palatable to some political leaders than alternative measures that challenge the underlying structural causes of forced labour or slavery. However, if slavery is to be ended, or at least reduced, there needs to be new policymaking and practice focused on ending its causes, not just addressing isolated symptoms. Hence, there must be much more frank discussion on policy on migration, international aid and trade, and diplomacy – that is, political conversations between nations about their relationships – which should be addressed in terms of how to reshape the international political economy away from one where unscrupulous political and business leaders are allowed to develop competitive advantage through their facilitation of, or use of, forced labour and slavery.

This political-corporate 'race to the bottom' is, of course, understandable, if still morally reprehensible. To address these issues, governments would have to risk confronting powerful vested interests in their own societies and across the world. For example, to break the deafening international silence on caste discrimination in South Asia, something that is foundational to slavery and exploitation across the subcontinent, governments like the UK would risk jeopardising their long-dreamt-of trade deals with the region. That is a tall order under normal circumstances. With, at the time of writing, the UK perched on a Brexit-shaped precipice, it is taller still as following its departure from the European Union, the UK is most likely to find itself an abject supplicant desperate for any trade deal that may allow it to escape from the economic nightmare into which it will otherwise plunge.

Caste-based apartheid afflicts over 300 million people, and is a system that not only undermines the very concepts of rule of law and democracy in South Asia, but also provides the social exclusion vital to establish a population that can be enslaved with impunity. This provides huge benefits to powerful vested interests across the region. However, the consumers of the northern hemisphere also benefit. For example, the use of the forced labour of girls and young women in garment manufacture in Southern India helps maintain a supply of cheap garments to the markets of Europe and North America. While the collapse of the Rana Plaza factory in Bangladesh, killing more than one thousand workers, was largely perceived as an issue requiring stronger government and trades union action against businesses in Bangladesh, what was initially overlooked was the complicity of many UK high-street brand names in sourcing cheap goods from this factory.

In the course of research for the report *Slavery on the high street* (Anti-Slavery International 2012), researchers spoke to the mother of one young 20-year-old woman who worked in one of the spinning mills. She described visiting her daughter:

> I spoke to her in a room provided for visitors, because visitors are not allowed to go inside the mill or hostel. My daughter told me that she was suffering with fever and vomiting often.... I met with the manager and requested him to give leave to my daughter because she was unwell. I told him that I would send my daughter back once she was better. But the manager refused saying that there was a shortage of workers therefore they cannot grant leave. He also assured me that they would take care of my daughter and asked me not to worry.

A week later, she received a call to say that she could now collect her daughter – she was dead.

Just as enslaved people were worked to death on the plantations of the US South in the 19th century, so, too, are they now worked to death in the garment factories of South Asia, the fishing boats of Thailand, on the World Cup building sites of Qatar and the rest of the Gulf, in agricultural fields from West Africa to North America, and in the servants' quarters of every major city of the world. Just as caste imperils lives and livelihoods in South Asia, xenophobia and anti-migrant prejudice fulfils a similar function in Europe. For example, perhaps the biggest single increase in the risk of human trafficking in Europe since the rise of the Islamic State has its origins in the refugee crisis in the Mediterranean.

As far back as 2006, Anti-Slavery International identified how people trafficked into Western Europe often entered perfectly legally but then had their migration status made irregular by their traffickers. This increased the power and control that the traffickers had over them. The corollary of this is that if a person's migration status is already irregular, they are already vastly more vulnerable to enslavement than they would be if their status was regular (Dwyer et al 2011). Hence, irregular migration status reduces the options for protection and support that exploited people can seek as doing so brings with it the risk, at least in the minds of those who may wish to seek help, of deportation. Moreover, if they risked being deported back to a place where their lives and those of their families would be at risk, then their dependency on their traffickers becomes all the more acute. So, the absence of a comprehensive approach to the refugee crisis in the Mediterranean, particularly the absence of safe migration options for vulnerable people fleeing war, has been a significant factor increasing the risks of human trafficking in Europe over the past two years.

The recent efforts to exclude so many desperate people from Europe, which have accelerated over the past few years, have led thousands to attempt the hazardous crossing to Europe's southern shores. For those that survive the arduous sea crossing, however, their troubles have not ended. Their irregular migration status can close down opportunities for decent work, and instead render them vulnerable to exploitation. To counter this effectively would require that the member states of the European Union fundamentally reshape their inadequate and inhumane response to this crisis, focusing on the safe passage and protection of refugees rather than simply excluding unwanted people from what is increasingly understood as Fortress Europe. This seems beyond the political pale for many, including some of the most vocal European leaders on the issue of slavery, hence rendering questionable their commitment to ending slavery (see McQuade, 2015, 2017a).

Transforming the global political economy

It may be classed as utopian to imagine a more focused, less muddled, approach to ending slavery given the ignorance and self-interest that marks so much of the contemporary political economies of slavery. However, utopian idealism has long been a hallmark of the struggle against slavery: Thomas Clarkson's 18th-century campaign was nothing if not idealistic. So, too, was St Patrick's Letter to the Soldiers of Coroticus, over a millennium before.[5] 'Unreasonable' idealism tends to change the world and may, as Margaret Mead once commented, be initiated by a relatively few thoughtful and committed people acting together. So, here are some more.

An appropriate international struggle against slavery should include attention to the need for safe migration; we should not tolerate, either in crisis or in any other circumstances, the establishment of rules on migration that facilitate the trafficking of vulnerable people. Countries that establish such rules, like Qatar, Saudi Arabia and the UK, should be treated as pariahs and the terms with which they trade with the rest of the world should be altered. There is a hypocrisy in how migrant workers are treated internationally. On the one hand, we, as an international community, tolerate circumstance of injustice and poverty that compel them to migrate. We will then sometimes go so far as to recognise the importance of remittances from these workers towards the development of their countries and reducing the poverty of their families. The economies of many countries benefit enormously from the presence of migrants, as debates about Brexit in the UK have revealed in relation to certain key industries such as food production and social care. However, the world still fails to ensure safe migration.

In addition to a more humane attitude towards migration in which immigration law and policy that maintains or increases an individual's vulnerability to exploitation and slavery is prohibited, there is a need to develop a much broader response to slavery that would begin to offer a real prospect of transforming the global political economy. To begin with, those states that have not done so must legislate to criminalise all forms of slavery. Slavery is a crime, but it needs more than a criminal justice approach to counteract it. Specifically, national and international systems of rule of law, which protect the human rights of all, must be established and enforced. These must be administered without fear or favour by a sufficient number of properly trained judges, supported by a similarly professional police force and labour inspectorate, so as to ensure that the promise of the laws to protect is not an empty one.

Furthermore, discrimination and racism must not only be prohibited, but actively challenged through political and police action, and states, businesses and civil society must take meaningful measures to eradicate dehumanising and discriminatory practices from every section of society, and to ensure true equality before the law. Measures must be enacted to uphold the rights of children and to protect them from child labour and enslavement. All nations must put in place, and implement, laws, policies and effective law enforcement to bring all forms of forced marriage, in particular, forced child marriage, to an end. Furthermore, all nations must ensure universal access to quality and appropriate education up to the age of 18, particularly for girls, for groups vulnerable to slavery such as Dalits and Adavasi, and for communities where child labour is endemic. Anti-Slavery International's work in Niger, for example, has shown how access to education can help to break the bonds of slavery across generations (Abdou and Sani 2001).

States must also advance access to decent work and pay particular attention to the specific needs of disadvantaged groups or individuals, such as women, children, migrants, people affected by disability and people affected by caste discrimination, to achieve equal access and treatment. Some states may protest that they would have difficulty doing all this – perhaps so. However, they can start, and if they guarantee freedom of association for workers and human rights activists, they will find willing allies in this endeavour.

It is essential for businesses to engage in this struggle in common cause with trades unions and human rights activists. Full transparency of national and international business supply chains must be established and enforced to identify where risks of slavery and forced and child labour are highest, and to help identify and expose the causes of these risks. Businesses must not become complicit in trade that allows states to benefit from shoddy protections for the human rights of workers. Indeed, goods tainted by slavery and forced and child labour should be denied access to markets, as President Obama asserted when he signed the Trade Facilitation and Trade Enforcement Act into law in 2016. This adds a direct commercial imperative to the moral imperative for businesses to address the issues of slavery in their supply chains and will have a much more obvious and positive effect than will, for example, the current weak provisions in the UK MSA.

By adopting a broader response to slavery, there would begin to be a real prospect for those most discriminated against and most vulnerable to slavery to begin to envisage a life of peace and prosperity for themselves and their families. Such an approach would also offer a route out of poverty for their countries rather than the continued violence of forced labour and poverty that describes their present, not to mention the risks to their futures.

Hence, the struggle to end slavery should become a central feature of aid and development policy and practice. The UK Department for International Development seems to be beginning this process, and there is a long way to go in an effort that must ultimately encompass non-governmental as well as governmental agencies. Without such considerations, there is a significant risk that anti-poverty interventions will either relatively or absolutely exacerbate the position of the most vulnerable groups in those communities. For example, in 2005, the Niger anti-slavery organisation Timidria identified that slaves were being used in some of the food-for-work programmes that had been set up in response to the West African famine of the time. The way this worked was that slave masters would send those that they had enslaved to toil all day on the programmes and, on their return, would confiscate the ration cards that they had been given in payment for their work.

It is certainly the case that humanitarian response is a fraught and vital business, but this should not detract from the invocation to 'first do no harm'. Increased awareness by humanitarian and development professionals of the institutions of contemporary slavery should lead policymakers and practitioners to routinely ask: 'How can my work impact upon slavery and non-gender-based discrimination in the area in which I am working?'. Asking such questions (and this process can start in schools with children) can help mainstream anti-slavery practice to development and humanitarian work and lead to the sort of qualitative improvement in practice that gender mainstreaming brought two decades ago. It is for this reason that Anti-Slavery International campaigned from 2007 for slavery eradication to be included in the United Nations Sustainable Development Goals. Its inclusion now forces attention to slavery onto the frequently unwilling agendas of all the development and aid agencies.

Conclusion

Two hundred years ago, people like Oluadah Equiano, Hannah More and Thomas Clarkson in Europe, and Sam Sharpe, Frederick Douglass, Nat Turner, Touissant D'Ouverture and the Maroons in the Americas, for diverse reasons, decided to try to end slavery, so morally repugnant did they find it. In doing so, they took on a system that Adam Hochschild (2005) has compared in terms of its power to the oil industry today. In ending the slave trade through force of arms and force of argument in a mere 20 years, they showed what could be achieved when there is the collective will and the audacity of ambition to do so.

Many of these, and the nascent trades unions, have been substantially written out of the history of that struggle, first by those claiming to inherit Wilberforce's mantle, and subsequently largely forgotten. That historiographical injustice contributes not just to the misremembering of what happened, but also to the misunderstanding of why it happened. The achievements of 200 years ago were a classic example, in Bobby Kennedy's phrase, of numberless acts of courage and belief shaping the history of the time (Heyman 1999: 409). There are no 'silver bullets' to end slavery; there is no single measure that will eliminate slavery from the world. However, if there is a clearer understanding of what slavery is, and how it is intertwined with the systems of law and policy that are used to govern human society, then perhaps those numberless diverse acts of courage and belief taken by citizens across the planet to resist the systems of slavery can be more efficiently and effectively delivered.

Notes

[1] *Siliadin v France*, 2005, https://ec.europa.eu/anti-trafficking/legislation-and-case-law-case-law/siliadin-v-france-application-no-7331601_en

[2] *CN and V v France*, 2012, https://ec.europa.eu/anti-trafficking/legislation-and-case-law-case-law/cn-and-v-v-france_en

3 *Rantsev v Cyprus and Russia*, 2010, https://ec.europa.eu/anti-trafficking/legislation-and-case-law-case-law/rantsev-v-cyprus-and-russia-application-no-2596504_en

4 *CN v the United Kingdom*, 2012, https://ec.europa.eu/anti-trafficking/legislation-and-case-law-case-law/cn-v-united-kingdom_en

5 In which he exhorts them, among other things, not to 'accept the gifts of evil-doers'.

References

Abdou, H. and Sani, M. (2011) 'Evaluation of community schools in Tchintabaraden', December, Anti-Slavery International. Available at: www.antislavery.org/wp-content/uploads/2016/12/Niger-school-project-evaluation-2011.pdf

Anti-Slavery International (2012) *Slavery on the high street*, London: Anti-Slavery International. Available at: www.antislavery.org/wp-content/uploads/2017/01/1_slavery_on_the_high_street_june_2012_final.pdf

Anti-Slavery International (2017) 'Anti-Slavery Charter'. Available at: www.antislavery.org/anti-slavery-charter/

Anti-Slavery International and Volunteers for Social Justice (2017) 'Slavery in India's brick kilns and the payment system'. Available at: www.antislavery.org/wp-content/uploads/2017/09/Slavery-In-Indias-Brick-Kilns-The-Payment-System.pdf

Anti-Slavery International et al (2006) *Trafficking for forced labour in Europe*, London: Anti-Slavery International. Available at: www.antislavery.org/wp-content/uploads/2017/01/trafficking_for_fl_in_europe_4_country_report.pdf

Anti-Trafficking Monitoring Group (2013) *Hidden in plain sight*, London: Anti-Trafficking Monitoring Group. Available at: www.antislavery.org/wp-content/uploads/2017/01/hidden_in_plain_sight.pdf

BBC (British Broadcasting Corporation) (2008) 'Niger ex-slave wins landmark case', 27 October. Available at: http://news.bbc.co.uk/1/hi/world/africa/7692396.stm

Bingham, T. (2010) *The rule of law*, London: Allen Lane.

Dominguez, G. (2015) 'Why Southeast Asia struggles to tackle modern-day slavery', *Deutsche Welle*. Available at: www.dw.com/en/why-southeast-asia-struggles-to-tackle-modern-day-slavery/a-18371333

Dwyer, P., Lewis, H., Scullion, L. and Waite, L. (2011) *Status matters: Forced labour and UK immigration policy*, York: Joseph Rowntree Foundation. Available at: www.jrf.org.uk/publications/forced-labour-and-uk-immigration

European Court of Human Rights (2017) *Guide on Article 4 of the European Convention on Human Rights: Prohibition of Slavery and Forced Labour*, Strasbourg: Council of Europe/European Court of Human Rights.

Grant, H. (2015) 'UK Immigration Bill will play into hands of traffickers, anti-slavery experts warn', *The Guardian*, 15 December. Available at: www.theguardian.com/global-development/2015/dec/21/uk-immigration-bill-trafficking-anti-slavery-experts-modern-slavery-act-2015

Heyman, C.D. (1999) *RFK: A candid biography of Bobby Kennedy*, London: Arrow Books.

HMICFRS (Her Majesty's Inspectorate of Constabulary and Fire and Rescue Services) (2017) *Stolen freedom*, London: Her Majesty's Inspectorate of Constabulary and Fire and Rescue Services.

Hochschild, A. (2005) *Bury the chains: The British struggle to abolish slavery*, New York, NY: Houghton Macmillan.

Kaye, M. (2005) *1807–2007: Over 200 years of campaigning against slavery*, London: Anti-Slavery International. Available at: www.antislavery.org/wp-content/uploads/2017/01/18072007.pdf

Kaye, M. (2008) *Arrested development: Discrimination and slavery in the 21st century*, London: Anti-Slavery International. Available at: www.antislavery.org/wp-content/uploads/2017/01/arresteddevelopment.pdf

Kelly, A. (2017a) 'World Bank funds linked to forced labour in Uzbekistan', *The Guardian*, 27 June. Available at: www.theguardian.com/global-development/2017/jun/27/world-bank-funds-linked-to-forced-labour-in-uzbekistan

Kelly, A. (2017b) 'Latest figures reveal more than 40 million people are living in slavery', *The Guardian*, 19 September. Available at: www.theguardian.com/global-development/2017/sep/19/latest-figures-reveal-more-than-40-million-people-are-living-in-slavery

Le Baron, G., Howard, N., Thibos, C. and Kyritisis, P. (2018) 'Confronting the root causes of forced labour: where do we go from here?', *Open Democracy*, January. Available at: www.opendemocracy.net/beyondslavery/genevieve-lebaron/confronting-root-causes-of-forced-labour-where-do-we-go-from-here-0

McQuade, A. (2015) 'Migrant crisis: smuggling or trafficking? Politicians don't seem to know', *The Guardian*, 22 April. Available at: www.theguardian.com/global-development/2015/apr/22/migrant-crisis-smuggling-trafficking-politicians-dont-seem-to-know

McQuade, A. (2016a) 'Aspiration and reality: how caste-blindness undermines UK anti-slavery efforts', 26 May. Available at: https://aidanjmcquade.com/2016/05/25/aspiration-and-reality-how-caste-blindness-undermines-uk-anti-slavery-efforts/

McQuade, A. (2016b) 'North Korean slavery demands robust action from Europe', *Left Foot Forward*, 9 August. Available at: https://leftfootforward.org/2016/08/north-korean-slavery-demands-robust-action-from-europe/

McQuade, A. (2017a) 'Ending the Dubs scheme will put child refugees at the mercy of traffickers', *The Guardian*, 14 February. Available at: www.theguardian.com/global-development/2017/feb/14/ending-the-dubs-scheme-will-put-child-refugees-at-the-mercy-of-traffickers

McQuade, A. (2017b) 'Xenophobic rhetoric created conditions for abusing migrants', 12 March. Available at: www.theguardian.com/commentisfree/2017/mar/12/xenophobia-exploitation-migrants-sicily-trafficking-slavery

McQuade, A. (2017c) 'Theresa May, anti-slavery crusader? Her craven quest for trade deals suggests not', *The Guardian*, 22 September. Available at: www.theguardian.com/global-development/2017/sep/22/theresa-may-anti-slavery-crusader-craven-quest-trade-deals-brexit

Pattisson, P. (2013) 'Revealed: Qatar's world cup "slaves"', *The Guardian*. Available at: www.theguardian.com/world/2013/sep/25/revealed-qatars-world-cup-slaves

Sloan, A. (2013) 'The domestic workers forced into modern slavery', *The Guardian*, 26 November. Available at: www.theguardian.com/society/2013/nov/26/domestic-workers-modern-slavery-visa-laws-tie-employers

The Guardian (2018) 'Seven UK police forces report zero charges under anti-slavery law', *The Guardian*, 22 January. Available at: www.theguardian.com/world/2018/jan/21/seven-uk-police-forces-report-zero-charges-under-anti-slavery-law

Upadhyaya, K.P. (2008) *Poverty, discrimination and slavery: The reality of bonded labour in India, Nepal and Pakistan*, London: Anti-Slavery International. Available at: www.antislavery.org/wp-content/uploads/2017/01/1-poverty-discrimination-slavery-final.pdf

TWO

The UK's response to modern slavery: law, policy and politics

Ruth Van Dyke

Research and policy: key influences

The UK government, despite its increasingly frequent assertions, has not been a world leader in terms of policy development in relation to modern slavery. Policy has actually developed in a fashion that is piecemeal, uneven and inconsistent. Moreover, different governments have been resistant to making policy more robust, and more victim-centred.

The UK's policy approach has also been shaped by different understandings of the problem. As Bacchi (1999) points out, governments can interpret issues in diverse ways, resulting in different solutions. I will explore three approaches underpinning policy and the agencies tasked with implementing the policy. The first is that modern slavery is defined as a crime and, as a result, requires a criminal justice response. Thus, law enforcement agencies play a central role in identifying victims and investigating cases, and the judicial system in holding offenders to account. The second is that modern slavery is considered an abuse of human rights and has to be rectified by meeting victims' needs, restoring dignity and enabling recovery and reintegration. In the UK, many non-governmental organisations (NGOs) have established appropriate services to meet short- and medium-term needs, supplemented by statutory provision. The third approach identifies modern slavery as arising from the abuse and exploitation of labour, which may be inherent in neoliberal economic policy and in changes in employment practices, such as growing demand for cheap and flexible labour (see Chapter Ten). This perspective suggests the need for a stronger regulatory framework, protecting labour rights and promoting the welfare of workers, as well as an enforcement arm ensuring that employers and labour suppliers comply with regulations.

Various factors have influenced policy development in relation to modern slavery in the UK since 2000. These include international

Conventions, obligations arising from membership of regional organisations, advocacy by pressure groups and think tanks, evidence provided by research, action taken by influential individuals, responses to scandal, and the identification of human trafficking and forced labour as social problems. For example, the role of United Nations (UN) and International Labour Organisation (ILO) Conventions and the UK's membership of regional bodies – the Council of Europe and the European Union (EU) – in shaping UK policy are significant, alongside the Group of Experts on Action Against Trafficking in Human Beings (GRETA) and the Anti-Trafficking Monitoring Group (ATMG) (see, eg, Chapter Four), which has monitored the UK response. Civil society organisations and researchers have played key roles in drawing attention to different forms of modern slavery[1] and to difficulties in supporting victims, as well as suggesting different remedies. They have used a variety of pressure group tactics (Grant 1989), including report writing, submitting evidence to parliamentary committees and engaging with Members of Parliament (MPs) and peers to raise awareness of or to seek support for important initiatives during the legislative process.

The Human Trafficking Foundation (HTF), established by a former MP, has provided a forum to share good practice and to campaign for improved legislation or ministerial action by drawing on its members' experiences of identifying and supporting victims, investigating cases, or raising awareness. It has an insider status as it supplies the administrative support to the All-Party Parliamentary Group (APPG) on Human Trafficking and Modern Slavery, a cross-party group of MPs and peers that seeks to enhance their understanding of modern slavery and how policy works in practice. They have used their voices to ask questions and contribute to parliamentary debate, employing their knowledge and power to affect Bills as they are discussed within Parliament.

Law enforcement bodies have also influenced the policy response. For example, the Modern Slavery Human Trafficking Unit, based in the National Crime Agency (NCA), and the National Policing Lead for Modern Slavery provide advice on policy and on practice. It is also apparent that law enforcement officers have contributed to various consultation exercises and policy reviews, where they have been able to share their knowledge and to express their views.

The Metropolitan Police Service (MPS) has been particularly influential through the operational lead for the MPS's response to human trafficking. It was a member of the Slavery Working Group that produced a seminal report on modern slavery in 2013 (Slavery

Working Group 2013), and the former head of the Human Trafficking Unit became the first Independent Anti-Slavery Commissioner and encouraged the-then Home Secretary, Theresa May, to participate in the Santa Marta Group, an international consortium sponsored by Pope Francis aimed at combating modern slavery. Law enforcement also plays a key role in policy implementation and, as we shall see, has been the subject of concern.

Research on the phenomenon of modern slavery, as well as on the policy response, has grown significantly in the 2000s. Some of this research has been commissioned by the government (Kelly and Reagan 2000; Wilcox et al 2009; Malloch et al 2017), and thus may be more influential if the findings chime with party ideology or political expediency. For example, research by the Chief Scientific Advisor for the Home Office produced what was regarded as a robust estimate of the scale of modern slavery in the UK (Silverman 2014). His estimate of 10,000 to 13,000 people trapped in modern slavery conditions is cited by the government to reflect the scale of the problem (although now overtaken by other higher estimates). Other research may also have an impact but perhaps in a more indirect fashion by enlightening those charged with developing policy and expanding their knowledge of different forms of modern slavery, its impact on individuals and society, its causes, or the effectiveness of particular policy measures (Skrivánková 2006; Craig et al 2007; ATMG 2010, 2012, 2013).

The chapter is organised as follows. The first sections explore the three different policy responses to human trafficking and forced labour: the criminalisation of modern slavery; the human rights approach to modern slavery; and regulatory mechanisms to protect workers' welfare and rights, from 2000 to now. It is suggested that there is an implementation gap between policy and practice caused by low levels of awareness, the priority attached to tackling modern slavery, inadequate organisational capacity or a lack of resources (Barton and Johns 2013). The chapter then focuses on the factors that influenced the development of the Modern Slavery Act 2015 (MSA), describing some strengths and weaknesses. It concludes by looking to the future and exploring current policy concerns relative to the criminal justice response.

The criminalisation of human trafficking, forced labour, slavery and servitude

At the start of the 21st century, there was no specific legislation in Britain that made modern slavery a criminal offence. Three developments in international law have driven the UK response: the 2000 UN Palermo Protocol, the 1948 Universal Declaration of Human Rights (enacted in the UK Human Rights Act 1998) and the 2005 European Convention on Action Against Trafficking of Human Beings. These laws, discussed elsewhere in this volume, alongside campaigning by civil society groups, court cases and evidence from research and reports, brought about significant policy development and promoted a criminal justice response to the phenomenon of modern slavery.

The most significant international Convention impacting on British legislation and policy development was the UN Convention on Serious Organised Crime, and specifically the 2000 Protocol to Prevent, Suppress and Punish Trafficking in Persons, Especially Women and Children, known as the Palermo Protocol. The Protocol had three important outcomes. First, it provided the first globally agreed definition of human trafficking, which has three elements: the act, the means and the purpose. (The Palermo Protocol is discussed in detail in Chapters Five and Six.) Second, the Protocol required countries that ratify the Convention to introduce legislation to make human trafficking a criminal offence. Third, it encouraged states to take action to identify victims of human trafficking and to protect and support them.

The *Global report on trafficking in persons*, produced periodically (in 2009, 2012, 2014 and 2016) by the UN Office of Drugs and Crime (UNODC), attests to the global significance of the Palermo Protocol. Between 2003 and 2016, the number of countries that had introduced legislation to criminalise human trafficking increased from 33 to 158, although the extent of coverage varied (UNODC 2016). These reports highlight the scale of human trafficking, and its global footprint, but also express concern about the number of victims identified and the small number of offenders prosecuted and convicted, despite law enforcement having obligations to enforce the law. The annual *Trafficking in persons report*, from the US State Department, offers another source of information on individual countries' anti-trafficking initiatives, underpinned by the Palermo Protocol (US Department of State 2017).

There are several aspects of the Palermo Protocol that have important repercussions for its implementation. As it is an adjunct to the UN Convention against Transnational Organised Crime, the focus of attention by law enforcement may be on individuals that are foreign nationals, that is, victims or traffickers that have crossed national borders. Internal trafficking may be ignored. The growing numbers of

UK nationals identified as potential victims of human trafficking since 2013 may reflect increased understanding that the recruitment and transport of individuals for exploitation can take place within Britain, and entail movement across county lines or even within a town.[2]

The Palermo Protocol is also attached to a Convention aimed at tackling organised crime. As a result, victims trafficked by individuals, family members or business practices that bring about criminal exploitation may not receive sufficient attention if the focus of investigations is on organised crime groups. Lee (2011) points to the much more complex typologies of trafficking groups. Some are highly organised criminal networks while others have developed a business approach that may incorporate a network of people who facilitate different elements entailed in human trafficking. CORE (2016), on the other hand, identified a number of business practices that place many people at risk of forced labour or trafficking for labour exploitation. These include companies engaged in subcontracting and with complex supply chains, with extended or complex employment relationships, or that require the presence of labour recruiters or sectors with low profits and highly flexible labour. The variety of practices indicated by this literature suggests that a more varied criminal justice response is required than can be delivered by law enforcement officers on their own.

Finally, the Palermo Protocol can be considered problematic because it privileges a criminal justice response. As we will see, subsequent developments acknowledged the human rights abuses arising from trafficking and modern slavery, and the need to provide adequate support to victims. Moreover, a victim–centred approach was seen as necessary to enhance criminal investigations and to aid prosecutions (Goodey 2008). After the Palermo Protocol came into effect in 2003, the UK included sections 57, 58 and 59 in the Sexual Offences Act 2003, which made the trafficking of humans into, within or out of the UK for sexual exploitation a criminal offence in England, Wales and Northern Ireland. In Scotland, section 22 of the Criminal Justice (Scotland) Act 2003 covered roughly the same issues. In the same year, Eaves[3] requested funds for a range of services to meet the needs of women victims. Through its Poppy Project, Eaves became the first government-funded agency to fulfil the protection and support elements of the Palermo Protocol (Home Office and Scottish Executive 2007). In 2004, section 4 of the Asylum and Immigration (Treatment of Claimants etc.) Act made trafficking people into, within or out of the UK for the purpose of exploitation a criminal offence, extending the previous sexual exploitation offence to all forms of exploitation.

Legislation to criminalise forced labour was less straightforward, and was influenced by the Universal Declaration of Human Rights, as well as the ILO Convention Concerning Forced or Compulsory Labour (1930 Forced Labour Convention). The 1948 Universal Declaration of Human Rights, followed two years later by the European Convention on Human Rights, was not transposed into UK law until Labour passed the Human Rights Act 1998. Significantly, the Act protected all persons in the UK, no matter their age, nationality, gender or immigration status, as human rights were considered inalienable. Article 4, based on the European Convention on Human Rights, provides that 'no one shall be held in slavery or servitude' or 'be required to perform forced or compulsory labour'. Unlike the Palermo Protocol, the legislation was rights-giving, rather than criminological, in intent. It could be used to hold the government, including the police, to account for failure to ensure that individuals were protected from forced labour.

Despite ratifying the 1930 Forced Labour Convention, the UK failed to meet its obligation in relation to this international Convention for 79 years. Finally, section 71 of the Coroners and Justice Act 2009 made slavery, servitude and forced labour a criminal offence in England, Wales and Northern Ireland. This offence gave law enforcement a tool to tackle serious forms of labour exploitation that did not meet the criteria required for human trafficking. There were a number of factors that produced this change. One relates to a case, brought by Liberty, a civil liberties and human rights organisation, against a police force that had failed to investigate an allegation of domestic servitude. The British court ruled that the police had breached its obligations under Article 4 of the Human Rights Act to offer real protection from servitude. It could also be argued that the Labour government had failed to give police the tools to ensure that people were adequately safeguarded. The second was pressure from Liberty, Anti-Slavery International (ASI) and other groups concerned about the incidence of servitude and forced labour in the UK, as well as Britain's inadequate policy response to its international and national human rights obligations. A third was research evidence, for example, Anderson and Rogaly's (2005) study on forced labour for the Trades Union Congress, Skrivánková's (2006) report on trafficking for forced labour in the UK for (ASI) and Craig et al's (2007) research on contemporary slavery, leading to a wide-ranging research programme commissioned by the Joseph Rowntree Foundation (JRF). These probably informed civil service understandings at the time, in particular, by highlighting the extent of forced labour and other forms of slavery-like practices and the means used to enslave people in 21st-century Britain.

The Council of Europe's 2005 Convention on Action against Trafficking in Human Beings (European Convention), and concern about the demand for sexual services, also had an impact on UK legislation. Article 6 of the European Convention called for measures to discourage 'the demand that fosters all forms of exploitation of persons', which might entail making it a criminal offence to use services provided by a trafficked victim. Respondents to the public consultation on a UK national action plan also suggested a criminal justice approach to reduce demand (Home Office and Scottish Executive 2006). In 2008, the Home Secretary commissioned a 'review to assess what further measures could be taken to reduce the demand for prostitution', making a case for initiatives that targeted the sex buyer. She commented that 'too little attention has been focused on the sex buyer, the person responsible for creating the demand for prostitution markets. And it is time for that to change' (Home Office 2008: 2). The review discerned support for criminal sanctions for those who pay for sex with persons forced to provide sexual services. The outcome was section 14 of the Policing and Crime Act 2009, which created a new offence of paying for the sexual services of a prostitute subjected to force, by amending the Sexual Offences Act 2003 (adding section 53A). As a result, the UK could show that it had met 'its international legal obligations to discourage the demand for sexual services in support of Conventions to suppress and prevent trafficking for sexual exploitation' (CPS no date), as well as responding to public interest to curb demand and to evidence that supported the policy response. However, research undertaken by Matolcsi (2017) found that this offence has rarely been used. Poor implementation was mainly attributed to police lacking relevant knowledge about this offence, in particular, that as a strict liability offence, they did not have to prove that the sex buyer was aware of the coercion or exploitation of the person selling sex.

By 2009, there was a legal framework that could be used to tackle modern slavery as a crime (Liberty and Anti-Slavery International 2009). Implementation was another matter and we must turn to evidence from the UK 'Human trafficking action plans' to discern the effectiveness of the policy response. The 2007, 2008 and 2009 action plans (see Home Office and Scottish Executive 2007, 2008, 2009) are largely descriptive and provide information on the actions taken by law enforcement to tackle human trafficking. They also document that an increasing number of victims were identified, but that the number of prosecutions resulting from criminal investigations remained low. The evidence in these action plans points to an implementation gap

(Barton and Johns 2013). Legislation that introduced new offences was not adequately transmitted to front-line police officers. In other words, they lacked awareness of the crime of human trafficking or of indicators that could be used to identify victims and thereby initiate criminal investigations. In addition, while the government was promoting a leading role for law enforcement, human trafficking had not become part of core police business at the local level. Recommendations to train staff and prioritise this work suggest that the 2005 Labour government sought to reduce the gap between its objective to tackle human trafficking and action on the ground.

The 2011 Human Trafficking Strategy (HM Government 2011) and 2014 Modern Slavery Strategy, produced by the 2010 Coalition government (HM Government 2014), also placed law enforcement at the heart of their response. However, continued reference to a lack of awareness of human trafficking and forced labour legislation, and a lack of engagement by police, illustrates the continued implementation gap. This gap was also noted in the ATMG's third report (ATMG 2012). It explored a number of obstacles impeding an effective criminal justice response to trafficking. One of the key barriers that they noted was the culture of policing targets, which meant 'that trafficking is not considered a priority and an investigation is often based on the goodwill and perseverance of individual officers' (ATMG 2012: 11). However, the Home Secretary was adamant that the law had to be enforced. Enhancing international cooperation, making greater use of asset seizure to reduce the financial gains from modern slavery, setting modern slavery as a priority for the NCA and developing intelligence and investigative capabilities were intended to operationalise the UK's commitment to stopping these crimes. The criminal justice approach to modern slavery was, however, not the only response being developed in the 2000s; a human rights approach was also being encouraged internationally and regionally.

The development of a human rights approach to modern slavery

Subsequent to the Palermo Protocol, in 2002, the UN High Commissioner for Human Rights highlighted the link between human rights and human trafficking. He recommended a number of principles and guidelines 'to promote and facilitate the integration of a human rights perspective into national, regional and international anti-trafficking laws, policies and interventions' (OCHR 2002: 2). The principles and guidelines document is important as it established human trafficking as a crime linked to human rights abuses. It suggested that victims of trafficking could be identified based on an infringement of their rights, for example, victims lacked freedom of movement, were subject to inhuman or degrading treatment or gendered violence, were denied access to health care, and/or experienced unjust conditions of work. Moreover, it stipulated that all states had a responsibility to identify victims in order to safeguard them from further abuse and to aid their recovery from the consequences of human rights violations. The principles and guidelines document also set out how a human rights perspective could be integrated within prevention strategies and criminal justice responses, as well as schemes to protect and support victims. From a law enforcement standpoint, adopting a human rights perspective in relation to how police interact with victims became recognised as a necessary condition for victims to be willing to participate in a criminal justice investigation and prosecution.

The 2005 European Convention and the 2011 EU Directive on Preventing and Combating Trafficking in Human Beings and Protecting Its Victims (EU Directive) display the influence of these principles as they both enshrine a human rights perspective. In fact, the European Convention (see also Chapters One and Ten) preamble states: 'trafficking in human beings constitutes a violation of human rights and an offence to the dignity and the integrity of the human being'. Article 12 of the Convention was clearly designed to respond to these violations as it placed an obligation on governments to adopt measures to assist victims in their physical, psychological and social recovery. It lists the forms of assistance that should be provided, including subsistence, appropriate and safe accommodation, access to emergency medical treatment, counselling, legal advice and access to education for children. However, the gateway to support was identification as a victim of human trafficking, and the European Convention proposed a legal framework with competent authorities capable of performing this task. The EU Directive includes similar Articles and thus places these duties on all EU member states.

These international instruments demonstrate policy change as they placed more attention on states' obligations in relation to victims, including their responsibilities to protect them and to meet their individual needs, than the framework provided by the Palermo Protocol. Gallagher (2013) argues that the UN High Commissioner for Human Rights pushed the Council of Europe to make the protection of victims obligatory, an approach endorsed by NGOs.

Citing concerns about support provisions acting as 'pull factors' to encourage human trafficking, the 2005 Labour government initially expressed reservations about signing the European Convention. However, pressure from stakeholders (Home Office and Scottish Executive 2006) was effective and the UK ratified the Convention in 2008. Following consultation with experts and a review of practices in other EU member states, the Home Office adopted a 45-day reflection and recovery period for victims instead of the minimum 30 days stipulated in the Convention, and allowed for an extension of the recovery period based on individual need. This support and the possibility to grant a one-year residence permit were used to 'demonstrate the Government's commitment to putting victim care and protection at the heart of our human trafficking strategy' (Home Office and Scottish Executive 2008: 3). The ATMG (2013) suggests that this was a rhetorical flourish as it identified significant flaws in the National Referral Mechanism (NRM) introduced to identify victims of human trafficking. It provided evidence of delayed and discriminatory decision-making, and of inadequate provision for victims, particularly after the 45-day reflection period. The UK's capacity to respond to potential victims' needs during police operations, as well as during the identification and recovery process, also required improvement. NGOs, including the Poppy Project, were identified to support victims in the short and medium term, and demonstrate the important role played by NGOs, continuing to this day.[4]

A further impetus to policy development in the UK came from the 2011 EU Directive. It reinforced the human rights approach set out in the European Convention, as well as adopting many of the Convention's measures. However, public and political pressure was necessary to get the Coalition government to sign the EU Directive. Tactics used included a petition signed by 47,000 people that was handed in to No. 10 Downing Street (ASI 2011).

Two Articles in the EU Directive are of particular importance in the UK context as they have enabled lawyers to hold the British government to account for inadequate provision for victims. Article 11 mandated that member states incorporate minimum standards of assistance into national law, and Article 12 stated that victims should have access to legal counselling and legal representation, including for the purpose of claiming compensation (see, eg, Leigh Day 2015).

Implementation of policy on support and assistance to victims

While there is some acceptance that the UK and devolved governments have an obligation to meet the needs of victims, in reality, it is NGOs that have played a significant role in providing services to support them.[5] NGOs not only deliver the government-funded 45-day reflection and recovery service (Salvation Army 2016), but also provide additional services, through charitable donations, volunteer time and expertise, illustrating public interest in modern slavery. However, there is evidence of an implementation gap, as GRETA (2012) noted, with a number of concerns about the quality and availability of services that the Council of Europe considered necessary to support victims of human rights abuses. They referred to a lack of appropriate accommodation and the difficulty in obtaining specialist services, including interpretation and legal assistance, stating that it was NGOs who often had to use their own funds to provide these services.

One of the factors that is likely to have influenced the quality and extent of statutory provision is the budget. In their second evaluation of the European Convention, GRETA (2016) noted the increasing number of victims receiving support in the UK, from 550 in 2012/13 to 1,097 in 2014/15. However, it also stated that the annual support contract of the Salvation Army remained at £4 million in the years 2013 to 2015. This evidence suggested that the government is not bearing the full cost of provision, but relies on NGOs to meet the shortfall for both immediate needs and longer-term support to help in the reintegration process. GRETA, as well as the HTF, which established care standards for survivors of modern slavery (Andreatta et al 2015), have pressed for improved provision.

The enhancement of a regulatory response

Trafficking for labour exploitation and forced labour have been made criminal offences. These practices can also be viewed as extreme forms of labour abuse and exploitation (see Geddes et al 2013). The UK developed a regulatory framework for this purpose that gives workers rights and should protect them from harm in the workplace. The framework is based on national labour standards, coupled with agencies responsible for promoting compliance and for enforcing the standards through civil and criminal remedies.[6]

An event, the drowning of 23 Chinese cockle-pickers in 2004 in Morecambe Bay, provided the impetus for further action. The deaths of these workers, supplied by a gangmaster, received headline news, and the resulting moral outrage created sufficient political momentum for Parliament to introduce additional regulation of the labour market in order to protect vulnerable workers. The Gangmasters (Licensing) Act 2004 established the Gangmasters Licensing Authority (GLA), with the aim of safeguarding the welfare of the worker. It was tasked with setting up a rigorous licensing system for labour providers in four sectors: agriculture, horticulture, shellfish gathering and associated processing and packaging. When it was set up, the GLA's main tool to ensure compliance with labour standards was to refuse a licence or to revoke it, which meant that labour providers were in breach of the law if they continued to supply labour. Where gangmasters operated illegally or infringed standards, which included trafficking for labour exploitation or engaging in forced labour practices, the GLA cooperated with the police to carry out a criminal investigation and use criminal justice remedies. Thus, the GLA had a range of civil as well as criminal sanctions aimed to prevent labour exploitation or act as a deterrent. However, Paul Broadbent, the first Chief Executive of the GLA, indicated that the sanctions used against people who engaged in modern slavery practices were insufficient to act as a deterrent. The fines were derisory in relation to the profits made from labour exploitation. As a result, the GLA lobbied the Crown Prosecution Service (CPS) 'to make sure that bosses who pay workers poverty wages and force them to work long hours in appalling conditions get more stringent sentences' (Dugan 2013).

Additional pressure on the Coalition government to take action to prevent practices that fuelled modern slavery came from GRETA and the Slavery Working Group set up by the Centre for Social Justice. GRETA identified the fragmentary nature of regulation, which meant that many workers in many sectors had limited recourse to protection, and, as a result, presented opportunities for labour exploitation. GRETA proposed extending the GLA's remit to cover other industries, like hospitality and construction, which posed a risk in relation to modern slavery. The report produced by the Slavery Working Group (2013) made a similar recommendation. It expressed concern that gangmasters would move away from food production and packaging and into sectors that were subject to much less scrutiny, particularly by the GLA. According to the GLA, criminal activity would be more difficult to identify and eradicate.

While licensing is the core business of the GLA, recognition of the scale of the problem, the downward pressure on suppliers in these sectors to reduce costs and concern about the operation of organised crime gangs have meant increased focus on joint operations with the police. These are intended to identify and protect vulnerable workers, instigate criminal justice measures to punish offenders, and act as a deterrent by increasing risk and reducing profit. The GLA informed the APPG in 2015 that four criminal business models were operating in relation to labour exploitation – the 'chancer', 'the employer', 'the intermediary' and the 'organised crime group' – suggesting that they would 'require a differing approach to prevention, protection, pursuance and preparedness' (GLA 2016: 2). One of these was extending their powers to search premises, to retain evidence, to detain suspects and to fully investigate instances of potential human trafficking and slavery. Members of the APPG (2015) agreed to propose appropriate amendments and their actions, alongside much wider lobbying, helped achieve the desired outcomes in the Immigration Act 2016, which transformed the GLA into the Gangmasters and Labour Abuse Authority (GLAA), with expanded powers and an expanded remit to cover other sectors that posed risks to vulnerable workers.

However, Focus on Labour Exploitation (FLEX 2015, 2016) and other organisations have expressed concern about other elements of the Immigration Act 2016 that make it a criminal offence for people to undertake work if they have an irregular immigration status. This contradictory policy makes some groups more vulnerable to labour exploitation and forced labour as their immigration status can be used as a means of coercing and controlling them to accept situations of abuse and exploitation.

As discussed, the UK developed three approaches to tackling the problem of modern slavery. However, evidence pointed to the inadequate implementation of policy, but also to poor policy design. As a result, there were a number of recommendations over the years to develop new legislation and non–legislative policy initiatives. The following section explores the factors and actors that encouraged policy change.

Development of the MSA

In 2011, the government undertook 'to review human trafficking legislation to ensure effective prosecution of traffickers' (HM Government 2012: 5). At the same time, GRETA (2012) asked the UK government in 2012 to consider the consequences of having numerous pieces of legislation covering human trafficking. Interestingly, at this time, the government did not feel that a new Bill was necessary or proportionate. The GRETA report might have helped build a case, pressure reinforced by the ATMG (2012) report. However, it was the report produced by the Centre for Social Justice (Slavery Working Group 2013), a think tank aligned to the Conservative Party, that had the most political traction, and was unsurprisingly acknowledged by Theresa May, the Home Secretary, as influential in her thinking and subsequent legislative action. The policy recommendations set out in the report were evidenced-based, arising from information provided by 180 individuals and organisations from across all sectors. The report proposed new legislation, the MSA, to consolidate all human trafficking and modern slavery offences, which 'would have both practical and symbolic significance' (Slavery Working Group 2013: 155).

It seems that, at this time, the problem, policy and political streams that create a window of opportunity to get an issue on the policy agenda came together (Dorey 2005). The problem had been identified in reports produced by GRETA (2012), the Inter-Departmental Ministerial Group on Human Trafficking (Secretary of State for the Home Department 2012) and the CSJ (Slavery Working Group 2013), as well as many of the JRF programme reports. Policy solutions had also been proposed by GRETA, the ATMG (2010, 2012, 2013) and the CSJ (Slavery Working Group 2013). The political appetite to take action gathered momentum based on the interest of the Home Secretary and supported by her special advisor, Fiona Hill. By October 2013, new legislation was in the planning stages but the Home Secretary took the unusual step of setting up an evidence review instead of asking the Home Office to produce a White Paper setting out the government's vision.

The evidence review heard from a wide variety of stakeholders, including NGOs, senior police officers, lawyers and international experts. While it supported the limited range of issues in the proposed Bill, which had mainly a criminal justice focus, it also sought to shift the emphasis to protecting victims of slavery (Butler-Sloss et al 2013). The evidence review did not impact the content of the Draft Modern Slavery Bill (Home Office 2013) as both were produced in December 2013; however, it is likely to have influenced the thinking of a number of MPs and peers who contributed to subsequent debates in Parliament.

The appointment of a joint committee to scrutinise the Draft Modern Slavery Bill, later acknowledged to be very weak, provided further opportunities to build cross-party support and to amend it. Significant lobbying took place during the 10 months that the Bill went through the parliamentary process. Parliamentary briefings by the ATMG (2015), FLEX (Robinson 2015) and Kalayaan (2015), and evidence submitted by a range of interests (eg FLMG 2014), attest to ongoing engagement to improve the Bill, as do briefings on the proposed transparency in supply chains clause produced for the House of Commons and the House of Lords by CORE (2014).

As a result of their evidence-gathering, the Joint Committee on the Draft Modern Slavery Bill (2014) recommended significant changes to the contents of the Bill. The initial draft focused on offences, prevention orders and the Anti-Slavery Commissioner, but the Joint Committee report sought to: put victim support and assistance on a statutory footing; create separate offences of exploiting and trafficking a child; ensure victims were not prosecuted for crimes that they were forced to commit while enslaved; strengthen the asset recovery regime to seize illicit gains made from modern slavery; ensure the independence of the Anti-Slavery Commissioner and broaden its functions to include victim protection and partnerships; and make it obligatory that businesses above a certain size audit modern slavery in their supply chains. The government did not accept a number of these recommendations, resulting in considerable debate in both the House of Commons and House of Lords. The wrangling was cut short by an agreement to a compromise made in order to pass the legislation before Parliament was dissolved for a general election in May 2015. Thus, while the Home Secretary considered the MSA to be 'world-leading', the lack of adequate support for victims, particularly child victims, the continued perilous position of overseas domestic workers, the persistence of a discriminatory and inadequate NRM, and the voluntary nature of tackling modern slavery in supply chains point to major shortfalls in the legislation. (Chapters Seven, Six and Eight, respectively, critically assess the implications of the MSA in terms of victim protection and the situation of overseas domestic workers, children, and transparency in supply chains.)

These inadequacies, of course, do not appear in the House of Commons Library Briefing Paper, which summarised key developments arising from the MSA, stating that it:

- Consolidates and clarifies the existing offences of slavery and human trafficking and increases the maximum penalty for these offences.
- Provides for two new civil preventative orders, the Slavery and Trafficking Prevention Order and the Slavery and Trafficking Risk Order.
- Creates new maritime enforcement powers, so that the police can pursue traffickers on ships.
- Sets up the Office of the Independent Anti-Slavery Commissioner.
- Brings in measures focused to support and protect victims, including a defence for slavery or trafficking

victims and special measures for witnesses in criminal
proceedings.
- Requires certain businesses to say what they are doing to
  eliminate slavery and trafficking from their supply chains
  and their own businesses. (Brown 2016: 3)

The majority of provisions only extend to England and Wales. Scotland
and Northern Ireland passed their own legislation on modern slavery
in 2015. Brotherton explores the different approaches taken by the
devolved governments, particularly in relation to victim protection
(see Chapter Four).

Current and future concerns about the criminal justice response

The MSA had a number of significant effects on the criminal justice
response. First, it harmonised human trafficking, forced labour, slavery
and servitude offences, and gave them the same sentencing protocol.
Second, it increased the sanctions that could be imposed against
those convicted from a maximum of 14 years to life imprisonment.
Third, it provided a clearer framework for police and the CPS to
determine modern slavery charges, and thus increase prosecution for
modern slavery offences. Fourth, it introduced Slavery and Trafficking
Prevention Orders (STPOs) and Slavery and Trafficking Risk Orders
(STROs), measures intended to prevent and deter modern slavery.

Nevertheless, there remain significant gaps in the Act that make it
harder to fulfil the aims of a criminal justice response. While some
police forces may be keen to prosecute offenders under the MSA,
the cooperation of victims in criminal investigations is often key to a
successful outcome. Victims may not be willing to engage with the
police in the early stages of their recovery and may not be willing to
receive a referral for support through the NRM as it may have negative
consequences for them. First, as recipients of NRM support, they are
not able to work and thus do not have the remittances that they need
to send home to their families. Second, they may be concerned about
retribution against their family by members of trafficking networks.
Third, they may be concerned about long-term outcomes as they
are likely to be deported at the end of the process, especially if they
are non-EEA nationals, which undermines their migratory aims of
helping their families. Thus, the MSA does not reflect the complexity
involved in aiding victim recovery and in engaging with a criminal
investigation.

Partnership is also a missing element within the Act as it emphasises the role of law enforcement at the expense of other agencies that have a role to play, for example, the GLAA, local authorities and Her Majesty's Revenue and Customs (HMRC). Changes proposed to widen the remit of the GLA and to enhance its powers were not included in the MSA. Subsequently, they were embedded in the Immigration Act 2016, which enables the reformed GLAA to work more effectively on its own to prevent labour exploitation or in conjunction with law enforcement to pursue criminal investigations for modern slavery offences.

The MSA also sidesteps the demand for sexual services and the problem of sexual exploitation. Northern Ireland, on the other hand, introduced a clause to make the buying of sex a criminal offence in their Human Trafficking and Exploitation Act 2015. It joined several countries, including Sweden, Norway, Iceland and France, in criminalising men who purchase sex, believing that this legislation will have a deterrent effect (Topping 2014).

It is evident that the MSA has strengths and weaknesses as a policy aimed at improving the criminal justice response. Caroline Haughey's (2016) review of the new criminal justice provisions, at the behest of Theresa May, then Home Secretary, raises questions about its implementation. Haughey found that the MSA raised the profile of modern slavery across law enforcement. Moreover, police officers indicated that the new offences brought clarity in relation to charging. However, Haughey noted that police lacked awareness of modern slavery, its indicators or how to respond, and there was thus inconsistency in the police response, a view confirmed in a recent inspection. Once again, the evidence suggests that policy implementation is the issue. While modern slavery is a key priority for the Prime Minister and the Home Office, and features as a key priority for the NCA, decisions about police priorities are actually made locally by Police and Crime Commissioners. They may not believe that modern slavery is a priority for their area, or may not feel that, in the face of policing cuts, putting resources into modern slavery investigations, which tend to be complex, time-consuming and costly, is the best use of resources.

In response to Haughey's concern about police engagement, the Home Secretary asked Her Majesty's Inspectorate of Constabulary, Fire and Rescue Services (HMICFRS) to undertake an inspection of all 43 English and Welsh police forces in terms of their response to modern slavery. Its report (HMICFRS 2017) contrasted the strengthening of legislation with the inconsistent and often poor response by law enforcement agencies charged with implementation. The NCA did not provide adequate leadership in the fight against modern slavery, nor were they effective in collecting and collating intelligence and transmitting it to the appropriate police forces for action. At a local level, the inspectors found that police officers lacked adequate understanding of the law and of indicators of modern slavery that would allow them to identify victims and thereby offer them protection and a chance to obtain justice. In addition, they expressed concern about the quality of criminal investigations, which meant that cases were not adequately investigated. They identified good victim support in some forces but also felt that this had to be attached to efforts to prevent 'the creation of future victims by dismantling the networks and holding offenders to account' (HMICFRS 2017: 11). Police forces tended to be reactive rather than proactive, and few had developed the kinds of partnership necessary to be more effective in their work. In fact, they found that some police officers felt that modern slavery was not a problem in their area or did not want to 'turn over the stone' because they were worried about the demand and resulting costs. The HMICFRS made a number of recommendations to improve leadership, intelligence, victim identification and initial response, crime reporting, investigation, prevention, and learning. There are plans for a follow-up inspection in order to review the extent to which the MSA review and HMICFRS recommendations are being implemented by law enforcement agencies.

There are costs attached to improving the capabilities of police forces in England and Wales to respond to modern slavery. Some of these have been borne by the Home Office, which awarded an £8.5 million grant from the Police Transformation Fund to Devon and Cornwall in 2016. Its national Modern Slavery Police Transformation Unit (MSPTU) has employed 50 dedicated analysts, specialist and investigators to develop and share intelligence, good practice in investigations and learning from police forces and academics. It is too early to determine what impact the MSPTU will have on victim identification, criminal investigations and prosecutions, and partnership working. However, a recent piece of investigative journalism adds to concerns about the effectiveness of the MSA in relation to facilitating a criminal justice response. While the number of reports related to modern slavery have increased substantially since the MSA was introduced, the numbers charged with these offences remains small (Marsh 2018).

Looking ahead, a big challenge is the impact of Brexit on the UK's ability to tackle modern slavery (also discussed in Chapters One and Ten). The UK's membership of the EU has played an important role in its criminal justice response to modern slavery as it has made use of a variety of information sharing and police cooperation mechanisms that the UK has been instrumental in developing over the past 10 years (House of Lords European Union Committee 2016). According to the Inter-Departmental Ministerial Group on Modern Slavery (HM Government et al 2016: 22), UK police forces are 'the most proactive in Europe in fighting trafficking and slavery', having submitted more intelligence and information to its databases, and established more Joint Investigation Teams (JITs), than any other EU member state. JITs have enabled UK police forces to work in conjunction with their counterparts in other EU countries to provide a joined-up approach and thus instigate action in countries of origin against those who recruit and transport victims of modern slavery, as well as those in the UK who harbour, control and exploit them. However, Brexit is likely to have an impact on the UK's inclusion in these EU institutions and mechanisms, which will undermine its capability to investigate transnational crime and to work effectively with EU member states (see also Chapters Four, Five and Ten). Not surprisingly, the law enforcement community and the CPS have made a strong case for continued participation or an adequate replacement during the Brexit process (House of Lords European Union Committee 2016).

The ATMG (2017) briefing paper on the consequences of Brexit argued that participation was necessary to ensure that the UK fulfilled its obligations under Article 32 of the European Convention. However, it noted that despite the government's desire to maintain collaborative arrangements, these may be difficult to negotiate as long as the UK seeks to withdraw from the EU Court of Justice. The ATMG also looked at the importance of the EU in protecting workers' rights and labour standards. They argued that the UK government's propensity to support deregulation of labour and to endorse a flexible labour market might result in Britain not continuing to support legislation protecting workers' rights. Workers might become more vulnerable to exploitative work practices, and this is particularly the case for migrants as the Immigration Act 2016 introduced the offence of illegal working. The pull of low-skilled jobs in the UK, combined with restricted means of legally migrating, will place citizens of the EU at greater risk of becoming victims of modern slavery. In the possible post-Brexit labour climate, labour inspection authorities like the GLAA, the National Minimum Wage enforcement teams and the Health and Safety Executive would need to have increased capacity and funding.

Evidence suggests that Brexit poses risks to international law enforcement cooperation based on a criminal justice approach to modern slavery. The ATMG also made a strong case that Brexit poses a threat to the UK's efforts to tackle modern slavery linked to labour exploitation and requires a stronger regulatory response.

Conclusion

It is evident that the UK has, over time, instituted a wide range of policy responses to the problem of modern slavery. International policy instruments – the Palermo Protocol, the ILO Forced Labour Convention and the European Convention – played key roles in promoting a criminal justice response to modern slavery, but also in developing victim-centred responses to reflect human rights abuses linked to these crimes. However, it is also clear that a wide range of stakeholders, like ASI, civil society organisations involved in supporting victims and monitoring bodies like GRETA and the ATMG, as well as some politically active academics, have pushed the government to sign up to relevant Conventions and to meet their subsequent obligations. The 2000s produced legislation giving the police tools to tackle modern slavery but human trafficking action plans point to an implementation gap, with police lacking sufficient awareness of what human trafficking entails or how to respond. Additionally, it has not been considered part of core police business. Recognition of the human rights abuses experienced by victims of human trafficking, alongside the development of service provision by NGOs, helped to facilitate the victim-centred approach promoted by the European Convention. However, there has been concern about the way in which the government has institutionalised victim care in the NRM. In addition, the ATMG and HTF have pointed to significant inadequacies in the support provided to victims. Moreover, unlike Scotland and Northern Ireland, the UK has not transposed victim support into legislation and lawyers have thus had to use the EU Directive to hold the government to account over its obligations under European law.

A third policy response related to regulatory mechanisms aims to protect workers' rights and to tackle labour abuse and exploitation. The scandal arising from the death of Chinese cockle-pickers led to the establishment of the GLA (now GLAA), which, alongside other regulatory bodies like the HMRC Minimum Wage Team, have played increasingly important roles in preventing modern slavery, in identifying victims and in investigating and sanctioning those found in breach of the law. However, the level of resources available to these bodies undermines their ability to be fully effective.

Criticism of UK policy and its implementation, by GRETA, ATMG and the CSJ, helped put new legislation on the political agenda. Modern slavery became a priority issue for the-then Home Secretary. While her Bill received much cross-party support, its weaknesses, reflecting its focus on criminal justice remedies, were partly amended during the parliamentary process. However, a number of criticisms remained after the Bill was pushed through before the elections in May 2015. Nevertheless, the MSA consolidated existing offences and harmonised support for victims of all forms of modern slavery. It also introduced two new civil preventative orders, which provided additional remedies for police in relation to offenders, and it sought to ensure that those compelled to commit offences under the duress of modern slavery were treated as victims.

The MSA promoted a criminal justice response to modern slavery but the evidence points to a big implementation gap, with the NCA and police forces failing to understand risk, to identify victims, to offer high-quality criminal investigations and to pursue charges through the courts. In fact, modern slavery is not something that the police can handle on their own as it requires partnership working. In addition, investigations are time-consuming and resource-heavy, which means that it is not a police priority in some areas, despite political advocacy. In the future, tackling the transnational nature of some modern slavery, particularly linked to the EU, is likely to become more difficult as a result of Brexit. The UK will not have the same access to or influence within Europol, nor will it be able to access a variety of intelligence databases. The possibilities for European law enforcement cooperation and partnerships that are significant for tackling modern slavery remain unclear.

Notes

[1] See, for example, the Joseph Rowntree Foundation programme on forced labour (available at: www.jrf.org.uk/search?query=forced+labour) and the reports by Kalayaan (available at: www.kalayaan.org.uk) on overseas domestic workers.

[2] Information about potential victims of human trafficking/modern slavery is recorded if they are referred to the National Referral Mechanism (NRM). NRM figures are available from the NCA – see, for example, 'National Referral Mechanism statistics end of year summary 2016' (available at: http://nationalcrimeagency.gov.uk/publications/national-referral-mechanism-statistics/2016-nrm-statistics/788-national-referral-mechanism-statistics-end-of-year-summary-2016) – but they are

substantial underestimates as not all potential victims consent to being referred.

3 A London-based feminist NGO aiming to empower women who were subject to violence, exploitation or discrimination.

4 Many NGOs expanded their remit to provide support to victims of modern slavery or were specifically created to provide support. These include the Salvation Army, Medaille Trust, Trafficking Awareness Raising Alliance in Scotland, Migrant Helpline for victims of labour exploitation, Love 146, Hope for Justice, Hestia, Unseen, Helen Bamber Foundation, Baobab, Barnardos and Rahab.

5 Government action plans and strategy documents published in 2007, 2008, 2009, 2011 and 2014 describe the support arrangements.

6 The agencies include the Health and Safety Executive (HSE), the Employment Agency Standards Inspectorate (EAS), Her Majesty's Revenue and Customs (HMRC) and the Gangmasters Licensing Authority (GLA). For a discussion of the strengths and weaknesses of these agencies, see Balch (2012) and Chapter Seven.

References

Anderson, B. and Rogaly, B. (2005) 'Forced labour and migration to the UK'. Available at: www.ituc-csi.org/IMG/pdf/Forced_labour_in_UK_12-2009.pdf (accessed 14 August 2017).

Andreatta, C., Witkin, R. and Robjant, K. (2015) *Trafficking survivor care standards* (2nd edn), London: Human Trafficking Foundation.

APPG (All-Party Parliamentary Group on Human Trafficking and Modern Slavery) (2015) 'Minutes', 1 December, House of Lords.

ASI (Anti-Slavery International) (2011) 'Anti-slavery campaign victory as the government signs up to the EU Trafficking Directive'. Available at: www.antislavery.org/campaign-victory-government-signs-eu-trafficking-directive/

ATMG (Anti-Trafficking Monitoring Group) (2010) *Wrong kind of victim? One year on: An analysis of UK measures to protect trafficked persons*, London: Anti-Trafficking Monitoring Group.

ATMG (2012) *In the dock: Examining the UK's criminal justice response to trafficking*, London: Anti-Trafficking Monitoring Group.

ATMG (2013) *Hidden in plain sight: Three years on: Updated analysis of UK measures to protect trafficked persons*, London: Anti-Trafficking Monitoring Group.

ATMG (2015) 'Modern Slavery Bill report stage briefing – House of Lords February 2015 victim protection & the NRM'. Available from www.antislavery.org

ATMG (2017) *Brexit & the UK's fight against modern slavery: A briefing by the Anti-Trafficking Monitoring Group*, London: Anti-Trafficking Monitoring Group.

Bacchi, C. (1999) *Women, policy and politics: The construction of policy problems*, London: Sage.

Balch, A. (2012) 'Regulation and enforcement to tackle forced labour in the UK: a systematic response?', JRF Programme Paper. Available at: www.jrf.org.uk/report/regulation-and-enforcement-tackle-forced-labour-uk-systematic-response

Barton, A. and Johns, N. (2013) *The policy-making process in the criminal justice system*, London: Routledge.

Brown, T. (2016) 'MSA 2015: recent developments', House of Commons Library Briefing Paper. Available at: http://researchbriefings.parliament.uk/ResearchBriefing/Summary/CBP-7656

Butler-Sloss, E., Field, F. and Randall, J. (2013) 'Establishing Britain as a world leader in the fight against modern slavery: report of the Modern Slavery Bill evidence review'. Available at: www.frankfield.co.uk/upload/docs/Modern%20Slavery%20Bill%20Evidence%20Review.pdf

CORE (2014) 'Briefing for report stage of the Modern Slavery Bill transparency in the supply chain', 3 November. Available at: http://corporate-responsibility.org/wp-content/uploads/2014/11/Coalition-briefing-for-MSB-Report-Stage-3-Nov-2014.pdf

CORE (2016) 'Beyond compliance: effective reporting under the MSA: a civil society guide for commercial organisations on the transparency in supply chains clause'. Available at: www.labourexploitation.org/publications/beyond-compliance-effective-reporting-under-modern-slavery-act

CPS (Crown Prosecution Service) (no date) 'Legal guidance: prostitution and exploitation of prostitution'. Available at: www.cps.gov.uk/legal/p_to_r/prostitution_and_exploitation_of_prostitution/ (accessed 21 August 2017).

Craig, G., Gaus, A., Wilkinson, M., Skrivankova, K. and McQuade, A. (2007) *Contemporary slavery in the UK: Overview and key issues*, York: Joseph Rowntree Foundation.

Dorey, P. (2005) *Policy making in Britain: An introduction*, London: Sage.

Dugan, E. (2013) 'It pays to use slave labour, says watchdog: Gangmasters Licensing Authority is dismayed at tiny fines levied on unscrupulous employers', *Independent*, 22 June. Available at: www. independent.co.uk/news/uk/home-news/it-pays-to-use-slave-labour-says-watchdog-8669797.html

FLEX (Focus on Labour Exploitation) (2015) 'Combating labour exploitation through labour inspection: policy blueprint'. Available at: www.labourexploitation.org/sites/default/files/publications/ Flex%20Labour%20Inspection%20Blueprint.pdf

FLEX (2016) 'FLEX briefing: Immigration Bill part one – January 2016'. Available at: www.labourexploitation.org/sites/default/files/ publications/FLEXImmBillBriefFINAL.pdf

FLMG (Forced Labour Monitoring Group) (2014) *What next for forced labour?*, Durham: Forced Labour Monitoring Group.

Gallagher, A. (2013) *The international law of human trafficking*, Cambridge: Cambridge University Press.

Geddes, A., Craig, G. and Scott, S. (2013) 'Forced labour in the UK', JRF Programme Paper. Available at: www.jrf.org.uk/report/forced-labour-uk

GLA (Gangmasters Licensing Authority) (2016) 'All Party Parliamentary Group – human trafficking and modern slavery', GLA briefing, January.

Goodey, J. (2008) 'Human trafficking: sketchy data and policy responses', *Criminology and Criminal Justice*, 8: 421–42.

Grant, W. (1989) *Pressure groups, politics and democracy in Britain*, London: Philip Allen.

GRETA (Group of Experts on Action against Trafficking in Human Beings) (2012) 'Report concerning the implementation of the Council of Europe Convention on Action against Trafficking in Human Beings by the United Kingdom: first evaluation round'. Available at: https://rm.coe.int/168067a080

GRETA (2016) 'Report concerning the implementation of the Council of Europe Convention on Action against Trafficking in Human Beings by the United Kingdom: second evaluation round'. Available at: https://rm.coe.int/16806abcdc

Haughey, C. (2016) 'The MSA review: one year on'. Available at: www.gov.uk/government/publications/modern-slavery-act-2015-review-one-year-on (accessed 24 August 2017).

HM Government (2011) *Human trafficking: The government's strategy*, London: TSO.

HM Government (2012) *Report on the internal review of human trafficking legislation*, London: TSO.

HM Government (2014) 'Modern slavery strategy'. Available at: www.gov.uk/government/uploads/system/uploads/attachment_data/file/383764/Modern_Slavery_Strategy_FINAL_DEC2015.pdf

HM Government, Ministry of Justice, The Scottish Government and Llywodraeth Cymru/Welsh Government (2016) '2016 report of the Inter-Departmental Ministerial Group on Modern Slavery'. Available at: www.gov.uk/government/uploads/system/uploads/attachment_data/file/559690/Modern_Slavery_IDMG_Report_2016.pdf

HMICFRS (Her Majesty's Inspectorate of Constabulary, Fire and Rescue Services) (2017) 'Stolen freedom: the policing response to modern slavery and human trafficking'. Available at: www.justiceinspectorates.gov.uk/hmicfrs/wp-content/uploads/stolen-freedom-the-policing-response-to-modern-slavery-and-human-trafficking.pdf

Home Office (2008) 'Tackling the demand for prostitution'. Available at: http://webarchive.nationalarchives.gov.uk/20100408141223/http://www.homeoffice.gov.uk/documents/tackling-demand2835.pdf?view=Binary (accessed 21 August 2017).

Home Office (2013) 'Draft Modern Slavery Bill', Cm 8770. Available at: www.gov.uk/government/uploads/system/uploads/attachment_data/file/266165/Draft_Modern_Slavery_Bill.pdf

Home Office and Scottish Executive (2006) 'Tackling human trafficking – summary of responses to the consultation on proposals for a UK action plan'. Available at: http://webarchive.nationalarchives.gov.uk/20100408132024/http://www.homeoffice.gov.uk/documents/cons-2006-tack-human-trafficking/cons-summary-210606-trafficking2835.pdf?view=Binary

Home Office and Scottish Executive (2007) *UK action plan on tackling human trafficking*, March, London: Home Office.

Home Office and Scottish Executive (2008) *Update to the UK action plan on tackling human trafficking*, July, London: Home Office.

Home Office and Scottish Government (2009) *Update to the UK action plan on tackling human trafficking*, October, London: Home Office.

House of Lords European Union Committee (2016) 'Brexit: future UK–EU security and police cooperation', 7th report of Session 2016–17, HL Paper 77.

Joint Committee on the Draft Modern Slavery Bill (2014) 'Report'. Available at: https://publications.parliament.uk/pa/jt201314/jtselect/jtslavery/166/16602.htm

Kalayaan (2015) 'Time to untie migrant domestic workers: briefing for report stage of the Modern Slavery Bill in the House of Lords'. Available at: www.kalayaan.org.uk/wp-content/uploads/2014/09/Kalayaan-Peers-briefing-Report-Stage.pdf

Kelly, L. and Regan, L. (2000) *Stopping traffic: Exploring the extent of, and responses to, trafficking in women for sexual exploitation in the UK*, Police Research Series Paper 125, London: Home Office Policing and Reducing Crime Unit.

Lee, M. (2011) *Trafficking and global crime control*, London: Sage.

Leigh Day (2015) 'High Court to hear case against government over "support duty" for trafficking victims'. Available at: www.leighday.co.uk/News/2015/December-2015/High-Court-to-hear-case-against-Government-over-su

Liberty and Anti-Slavery International (2009) 'Joint briefing on the Coroners and Justice Bill for the report stage of the House of Lords: servitude and forced labour amendment'. Available at: www.liberty-human-rights.org.uk/sites/default/files/joint-liberty-asi-report-stage-briefing-on-forced-labour-lords.pdf

Malloch, M., Robertson, L. and Forbes, E. (2017) *Evidence assessment of the impacts of the criminalisation of the purchase of sex: A review*, Scottish Centre for Crime and Justice Research, Edinburgh: The Scottish Government.

Marsh, S. (2018) 'Seven UK police forces report zero charges under anti-slavery law', *The Guardian*, 21 January. Available at: www.theguardian.com/world/2018/jan/21/seven-uk-police-forces-report-zero-charges-under-anti-slavery-law

Matolcsi, A. (2017) 'Section 53A of the Sexual Offences Act 2003 (inserted by section 14 of the Police and Crime Act 2009) on "paying for the sexual services of a prostitute subject to coercion etc": implementation and the views of practitioners', PhD thesis, University of Bristol.

OHCR (Office of the High Commissioner for Human Rights) (2002) 'Recommended principles and guidelines on human rights and human trafficking'. Available at: www.ohchr.org/_layouts/15/WopiFrame.aspx?sourcedoc=/Documents/Publications/Traffickingen.pdf&action=default&DefaultItemOpen=1

Robinson, C. (2015) 'Claiming space for labour rights within the United Kingdom modern slavery crusade', *Anti-Trafficking Review*, 5: 129–43.

Salvation Army (2016) 'Supporting adult victims of modern slavery: update on the fifth year of the Salvation Army's victim care & coordination contract'. Available at: www.salvationarmy.org.uk/sites/default/files/media/year_5_report_1.pdf

Secretary of State for the Home Department (2012) 'First annual report of the Inter-Departmental Ministerial Group on Human Trafficking', Cm 8421. Available at: www.gov.uk/government/uploads/system/uploads/attachment_data/file/118116/human-trafficking-report.pdf

Silverman, B. (2014) 'Modern slavery: an application of multiple systems estimation'. Available at: www.gov.uk/government/uploads/system/uploads/attachment_data/file/386841/Modern_Slavery_an_application_of_MSE_revised.pdf

Skrivánková, K. (2006) *Trafficking for forced labour: UK country report*, London: Anti-Slavery International.

Slavery Working Group (2013) *It happens here: Equipping the United Kingdom to fight modern slavery*, London: Centre for Social Justice. Available at: www.centreforsocialjustice.org.uk/library/happens-equipping-united-kingdom-fight-modern-slavery

Topping, A. (2014) 'Northern Ireland prostitution ban divides opinion', *The Guardian*, 23 October. Available at: www.theguardian.com/society/2014/oct/23/northern-ireland-prostitution-ban-reaction

UNODC (UN Office of Drugs and Crime) (2016) *Global report on trafficking in persons*, Vienna: UNODC.

US Department of State (2017) 'Trafficking in persons report June 2017'. Available at: www.state.gov/documents/organization/271339.pdf

Wilcox, A., Christmann, K., Rogerson, M. and Birch, P. (2009) 'Tackling the demand for prostitution: a rapid evidence assessment of the published research literature', Home Office Research Report 27.

THREE

Defeating 'modern slavery', reducing exploitation? The organisational and regulatory challenge

Alex Balch

Introduction

Are political promises to eradicate modern slavery, and to stamp out the criminals that Theresa May referred to as 'slave-drivers' (May 2017), empty and doomed to fail? Will they do nothing to reduce severe forms of exploitation? This would be the likely verdict of a growing group of scholars and activists who reject the political agenda on modern slavery, dismissing the UK's approach from first principles and denouncing it as reactionary and undermining human rights (O'Connell Davidson 2010, 2015). Others have questioned the appropriateness of the language of slavery (Dottridge 2017), rejecting, in particular, the equation with the historical (transatlantic) slave trade (Beutin 2017). This chapter focuses on the more practical question of the agenda's implementation and its effectiveness in addressing labour exploitation. It explores the shift from the pre- to the post-Modern Slavery Act (MSA) era. It examines the new enforcement practices and regulatory system in the context of the institutional and organisational environment that preceded it.

A significant indication of some of the problems of delivery was given by the recent National Audit Office (NAO 2017) report regarding the UK's strategy on modern slavery. This concluded that, in its current form, the system would be unlikely to achieve its main aim of significantly reducing modern slavery. It also noted the allocation of increasing funds, the growing thousands of individuals identified as victims and offered support, and the creation of a panoply of advisory bodies and stakeholder forums to execute the government's aim to eradicate it.[1] The question, then, becomes: what difference does the MSA, and associated policy, make, and to whom? To begin answering this question, we need to work out how to assess the main innovations and distinguish between the key outputs and outcomes of the modern slavery agenda, the former being the actions of government, the institutions created and the policy changes announced, and the latter being the effects of these actions. Only in this way, it is argued, can we place the new system against the criticisms and failings that beset previous approaches designed to tackle human trafficking (eg ATMG 2010, 2013).

The focus here is the system of regulation and enforcement constructed around modern slavery, and the wider context of the UK labour market perspective. This is slightly different from the NAO approach, which assesses the policy on its own terms. Hence, we will not explore whether the modern slavery agenda will actually eradicate modern slavery. The assumption here is that the answer to that question, as explained in other chapters in this book (see, eg, Chapters Four, Five and Nine), is a fairly resounding 'no'.

However, there are broader potential consequences of the intensification of political rhetoric around anti-slavery. There is a strong case for evaluating such consequences with the interests of all workers in global production networks in mind (these are, after all, the lofty ambitions of some of the supporters of the modern slavery agenda). However, in the space afforded by a single chapter, and given the UK focus of this book, it makes sense to narrow this analysis to organisations with the responsibility and the powers to regulate and enforce the legislation designed to counter modern slavery in the UK. Among other things, the chapter aims to pay close attention to implementation and the ways in which those implicated in this process have developed techniques according with their own organisational identity and interests while setting out to achieve the politicians' aims.

We first chart the short history from the early anti-trafficking strategy put in place by the Labour government in 2007 through the changes and reorganisations of the subsequent 10 years, including the launch of the modern slavery strategy in 2015 under then Home Secretary May. While focusing on the impacts felt by workers in the UK, this part will also take into account the position adopted by the UK in relation to international frameworks. The second section then focuses on the importance and potential impact of the creation of the most recent governance and enforcement structures – for example, the Director of Labour Market Enforcement (DLME) and the evolution of the Gangmasters Licensing Authority (GLA). As of May 2017, the GLA was rebranded as the Gangmasters and Labour Abuse Authority (GLAA) and has new powers to investigate serious exploitation across the whole UK labour market. The third section moves from outputs to outcomes, asking how we can best assess and evaluate the effectiveness of the modern slavery agenda.

Trafficking, forced labour or business and human rights?

In 2007, the UK government announced its first national strategy to tackle human trafficking. The approach was to treat the issue as serious organised crime, mainly affecting immigrants (HMG 2007). It came at a time of crisis for the Home Office following a number of scandals on the topic of immigration. As such, it can be seen as both a result of the opportunities that this created and a public relations (PR) exercise to restore a moral purpose for the government's internal security ministry (Balch and Geddes 2011). The strategy document included a long list of priorities, among them the pledge that tackling human trafficking would become a part of 'core policing' and that efforts would move forward with implementation characterised by a collaborative 'multi-agency' approach. The main agencies charged with implementing the strategy and regulating and enforcing the new rules were not dispersed across government, however. Those charged with the job were squarely within the security focus of the Home Office, with police and immigration services centre stage. The effectiveness of the resultant anti-trafficking regime was a function of the capacity of these two Home Office directorates to work together.

The exception to this was the GLA, an enforcement agency initially based in the Department for Environment, Food and Rural Affairs (DEFRA). The GLA had been set up in 2006, partly in reaction to the Morecambe Bay tragedy. The deaths of 23 cockle-pickers demonstrated that migrants were being ruthlessly exploited by labour providers in the shellfish sector, adding to evidence of exploitation of migrants in other parts of the UK's food supply chain (Scott et al 2013; TUC 2007). The GLA was therefore explicitly designed to deal with labour market exploitation, although it was immediately limited to a few sectors relating to food supply. The agency largely recruited inspectors from the ranks of retired police officers and set up intelligence and other systems in ways very closely reflecting standard police methods. It cooperated closely from the start with Her Majesty's Revenue and Customs (HMRC) (the taxation authority), with the collection of lost tax revenue a priority for the GLA (and its claims regarding value for money). Its focus on employment standards, and the licensing of labour providers to prevent labour exploitation, meant that the GLA aligned itself with the International Labour Organisation's (ILO's) large body of work on forced labour (and how to deal with the problems associated with brokers, middlemen and temporary agency working).

The ILO perspective on how to address labour exploitation was initially quite distinct from the anti-trafficking regime and the solutions it set out, based on the agreements of Palermo and the United Nations (UN) Convention against Transnational Organised Crime (hereafter, the Convention). Although the fight against 'human trafficking' has a long history, the definition agreed under the Palermo Protocol launched the so-called 'war on trafficking' in the 21st century (Balch 2015). Efforts to tackle forced labour have a tradition stretching back well before the start of the Cold War and can be seen as part of wider international cooperation to improve working conditions, albeit with a strong colonial flavour (Maul 2012). The contemporary linkage between trafficking and forced labour was forged when forced labour was included as one of the potential destinations or 'outcomes' for trafficked persons in the Palermo Protocol (for further discussion, see the Introduction and Chapter Two), thus opening a conduit to the ILO's substantial body of work around forced labour. The ILO had come to conceptualise forced labour as one extreme end of a continuum where decent work was at the other end (Scott 2017). However, the political attention drawn by the international anti-trafficking regime provided a new platform for the ILO's expertise. It became expedient for the ILO to intervene in the growing anti-trafficking movement, suggesting that forced labour could be used as an umbrella concept, covering all forms of trafficking.

Regardless of the organisational interests behind these manoeuvres, the arrival of the ILO in the anti-trafficking field provided a methodological contrast when one considers the kinds of state-led cooperation and security-based solutions suggested by the Palermo agreement. The ILO approach has always been to emphasise regulation of the labour market, chiefly via proactive labour inspections. It was natural, then, that the police and immigration service followed the Palermo 'recipe' to address human trafficking as serious organised crime – a pathological, rather than structural, diagnosis. The GLA's approach recognised that there were structural issues within the labour market that needed addressing; their inspectors used ILO indicators of forced labour to identify labour exploitation in their sectors (for the ILO indicators, see the Introduction). Moreover, this was in marked contrast to the previous labour market mechanism to deal with problematic or exploitative practices in the realm of temporary agency work, the Employment Agency Standards Inspectorate (EASI). EASI had around a dozen inspectors to cover the whole economy (where there are at least 17,000 recruitment agents) and could only mount reactive intelligence-led enforcement operations against the very worst offenders, leaving disreputable or exploitative labour providers unencumbered by threats of pre-emptive inspections or the prospect of legal enforcement action. Pronouncing its acronym exemplified the 'light-touch' approach of the UK.

At first sight, the GLA's creation in an otherwise anti-regulation, pro-business political environment is a puzzle. On reflection, however, it could be argued to be a classic case of what political scientist Kingdon (1984) described as a convergence of multiple political and policy 'streams' leading to a window of opportunity for unexpected change to occur. The insistence on those drafting the Palermo Protocol to include labour exploitation (*qua* forced labour), as well as sexual exploitation, as an outcome of human trafficking had laid the groundwork. At the international level, labour rights activists subsequently joined the growing anti-trafficking movement to push for broader changes to improve conditions for all workers. In the UK, this gained some traction with the Blair Labour government, which, while avowedly pro-business, still needed to appease its traditional base of trades union support. The Morecambe Bay tragedy thus provided a crisis and requisite level of uncertainty to create a moment of opportunity for the GLA to be created. It was fortuitous that, in that window of opportunity, a system of licensing for rogue labour providers was ready to be taken 'off the shelf' in draft Bill form as a Private Members' Bill.

Almost in parallel with this regulatory innovation was the development of anti-trafficking enforcement methods by the police with the immigration service, alongside the government's first strategy on human trafficking. This was released in the same year that the UK government signed the Council of Europe Convention against Trafficking in Human Beings. It also happened to coincide with the 200th anniversary of the 1807 Act to end the slave trade. Needless to say, politicians were keen to highlight the UK's anti-slavery heritage, with then Home Secretary John Reid signing the document on William Wilberforce's desk. The timing was a neat PR stunt, concealing the fact that, up until this point, the UK had been very reluctant to sign up to European anti-trafficking efforts. A key reason for this was the concern expressed by police and immigration services about the 'pull effect' that offering a quasi-humanitarian immigration status for potential victims would lead to, that is, an open door for those allegedly wishing to 'abuse' the system (Balch and Geddes 2011). Less publicised were the requirements of the

Convention to set up a National Referral Mechanism (NRM) to provide a period of rest and reflection for potential victims, and the demand for non-governmental organisations (NGOs) to be included as part of the national response. The UK's initial framing of the issue can be directly traced to its identification as an immigration problem. The fear of migrants abusing the system also reflected the extent to which the immigration agency was mired at that point in various scandals over the supposed exploitation of the asylum system (Balch 2010).

If immigration concerns provided the narrative or 'framing' of anti-trafficking, it was national police tactics that would dominate enforcement operations. The Pentameter operations (I and II)[2] demonstrated the kind of enforcement activity that the government imagined most appropriate to deal with human trafficking. They were deliberately dramatic, theatrical and highly visible: a short, sharp, but massive coordinated programme of raids on brothels across all police forces. The message was clear: human trafficking was seen as a form of sexual exploitation mainly affecting women (and perhaps children) and the best way to address this would be targeted police operations or 'raids'. The criteria for success would be the numbers of individuals 'rescued' from situations of trafficking and the number of eventual prosecutions and convictions of the traffickers.[3]

Ultimately, while the Pentameter operations, in many ways, inaugurated the implementation of the UK's anti-trafficking strategy, and generated significant press coverage, they also crystallised a number of negatives, including the lack of effectiveness in government anti-trafficking enforcement. The initial figures, in terms of numbers of operations, appeared impressive. However, a report later made public by *The Guardian* found that after raiding 822 premises, only 15 individuals were convicted of trafficking (Davies, 2009). A key benefit in terms of the human trafficking strategy was to place the issue on the radar of police chiefs at a national level – no mean feat in the UK's notoriously fragmented patchwork of 43 police services. However, as many have pointed out, there are a number of problems with the enforcement model predicated upon the 'rescue' of foreign victims in the sex industry (see also Chapter Nine). State enforcement actions that target female migrants tend to have a predictable impact in societal terms, reinforcing conservative ideas about victimhood and neo-colonialist constructions of good and bad migrants (Agustín 2007). In addition to this, the secondary goal of raising awareness has also been questioned as a sufficient strategy in reducing human trafficking (Quirk and Shih 2017).

Interestingly, what the police-led human trafficking strategy and the nascent forced labour approach of the GLA together highlighted was the absence of any economy-wide labour market regulator with appropriate authority or reach. It demonstrated the lack of a unified labour inspectorate and revealed the problems created by a steady erosion by successive governments (of all political persuasions) of regulatory power or enforcement practices governing the UK labour market (Balch 2012). This uneven level of protection for vulnerable individuals and workers in different parts of the economy and different areas of the country could only ever be papered over with the anti-trafficking rhetoric. There were innovations around a 'joined-up' approach and multi-agency working, for example, with immigration officers working on police forces through the REFLEX teams,[4] or the specialist approach of the Metropolitan Police, the first force to create a dedicated anti-trafficking unit (see also Chapter Three).[5] However, these kinds of units and the operations that they conducted simply served to underline the general problem of weak labour market regulation.

In one sense, the underlying institutional and organisational objectives of the Pentameter operations were probably achieved. Alongside the high level of publicity, they served to support a broader argument being made by central government for more coordination and centralisation to control the fragmented police service. There was a national centre, the UK Human Trafficking Centre (UKHTC), created in 2006 to oversee the national strategy, later subsumed under the Serious Organised Crime Agency (SOCA). Partly thanks to the success of the GLA and the creation of the UKHTC, several large genuinely multi-agency operations were mounted to tackle labour exploitation. An example would be Operation Ruby, developed following previous operations involving police and immigration. For all the good practice in terms of collaboration between different agencies, Operation Ruby resulted in acquittals and comments from the agencies involved about the difficulties of enforcement in the context of the UK's complex anti-trafficking laws (Balch 2012).

The number of cases of labour exploitation discovered by the GLA confirmed that weak labour market regulation, combined with a ready supply of cheap migrant labour, had left many vulnerable to exploitation in the UK economy (Geddes and Scott 2009; Lewis et al 2015). In contrast to the criticisms of the police-led anti-trafficking enforcement paradigm, with its 'rescue' focus, the GLA's licensing approach and its claim to protect workers appeared to offer one solution to the absence of a national labour inspectorate. However, the potential for the GLA to genuinely lead UK efforts to deal with exploitation was limited by the agency's sectoral remit and narrow focus on labour providers. Even within these sectors, some unlicensed operators continue to exist long after its establishment (Poinasamy and Bance 2009). A series of political campaigns to expand the GLA to other sectors came to nothing as the Labour government's later years became dominated by the economic crisis. Previous attempts to expand the GLA tended to focus, logically, on those parts of the economy perceived to have a problem with the exploitation of migrant labour, where intermediaries, or 'gangmasters', exerted control over workers and where there was a demand for cheap, seasonal labour.

While calls for the GLA's expansion went unheeded, the creation of a new stand-alone forced labour offence in 2009 created another opportunity (section 71 of the Coroners and Justice Act 2009). The argument was made that the GLA could use the new law to expand its operations to cover the whole economy. With its experience in identifying and prosecuting cases of forced labour, the case was (unsuccessfully) made that the agency was uniquely well placed to spearhead efforts to tackle forced labour with increased powers to investigate cases beyond its licensed sectors (eg by the Equalities and Human Rights Commission) (EHRC 2010).

As well as the GLA's approach on worker protection and the UKHTC's leadership on anti-trafficking, one could add a third approach, which emerged in the second decade of the 21st century. This was the launch of the Guiding Principles on Human Rights and Business (GPs) under the auspices of the UN's special envoy, John Ruggie (see also Chapter Eight). Although the ILO approach had naturally developed with the inclusion of the voice of business through its tripartite structure,[6] there was a clear contrast with the ideas contained in the UN GPs. Rather than suggesting that abuse of workers could be blamed on rogue operators – whether they were called 'gangmasters' by the GLA or 'traffickers' by the police and immigration authorities – Ruggie's approach placed business alongside government as jointly responsible for upholding human rights.

As has been well documented, by the second decade of the 21st century, the framework of regulation for the UK labour market, even before anti-trafficking or forced labour approaches were applied, was considered inadequate and insufficient (Balch 2012; Scott 2017). The verdict five years after the ratification of the 2005 Council of Europe Convention on Action against Trafficking in Human Beings, and after a series of multi-agency operations across the country with the combined forces of UKHTC and GLA (among others), was of a system 'not fit for purpose'[7] (Slavery Working Group 2013). The UK, like most 'friendly' states, could rely on a favourable rating from the US State Department's annual 'Trafficking in persons report'. However, a series of reports from the Anti-Trafficking Monitoring Group (a coalition of nine NGOs) condemned the UK's enforcement approach, its obsession with immigration controls and its weak regulatory structures enabling exploitation to flourish and grow (ATMG 2010, 2014). As noted elsewhere (see Chapter Two), the 2012 evaluation of the UK's approach by the Group of Experts on Action Against Trafficking in Human Beings (GRETA) pointed out that measures to protect victims were inadequate, and some of these problems remained unaddressed by the time of the same group's 2016 report.

To summarise, in the decade following the first strategy to tackle human trafficking, there were mixed impacts. Awareness about severe exploitation in the UK labour market was significantly increased. After the creation of new structures such as the UKHTC and GLA, there was a struggle over the framing of the issue in the policy community, connecting with the parallel development of competing approaches taken by regulators and enforcement agencies. Immigration authorities and the police maintained a focus on raids and high-profile operations to target trafficking for sexual exploitation and/or irregular migrant workers, while the GLA developed its standards-based licensing scheme, with proactive compliance inspections using ILO indicators on forced labour. Despite the obvious lack of teeth in the UN process led by Ruggie, from a human rights perspective, this can still be seen as a promising approach, siding with the structural, rather than pathological, understanding of the problem. However, this third line of approach did not immediately develop in the UK context in terms of any kind of new regulation/enforcement paradigm, and would not be picked up again significantly until the MSA and its (albeit weak) demands for transparency in supply chains. This would be one of many regulatory, legislative, policy and organisational changes applied in the name of improving the UK's enforcement response from 2014/15. We now turn to this new 'era'.

Joined up or papering over the cracks? Addressing labour exploitation post-MSA

Since the prospect of a modern slavery Act was first mooted by then Home Secretary May in 2013, a central argument has been that what went before (under the anti-trafficking regime) was inadequate and insufficient to deal with the scale of the problem. Of course, there are widely diverging definitions of 'the problem' when it comes to exploitation in the UK labour market. A key plank of the evidence base supporting a new Act was the research conducted by the Home Office's Chief Scientific Adviser, Professor Bernard Silverman, and colleagues. This used a multiple systems approach to estimate the number of victims of modern slavery and found a much larger figure than previously thought: between 10,000 and 13,000 (in 2013) (Bales et al 2015). While not the focus of this chapter, elsewhere, there has been speculation as to the real political calculation behind the modern slavery policy launch (Balch 2016), as in 2007, the Home Office was under pressure about immigration (in this case, the inability to meet the '10s of thousands' target), and the relationship between the initiative and May's ambitions to be Prime Minister were widely discussed (Balch 2016).

Since this point, the Coalition and subsequent Conservative governments have been enthusiastically reshaping the UK's response to meet the challenge of defeating what they call 'modern slavery'. This was partly a straightforward renaming and rebranding of the existing anti-trafficking strategy launched under the Labour government in 2007, which had often been referred to as modern-day slavery. Indeed, the shift away from talking about human trafficking and the insistence on the terminology of 'modern slavery' can be traced to the Centre for Social Justice (Slavery Working Group 2013) report *'It happens here'*. It also, however, became much more closely intertwined with immigration law in the Immigration Act 2016. Part 1 of that Act contained many of the key provisions to deal with exploitation in the labour market, such as the creation of the post of DLME.

Together, the new MSA and Immigration Acts came only a few years after a series of legislative and policy changes over human trafficking and forced labour. The Immigration Acts 2014 and 2016 were claimed to complement the MSA by bringing in changes to labour market enforcement (LME), criminalisation of illegal working and employer penalties. This had led to a complex and sometimes confusing array of instruments and organisational structures, which has been argued will increase susceptibility to modern slavery (see Chapter Nine). However, there was some agreement within the policy community that the gaps and weaknesses in the existing system were significant and meant that those who fell victim to such crimes were not being treated properly (ATMG 2010). This was not exactly the same as the reasons given by Home Secretary May in her case for a modern slavery Act (May 2013). Interestingly, one of the main arguments that later emerged for the Act was quite technical: the need to simplify and consolidate the sprawl and spread of laws around human trafficking and other forms of serious exploitation. Regardless of the underlying rationale, the two new Acts heralded a rise up the political agenda for labour exploitation and a significant increase in the allocation of resources.

When the MSA was passing through Parliament in 2014/15, it became an opportunity for all sides to demand those changes that they believed would improve the system. Those interested in reducing labour exploitation focused on the possibility of extending the GLA to other sectors, such as hospitality, care and construction. After potential changes for the GLA were again delayed, these demands were repeated during the passage of the Immigration Act 2016,[8] and this time, there was a response. Following the MSA and Immigration Acts, it could be argued that the government had created a whole new system to deal with labour exploitation. It is an open question whether this will have any demonstrable impact on working conditions and workers' rights.

One of the innovations claimed to be 'world-leading' by the government was the inclusion of section 54 of the MSA. Containing little detail, the clause simply required that (as of 1 April 2016) 'large' companies doing business in the UK make a 'Slavery and Human Trafficking Statement'. The statement needs to be signed by a director, approved by the board and then displayed on the company's website (if it has one). The government claimed that the new requirements on business would open up opportunities for civil society, customers and shareholders to place pressure on companies to reduce exploitative practices in their business. However, there is no extension of liability in terms of parent companies becoming more responsible for poor practices down their supply chains, and there is little compulsion for action to be taken (beyond the requirement to make a statement) (LeBaron et al 2018). An evaluation of a sample of the statements found that very few companies (11%) had disclosed any concrete steps taken, and there was little discernible improvement in companies' reporting of due diligence processes and significant levels of non-compliance (Ergon 2017; see also Chapter Eight). Supporters maintain that the real benefit will be apparent only in the fourth and fifth years (Berman 2017).

The government argued that the changes brought together under the MSA and Immigration Act 2016 constituted a 'coherent enforcement strategy to crack down on serious exploitation of workers'. Alongside the new DLME, which has an economy-wide remit, the function and powers of the GLA were changed, expanding its remit to cover 'labour abuse' across all sectors. In addition to this, new instruments were introduced for enforcement agencies to tackle exploitation, including LME 'undertakings' and 'orders'.[9]

One could see the new system as a response to many of the criticisms of the UK's regulation of its labour market: national regulators and agencies have now been created and charged with the task of reducing labour exploitation across the economy. However, the fact that this was introduced via immigration legislation has raised serious concerns. The government response to the consultation on the Immigration Act 2016 made a number of references to modern slavery.[10] It formalises the fusion of the enforcement of labour standards with the enforcement of immigration controls. Among the areas of concern are that those workers most likely to be subject to intimidation and exploitation in the labour market (particularly irregular migrants) will be less willing to report problems if that information might lead to immigration enforcement action (FLEX 2017).

Perhaps more importantly, considering that migrants are disproportionately affected by problems of exploitation in the UK labour market (see Chapter Nine), it should alert observers to the important changes taking place within immigration legislation that could undermine the regulatory innovations occurring through the modern slavery agenda. These include the criminalisation of irregular work through the Immigration Act 2016 (for the first time, irregular migrants found working without permission can be imprisoned and their earnings treated as proceeds of crime). There is also the gradual tightening of the restrictive 'hostile environment' for migrant workers created by successive pieces of legislation. These include several measures that actively reduce the chances for those' experiencing exploitation to act in order to free themselves from that situation, for example, the removal of legal aid for migrants and increased fees for employment tribunals (Balch 2016). A typical example of some of the problematic connections between the modern slavery and immigration agendas is illustrated by Operation Magnify.[11] Trumpeted as part of the fight against modern slavery, a series of targeted raids on 'nail bars' led to 97 arrests but only 14 identified victims, and with a larger number detained for immigration offences. This raises questions over the compatibility of the immigration and modern slavery objectives within the Home Office.

The ubiquity of the language of modern slavery, replacing other terms covering labour market exploitation (such as 'forced labour' or 'human trafficking') is a further step towards what Chuang (2009) refers to as the problem of 'exploitation creep'. This is where different types of labour market exploitation become reclassified as 'modern slavery' – to heighten moral condemnation and impose an organised crime paradigm – thereby ignoring the structural causes of exploitation. Through the Immigration Act 2016,[12] the GLAA was granted new powers to investigate forced labour while retaining its regulatory functions in its licensed sectors. However, it did not gain the power to inspect all businesses for compliance with labour standards in the same way as it does in its licensed sectors.

The creation of the DLME and GLAA raises the potential of the system to address exploitation because of the economy-wide remit and clear focus. However, without an extension to licensing beyond the GLA sectors, or a significant increase in resources and inspectors, there is a risk that the broader scope of regulators will produce few different outcomes, especially if the approach is taken to limit enforcement activity to a small number of high-profile operations in high-risk sectors. This would be one step forwards, but several steps backwards. If licensing is watered down or not extended into new sectors, the GLAA risks resembling the system that it was designed to improve upon (ie the EASI). The GLA introduced a more proactive approach with a slightly better ratio of inspections to businesses, largely because it was limited to some sectors. The real step-change represented by the GLA was the creation of specific powers around licensing for labour suppliers, although the GLAA is steadily identifying new industrial sectors where there is a high risk of slavery, such as construction, hospitality and social care.

The way in which the system has been set up, the prospect of real, radical change in LME depends on the vision, resources and independence granted to the DLME, which will oversee agencies such as the GLAA. There is a danger that the post-holder will be tempted to indirectly weaken protections by rationalising and pruning existing enforcement activities. It also remains to be seen what the impact of the GLA's transformation into the GLAA will be. When it was originally formed, the GLA and its licensing system for labour providers in the farming, food and fisheries sectors were created to address catastrophic failures to protect workers. In the decade or so since then, it has scored some significant successes in stopping unscrupulous businesses from exploiting workers, but it has always needed to balance this against pressures to prove value for money while reducing the 'burdens' of regulation on business. If licensing is not extended to any new sectors, it will become even more complicated to assess the impact and added value of the GLAA in terms of reducing labour exploitation.

From outputs to outcomes?

The NAO report demonstrates the difficulty of policy evaluation and measuring the success of the modern slavery agenda. This is especially when, as it noted, the government 'does not have a measure of success for its objectives nor a definition of what success looks like' (NAO 2017: 18). The empirical basis upon which the NAO evaluation was conducted amounted to relatively few sources of data, most of which were already publicly available. These were roughly divided into two columns: the amount spent by government on its modern slavery agenda versus 'results'. The first column included money spent, the numbers of civil servants employed, contracts paid for and investment in processes and funds made available. The second column covered the number of individuals identified and supported (total estimated population versus those who go through the NRM), and the recordable activities of the police (number of recorded crimes, investigations, prosecutions, etc).

This approach has the problem of creating a 'price per victim' ratio, which is a highly undesirable method of assessing policy outcomes. Indeed, it measures inputs against outputs rather than outcomes – the qualitative change or difference that the policy has made. There are interesting research questions not asked about the impact of the modern slavery agenda in different parts of the economy, or among different groups in society – all of which potentially go far beyond money spent correlated with numbers 'rescued'. For example, what are the longer-term labour market effects of targeted 'anti-slavery' enforcement activities for different kinds of workers and employers? How are employment relations and rates of pay affected? How can a modern slavery agenda contribute to changes in broader indicators around decent work? Even if there is supposed to be a focus on well-being for the narrow population who go through the NRM, there has been no concerted government effort to monitor or assess what happens to these individuals in the longer term (HTF 2015). This is counter-intuitive considering that policymakers would presumably be eager to see strong evidence of positive life-changing impacts as a result of the modern slavery agenda.

In its otherwise damning report, the NAO conceded that the legal and policy frameworks to tackle modern slavery have not long been in place. Even if we trace the inception of a 'modern slavery framework' to the first anti-trafficking strategy published in 2007, it was not until 2010 that a law creating a specific forced labour offence became active, or late 2014 that an Independent Anti-Slavery

Commissioner was appointed. By the time the MSA became law in 2015 and the Immigration Act created new structures in 2016, there had been a succession of new pieces of legislation, developing international obligations and changes in government. Given this, it is hardly surprising that it remains unclear what the outcomes will be in the medium and long term. Aside from the dynamic political context, this is because questions of evaluating policy 'success' or 'effectiveness' are notoriously fraught and depend on the choice of criteria, measure and context, and a host of other endogenous and exogenous factors.

Likewise, in the context of general labour market regulation, the new DLME sets out a fairly limited set of metrics to assess the different agencies charged with enforcement and to evaluate their relative value for money. Effectiveness is again presented as a rough equation of financial investment and number of staff against enforcement activity (Metcalf 2017: 18). Using this logic, the number of actions taken by the HMRC's Minimum Wage Compliance Unit is impressive (363 staff, 2,667 cases in 2015/16) as compared with the GLAA (70 staff, 335 cases). Interestingly, EASI comes out most strongly, with 11 staff and 924 cases. However, major reports on human trafficking in the UK have argued for an extension of the GLA/A, finding it a more effective actor than the other regulators when it comes to severe forms of exploitation (GRETA 2016: 25, US Department of State 2016: 385). The 'cases' of each agency compared by the DLME are likely to vary considerably – from instances where criminal proceedings are initiated, right through to formal letters sent to employers.[13] There is also the question of in what context, or sector of the labour market, regulators are operating when assessing what impacts they might achieve in terms of reducing labour exploitation.

If the modern slavery agenda is relatively new, the problem of labour exploitation is, of course, as old as work itself. The new interventions and the increasing numbers of people identified and supported through the modern slavery agenda need to be balanced against other developments, for example, increasing restrictions on migrant workers or the reduction in the numbers being able to seek redress through older, more traditional, means such as employment tribunals (Balch 2016). However, the NRM provides an important, albeit partial, source of data about exploitation and how it impacts upon individuals and communities. It remains to be seen whether this information can be used by researchers to more accurately describe and explain why and where exploitation is taking place in the UK labour market. A logical next step would be to investigate longer-term outcomes for workers in sectors where there are problems of exploitation (ie going beyond just those who are identified as potential 'victims of slavery').

Conclusions

This chapter set out to assess the modern slavery agenda from the perspective of how it might address labour exploitation. As should be clear from the preceding sections, this is but one 'framing' among many, meaning that following the landmarks of Palermo and the later European Convention, the expanding understanding of human trafficking as something that encompasses not just sexual exploitation, but also labour exploitation, was something very visible at the international level, resulting in a series of 'turf wars' over definitions between the UN and US. This is one of the reasons why there has been such emphasis on headline statistics. Ever since the ILO's release of statistics in 2012 estimating 20.9 million people in conditions of forced labour, there has been a fight over who can generate the best, largest and most comprehensive figure for the problem – and thereby define what that problem is. The Global Slavery Index created by the Walk Free Foundation has been heavily criticised (Gallagher 2016). The latest (2017) estimate produced in collaboration with the ILO has nearly doubled the latter organisation's previous estimate (in 2012), coming in at 40 million.[14] However, this new index included an expansion of definitions to incorporate forced marriage for the first time.[15]

This international struggle over how to define and frame, or reframe and redefine, severe forms of exploitation is strongly echoed in the case of the UK. Yet, this goes beyond conceptual, or academic, arguments: there is a reality for individuals who have experiences that the state deems worthy of intervention. Whatever the criticisms of the modern slavery agenda, and the anti-trafficking strategy that preceded it, rapidly rising numbers of individuals have been identified and provided with assistance through the UK's NRM since 2009. The vast majority of these have experienced severe forms of exploitation in the UK labour market. There are important questions about who is not included in this group, and why. However, those who have been identified and supported provide an important window into the dark corners of the UK labour market where there is virtually no regulatory authority. It is a significant oversight by the government not to monitor what happens to these individuals following their identification. Even if they accept NRM support and their cases are confirmed by the decision-making process, after 45 days[16] they may simply return to their original situation (HTF 2015; Balch 2017).

Writing in early 2018, amid the volatility and uncertainty created by Brexit and in the context of a series of disasters revealing the inadequacy of the UK's regulatory paradigms,[17] the modern slavery agenda has emerged as a touchstone for debates about what the state does, and what it is for. This is reflected in the polarisation among scholars who are interested in the expansionary potential of the concept to sustain a new global anti-slavery movement drawing on the history of 19th-century abolitionism (Bales 2007), while others fear precisely the same thing, pointing to its neo-colonial, patriarchal and racist resonances (O'Connell Davidson 2015). This chapter has argued that evaluation of the UK system of regulation and enforcement regarding modern slavery needs to contextualise policy implementation with respect to wider labour market governance. An important question is how it has impacted the general situation in relation to labour conditions, workers' rights (particularly those of migrants) and labour market exploitation that is 'below the line'.[18] Existing assessments of the agenda fall short of providing a realistic assessment of outcomes because they focus too narrowly on a basket of easily identifiable outputs rather than outcomes.

One thing that we can be certain about is that the UK's modern slavery strategy has developed rapidly and expanded to draw in ever-larger numbers of civil servants, civil society and the private sector. Engagement from the top downwards is evidenced by the number of speeches and interventions on the topic by central government and the expansion of both the Home Office's Modern Slavery Unit and the Office of the Independent Anti-Slavery Commissioner. As with all new laws and policies, implementation is another matter. The evidence here demonstrates that it has not been straightforward and has led to significant organisational and institutional change. While the stated aim of the government's strategy is clear, there will always remain questions about hidden, or conflicting, agendas around broader immigration and labour market policies (Andrijasevic and Anderson 2009). While we may never know the true motives of some politicians, any assessment of policy impact needs to consider the unintended consequences of the different legal and policy regimes that have been put in place. As is well known, reforms tend to meet resistance, and intended results can be confounded by path-dependent effects and exogenous factors. All of this underlines the need to expand the research agenda to the broader outcomes of the modern slavery framework. It also means that any such assessment needs to be clear about on what basis, and from which perspective, success is measured, and what the indicators of success might be.

Notes

1. For more detail on these developments, see, for example, HMG (2014, 2017) and GRETA (2016).

2. Two nationwide police-led anti-trafficking operations run in 2006 and 2007/08.

3. While the PR nature of these exercises can be challenged, they did profile the issue strongly. One senior officer leading a Pentameter exercise discovered 53 brothels in a city where the local Chief Constable had insisted there was only one (private communication to editor).

4. REFLEX was an initiative launched in 2000 seconding immigration officers to work in police forces.

5. Headed by the man later to become the first Anti-Slavery Commissioner.

6. The ILO describes itself as built upon the 'principle of tripartism' – including representatives from government, employer and worker groups.

7. Interestingly, this line echoed the time of the first human trafficking strategy, when the phrase was used to argue for a radical reorganisation of the Home Office under then Home Secretary John Reid.

8. See, for example, 'Immigration Bill: Part 1 – labour market enforcement' (Business, Trade Body & NGO Briefing). Available at: www.labourexploitation.org/sites/default/files/publications/Briefing%20on%20Immigration%20Bill%20-%20Business%2C%20Trade%20Union%20%26%20NGO.pdf

9. These can be used for 'serious or persistent' offenders engaging in exploitation (or 'labour abuse' in the government's terminology) to prevent further labour market offences and can impose specific requirements or prohibitions on businesses.

10. See: www.gov.uk/government/uploads/system/uploads/attachment_data/file/491260/BIS-16-11-government-response-to-tackling-exploitation-in-the-labour-market.pdf

11. A week-long operation carried out November 2016.

12. Commencing on 30 April 2017.

13. In parallel, recent commentary on police action has demonstrated that despite increasing levels of activity, these have rarely resulted in charges or prosecutions, see, for example: www.theguardian.com/world/2018/jan/21/seven-uk-police-forces-report-zero-charges-under-anti-slavery-law

[14] See: www.ilo.org/global/about-the-ilo/newsroom/news/WCMS_ 574717/lang--en/index.htm

[15] The earlier Home Office estimate has also been thoroughly undermined by a recent claim from the National Crime Agency that those in modern slavery number in the 'tens of thousands'.

[16] This is usually much longer – as high as 251 days according to the NAO report.

[17] From the weaknesses in financial regulation demonstrated by banking scandals following the 2007/08 economic crash, to building regulations blamed for the fire that killed 71 in Grenfell Tower.

[18] That is, exploitation that does not meet narrow criteria to be considered a criminal offence, such as forced labour or human trafficking.

References

Agustín, L. (2007) *Sex at the margins: Migration, labour markets and the rescue industry*, London and New York, NY: Zed Books.

Andrijasevic, R. and Anderson, B. (2009) 'Anti-trafficking campaigns: decent? Honest? Truthful?', *Feminist Review*, 92(1): 151–6.

ATMG (Anti-Trafficking Monitoring Group) (2010) *Wrong kind of victim? One year on: An analysis of UK measures to protect trafficked persons*, London: Anti-Trafficking Monitoring Group.

ATMG (2013) *In the dock: Examining the UK's criminal justice response to trafficking*, London: Anti-Trafficking Monitoring Group.

ATMG (2014) *Modern Slavery, Human Trafficking and Human Exploitation Bill (alternative to the Modern Slavery Bill)*, London: Anti-Trafficking Monitoring Group.

Balch, A. (2010) *Managing labour migration in Europe: Ideas, knowledge and policy change*, Manchester: Manchester University Press.

Balch, A. (2012) *Regulation and enforcement to tackle forced labour in the UK: A systematic response?*, York: Joseph Rowntree Foundation.

Balch, A. (2015) 'Assessing the international regime against human trafficking', in L. Talani and S. McMahon (eds) *Handbook of the international political economy of migration*, Cheltenham: Edward Elgar, pp 98–119.

Balch, A. (2016) 'Tightening the grip: the Coalition government and migrant workers', in S. Williams and P. Scott (eds) *Employment relations under Coalition government: The UK experience, 2010–2015*, London: Routledge.

Balch, A. (2017) *Fresh start: Integrating survivors of modern slavery*, Liverpool: Liverpool University.

Balch, A. and Geddes, A. (2011) 'Opportunity from crisis? Organisational responses to human trafficking in the UK', *British Journal of Politics and International Relations*, 13(1): 26–41.

Bales, K. (2007) *Ending slavery*, Berkeley: University of California Press.

Bales, K., Hesketh, O. and Silverman, B. (2015) 'Modern slavery in the UK: how many victims?', *Significance*, 12(3): 16–21.

Berman, C. (2017) 'Modern slavery statements: seeing evidence of company action', *Ethical Trading Initiative*. Available at: www.ethicaltrade.org/blog/modern-slavery-statements-seeing-evidence-company-action

Beutin, L.P. (2017) 'Black suffering for/from anti-trafficking advocacy', *Anti-Trafficking Review*, 9: 14–30. Available at: www.antitraffickingreview.org

Davies, N. (2009) 'Inquiry fails to find single trafficker who forced anybody into prostitution', *The Guardian*, 20 October. Available at: www.theguardian.com/uk/2009/oct/20/government-trafficking-enquiry-fails

Dottridge, M. (2017) 'Eight reasons why we shouldn't use the term "modern slavery"'. Available at: www.opendemocracy.net/beyondslavery/michael-dottridge/eight-reasons-why-we-shouldn-t-use-term-modern-slavery

EHRC (Equalities and Human Rights Commission) (2010) 'Inquiry into recruitment and employment in the meat and poultry processing sector', Equalities and Human Rights Commission. Available at: https://web.archive.org/web/20120603095726/http://www.equalityhumanrights.com/uploaded_files//Inquiries/meat_inquiry_report.pdf

Ergon (2017) 'Modern slavery statements: one year on', Ergon Associates. Available at: http://ergonassociates.net/wp-content/uploads/2016/03/MSA_One_year_on_April_2017.pdf?x74739

FLEX (Focus on Labour Exploitation) (2017) *Risky business: Tackling exploitation in the UK labour market*, research paper, London: Focus on Labour Exploitation.

Gallagher, A. (2016) 'Unravelling the 2016 Global Slavery Index'. Available at: www.opendemocracy.net/anne-gallagher/unravelling-2016-global-slavery-index

Geddes, A. and Scott, S. (2009) *Gangmasters Licensing Authority annual review*, Nottingham: GLA.

GRETA (Group of Experts on Action Against Trafficking in Human Beings) (2016) *Report concerning the implementation of the Council of Europe Convention on Action against Trafficking in Human Beings by the United Kingdom: Second evaluation round*, Strasbourg: Council of Europe. Available at: https://rm.coe.int/16806abcdc

HMG (Her Majesty's Government) (2007) *Action plan on tackling human trafficking*, London: Home Office.

HMG (2014) *Modern slavery strategy*, London: Home Office. Available at: www.gov.uk/government/uploads/system/uploads/attachment_data/file/383764/Modern_Slavery_Strategy_FINAL_DEC2015.pdf

HMG (2017) *2017 annual report on modern slavery*, London: Home Office. Available at: www.gov.uk/government/uploads/system/uploads/attachment_data/file/652366/2017_uk_annual_report_on_modern_slavery.pdf

HTF (Human Trafficking Foundation) (2015) *Life beyond the safe house*, London: HTF.

Kingdon, J. (1984) *Agendas, alternatives and public policies*, New York, NY: Harper Collins.

LeBaron, G., Howard, N., Thibos, C. and Kyritsis, P. (2018) 'Confronting root causes: forced labour in global supply chains', openDemocracy, Sheffield Political Economy Research Institute (SPERI), University of Sheffield.

Lewis, H., Dwyer, P., Hodkinson, S. and Waite, L. (2015) *Precarious lives*, Bristol: Policy Press.

Maul, M. (2012) *Human rights, development and decolonization. The International Labour Organization, 1940–1970*, Basingstoke: Palgrave.

May, T. (2013) 'Speech on modern slavery', 4 December, Thomsons Reuters Conference.

May, T. (2017) 'My government will lead the way in defeating modern slavery', *The Daily Telegraph*, 30 July. Available at: www.telegraph.co.uk/news/2016/07/30/we-will-lead-the-way-in-defeating-modern-slavery/

Metcalf, D. (2017) *United Kingdom labour market enforcement strategy – introductory report*, London: Director of Labour Market Enforcement.

NAO (National Audit Office) (2017) *Reducing modern slavery*, London: National Audit Office.

O'Connell Davidson, J. (2010) 'New slavery, old binaries: human trafficking and the borders of "freedom"', *Global Networks*, 10(2): 244–61.

O'Connell Davidson, J. (2015) *Modern slavery: The margins of freedom*, Basingstoke: Palgrave Macmillan.

Poinasamy, K. and Bance, A. (2009) *Turning the tide: How best to protect workers employed by gangmasters, five years after Morecambe Bay*, Oxford: Oxfam.

Quirk, J. and Shih, E. (2017) 'Introduction: do the hidden costs outweigh the practical benefits of human trafficking awareness campaigns?', *opendemocracy*. Available at: www.opendemocracy.net/beyondslavery/joel-quirk-elena-shih/introduction-do-hidden-costs-outweigh-practical-benefits-of-huma

Scott, S. (2017) *Labour exploitation*, Bristol: The Policy Press.

Scott, S., Craig, G. and Geddes, A. (2013) *The experience of forced labour*, York: Joseph Rowntree Foundation.

Slavery Working Group (2013) *'It happens here': Equipping the United Kingdom to fight modern slavery*, London: Centre for Social Justice.

TUC (Trades Union Congress) (2007) *COVE – Committee on Vulnerable Employment, final report*, London: Trades Union Congress.

US Department of State (2016) 'Trafficking in persons report, 2016'. Available at: www.state.gov/documents/organization/258876.pdf

FOUR

Class Acts? A comparative analysis of modern slavery legislation across the UK

Vicky Brotherton

Introduction

In June 2013, the Human Trafficking and Exploitation (Further Provisions and Support for Victims) Bill was introduced into the Northern Ireland Assembly. Its introduction was shortly followed by an announcement[1] in the autumn of 2013 by the-then Home Secretary, Theresa May, of plans to introduce a modern slavery Act in England and Wales, and the launch of Jenny Marra MSP's consultation[2] on a Human Trafficking Bill in Scotland. By the following year, draft Bills on human trafficking and related forms of exploitation were being scrutinised by the respective Parliaments in each of the UK's three jurisdictions (England and Wales, Northern Ireland, and Scotland), and by 2015, three new Acts had passed into law: the Modern Slavery Act (MSA),[3] the Human Trafficking and Exploitation (Criminal Justice and Support for Victims) Act (hereafter, Northern Ireland Act),[4] and the Human Trafficking and Exploitation (Scotland) Act[5] (hereafter, the 'Scotland Act').

The introduction of the legislation was widely welcomed by non-governmental organisations (NGOs) and legal professionals involved in anti-trafficking work. The Anti-Trafficking Monitoring Group (ATMG 2013) highlighted the need for improved legislation and called for the introduction of a new, comprehensive anti-slavery law. Given the importance of this new legislation, a significant amount of time and expertise was dedicated to scrutinising and strengthening the Acts. Through collaborative working and the commitment of parliamentarians, the government and NGOs, the legislation was very significantly improved. The three Acts are comprehensive in scope and include: a raft of new criminal offences; measures aimed at preventing modern slavery; support provisions for child and adult victims; and, in the MSA, the role of an Independent Anti-Slavery Commissioner and a 'Transparency in Supply Chains' provision, aimed at improving businesses' response to slavery and exploitation.

The MSA was heralded – at least in government – as 'world-leading'[6] and the 'first legislation of its kind in Europe'.[7] While it may be true that the Scotland and Northern Ireland Acts are not as broad in scope as the MSA, due to the reserved powers of the UK Parliament, closer inspection of comparable provisions across the three Acts shows that the MSA is, in a number of areas, weaker than its counterparts, let alone legislation in jurisdictions outside the UK.

The aim here is to consider the key, comparable provisions across the three Acts – assessing if and how they differ from each other and from standards in international law. The chapter also details the extent of their implementation and impact to date. Provisions that are unique to only one Act, such as section 53 of the MSA (Overseas Domestic Workers), are not covered in this chapter; however, further analysis of such provisions in UK modern slavery law can be found within the ATMG (2017) report (see also Chapters Three and Five).

Examining the Acts

This chapter will consider the following major provisions from the three Acts in turn: criminal justice measures, including offences, and prevention and risk orders; adult support entitlements; child guardianship; and the non-criminalisation of victims. It is argued that there are key differences in the drafting of the human trafficking offence across the Acts that will impact on related policy and training. While the introduction of the legislation has triggered the creation of various national and regional bodies, as well as greater funding commitments, little improvement has been seen to date in the operational response at the local level. It is further argued that data collection and analysis remain inadequate; as such, it is difficult to calibrate the overall success of the criminal justice response.

Despite the survivor-focused rhetoric of the UK government, little has changed on the front line in terms of the support provided to adult and child victims of modern slavery. Numerous provisions relating to victim support, such as the Statutory Guidance on victim identification and assistance (section 49 of the MSA) and Independent Child Trafficking Advocates, are yet to be fully implemented. In terms of content, victim support and protection provisions in the Scotland and Northern Ireland Acts are, on the whole, significantly more progressive than those in the MSA.

Criminal justice measures

Offences

The MSA and Scotland and Northern Ireland Acts each introduce new offences of human trafficking, slavery, servitude and forced or compulsory labour, replacing earlier offences that were dispersed across a number of different laws. The Northern Ireland Act also includes a new offence of paying for the sexual services of a person (Part 2, section 15) and the offence of forced marriage (Part 2, section 16). All three Acts provide an explanation of the meaning of 'exploitation' and define a child as any person under the age of 18 years. The drafting of the offence of human trafficking is broadly the same in the MSA and the Northern Ireland Act, but is significantly different in the Scotland Act. When comparing the Acts' offences, the majority of differences can be found in the wording of the human trafficking offence. The key differences are set out in Table 4.1.

Each of the Acts must take into consideration the related laws in their respective jurisdictions but, notwithstanding that, there are differences in wording that will impact on policy and training. For example, in section 2(2) of the MSA, it states: 'It is irrelevant whether V consents to the travel (whether V is an adult or a child)'. Yet, in the trafficking offences in the Northern Ireland and Scotland Acts, 'consent' is applied more widely and relates to any relevant action named in the Act.

The Northern Ireland Act, at section 25(1)(c), provides a clear and comprehensive definition of a 'vulnerable adult'. The MSA and the Scotland Act also set out a list of factors that could result in an individual being determined to be a 'vulnerable person'. However, they also both state that the courts must consider, when determining whether an offence of human trafficking, slavery, servitude or forced or compulsory labour has taken place, if a person who was not a 'vulnerable person', according to the definition, would have been able to refuse to be used for the purpose of exploitation.

The 2005 Council of Europe Convention on Action against Trafficking in Human Beings (hereafter, the 'Trafficking Convention') (CoE 2005) makes clear that children cannot consent to any of the trafficking acts *or* the exploitation itself. This is not clear in the drafting of the MSA, and, as such, it could be deemed to be out of line with the spirit of the Trafficking Convention. This has the potential to confuse and mislead practitioners in their understanding of the issue of consent in cases involving children.

Table 4.1: Key differences in anti-slavery legislation: UK jurisdictions

	MSA (England and Wales)	Northern Ireland Act	Scotland Act
Definition of human trafficking	**Section 2(1) –** A person commits an offence if the person arranges or facilitates the travel of another person ('V') with a view to V being exploited.	**Section 2(1) –** A person ('A') commits an offence if A arranges or facilitates the travel of another person ('B') with a view to B being exploited.	**Section 1 –** A person commits an offence if the person – (a) takes a relevant action, and (b) does so with a view to another person being exploited. *(This differs from the definition of 'arranges or facilitates the travel' in the other Acts.)*
Securing services from vulnerable persons	**Section 3(6) –** … (a) he or she is a child, is mentally or physically ill or disabled, or has a family relationship with a particular person, and (b) an adult, or a person without the illness, disability, or family relationship, would be likely to refuse to be used for that purpose.	**Section 1(4) –** … regard may be had to any of B's personal circumstances which may make B more vulnerable than other persons such as, for example – (a) that B is a child or a vulnerable adult; or (b) that A is a member of B's family. *(The definition of a 'vulnerable adult' can be found at section 25 (1)(c))*	**Section 3(8) –** … Another person uses or attempts to use the person for any purpose … where – (a) the person is – (i) a child, or (ii) an adult whose ability to refuse to be used for a purpose within subsection (7)(a), (b) or (c) is impaired through mental or physical illness, disability, old age or any other reason (a 'vulnerable adult'), and (b) a person who is not a child or a vulnerable adult would be likely to refuse to be used for that purpose.

(continued)

Table 4.1: Key differences in anti-slavery legislation: UK jurisdictions (continued)

	MSA (England and Wales)	Northern Ireland Act	Scotland Act
Consent	Section 2(2) – It is irrelevant whether V consents to the travel (whether V is an adult or a child). *(The focus here is on consent to travel.)*	Section 1(5) – The consent of B to any act which forms part of an offence under this section is irrelevant. *(This is not just 'consent to travel', it encompasses all acts, and is therefore different to the MSA)*	Section 1(3) – It is irrelevant whether the other person consents to any part of the relevant action. *(This is not just 'consent to travel', it encompasses all acts, and is therefore different from the MSA)*
Aggravated factors		Part 1, section 6 An offence is aggravated if: – the offender is a public officer – the offender is a family member of the victim – the offender was in a position of trust – it involves a child – it involves a vulnerable person – was committed by use of threats against a family member of the victim – the offence caused serious harm to the victim – the offender has previous convictions for offences of the same type whether committed in Northern Ireland or anywhere else	Part 1, sections 5–7 An offence is aggravated if: – It is connected to human trafficking* – Involves a child. – If the offender is a public officer. *(*This relates to an offence separate from but connected to the human trafficking offence)*

Unlike the MSA, the Scotland and Northern Ireland Acts also include a list of 'aggravating factors' that can be taken into account by the courts at the point of sentencing, including whether the offence was committed against a child, or committed by a member of the victim's family. The Scotland Act is unique in including an aggravation for offences committed that are separate from but connected to the human trafficking offence. Given the known difficulties in securing trafficking convictions, this particular aggravation may be important in ensuring that traffickers are appropriately punished for these linked offences, such as sexual assault or kidnapping, and receive sentences commensurate to the harm that they have caused to the victim.

Prevention and risk orders

In addition to the criminal offences, new civil orders were introduced in all jurisdictions designed to prevent future harm based on current risk. The titles of the civil orders across the jurisdictions reflect the different names of the legislative Acts, as set out in Table 4.2.

The new prevention and risk orders mirror the Sexual Harm Prevention Orders and Sexual Risk Orders introduced in England and Wales in March 2015.[8] The new prevention orders are not intended as a substitute for prosecution when sufficient evidence is available. They are intended as an additional tool available to law enforcement agencies to control the behaviour of individuals who may cause harm through committing slavery and human trafficking offences. Upon the granting of an order, the court can impose certain restrictions, including restrictions on travel and requirements for reporting bank accounts, address changes and other details. The main difference between the types of order is that a 'risk order' restricts the activity of individuals who have not been convicted of a relevant offence, but who pose a risk of committing any such offence, and a 'prevention order' restricts the activity of those who have already been convicted of a relevant offence.

Table 4.2: Types of anti-slavery order: UK jurisdictions

MSA 2015	Northern Ireland Act	Scotland Act
England/Wales	*Northern Ireland*	*Scotland*
Part 2: sections 14–34 Slavery & Trafficking Prevention Orders (STPOs)	Part 1: section 11 Schedule 3: Slavery and Trafficking Prevention Orders (STPOs)	Part 4: sections 16–34 Trafficking and Exploitation Prevention Orders (TEPOs)
Slavery & Trafficking Risk Orders (STROs)		Trafficking and Exploitation Risk Orders (TEROs)

There are some differences between the three Acts, notably, there is no 'Risk Order' in Northern Ireland, only a single Slavery & Trafficking Prevention Order (STPO). In Scotland, the name of orders reflect the offences in the Scottish Act and are called Trafficking & Exploitation Prevention Orders (TEPOs) and Trafficking & Exploitation Risk Orders (TEROs), whereas in the MSA, they are called Slavery and Trafficking Prevention Orders (STPOs) and Slavery and Trafficking Risk Orders (STROs). It might be suggested that it is not very helpful to have differing names within the different jurisdictions as this can only lead to confusion.

Implementation of criminal justice measures

The introduction of the three legislative Acts and the new offences resulted in revisions to police and prosecution service guidance,[9] and triggered the creation of the Modern Slavery Threat Group and the Modern Slavery Taskforce. The Modern Slavery Threat Group brings together senior operational law enforcement officers and is chaired by the current national policing lead for modern slavery, Chief Constable (of Devon and Cornwall Police) Shaun Sawyer. The Modern Slavery Taskforce, made up of government ministers and intelligence and policy experts, was established to spearhead the operational response. Further funding has been allocated by the UK government to improve the criminal justice response; for instance, in October 2016, the Home Secretary announced[10] an £8.5 million 'police transformation fund' to help reform and strengthen the operational response to modern slavery.

In October 2017, the UK government published its *Annual report on modern slavery* (Home Office 2017) (in lieu of the Inter-Departmental Ministerial Group's [IDMG's] annual report[11]), which reported that in 2016, 80 defendants were proceeded against for a total of 155 modern slavery offences, as provided for in the MSA. It also reported that in Scotland, since the introduction of their legislation, the Crown Office and Procurator Fiscal Service (COPFS) has appointed a national lead and local lead prosecutors for human trafficking to assist with all aspects of investigation and prosecution. Thirteen individuals were prosecuted in Scotland in 2016 for human trafficking offences, or where offences had a human trafficking aggravation added to them under section 5 of the Scotland Act 2015. In Northern Ireland, the Public Prosecution Service (PPS) was also reported to have appointed a lead prosecutor for human trafficking offences. Between January 2015 and June 2017, only four individuals were convicted for human trafficking offences in Northern Ireland.

Within the first year of the MSA being in force, applications for STPOs and STROs had been made in England and Wales. The UK *Annual report on modern slavery* (Home Office 2017), published in October 2017, reported that between July 2015 and March 2017, 56 orders were issued in total, consisting of 37 STPOs on conviction and 19 STROs. It also reported that since the regime for STPOs under the Northern Ireland Act commenced on 1 April 2016, two STPOs have been applied for and await the sentencing outcome. In Scotland, TEPOs have been available to courts, police and prosecutors since June 2017 and TEROs since October 2017. To date, none have been applied for.

Impact of the criminal justice measures

Despite the introduction of these new offences and prevention and risk orders in 2015, the related changes to policy and guidance, and the introduction of new operational and strategic bodies, the impact of this legislation has been limited, and the positive impact that it has had to date has been felt in some areas more than others. The first MSA review,[12] commissioned by the Home Secretary and written by barrister Caroline Haughey, was published on 31 July 2016. Ms Haughey reported that the number of modern slavery investigations instigated had increased, and that there had been a total of 289 offences prosecuted in 2015: 27 offences under the MSA (cases ongoing) and 262 under previous slavery and trafficking legislation. However, the review also noted that modern slavery was introduced as a separate crime-recording category by the Home Office in April 2015, so it is not possible to compare the statistics to previous laws before the introduction of the MSA.

The review concluded that the operational response to modern slavery was improving: however, '[d]espite stand-out examples of good practice, there is a lack of consistency in how law enforcement and criminal justice agencies deal with modern slavery' (Home Office 2016: 3). Furthermore, an inspection of police activity undertaken by Her Majesty's Inspectorate of Constabulary and Fire and Rescue Services between November 2016 and March 2017 (HMICFRS 2017: 5) found similar results, stating that the strengthened legislation had 'not as yet resulted in the development of a concerted overall response on the part of the police service'. Due to this, it stated, victims were being let down by the police 'at every stage'.

Both the modern slavery review and the HMICFRS report recommended the roll-out of quality-assured training for police, better strategic leadership and governance at the regional and national level, and measures to improve data collection and intelligence sharing. The issue of inadequate data collection has been raised repeatedly by key actors within the anti-trafficking sector, in particular, that the current recording and reporting of criminal offences and perpetrators is inadequate to provide a comprehensive picture of the nature and scale of modern slavery in the UK. For instance, the Crown Prosecution Service (CPS) case-recording process does not allow for concise reporting on the number of traffickers who are convicted for the specific offence of human trafficking. The CPS continues to publish only the number of charges for trafficking and slavery offences, rather than the number of defendants charged, and this fails to bring insight into how many perpetrators have been brought to justice or how well the laws are being used. Burland (in Chapter Seven) shows how, in one limited area, the criminal justice system is failing victims and failing to pursue perpetrators. The PPS in Northern Ireland does record the number of charges laid against each person; however, they do not routinely publish these figures. There is also no reporting across the UK on the age of the victims of the offences, making it impossible to know how many children's cases are being prosecuted. While extensive data is collected on victims through the National Referral Mechanism (NRM), data collection on perpetrators is still limited. To date, data on victims and criminals have been collected in silos by different authorities and no comprehensive assessment is undertaken to assess if and how one data set informs the other.

It is to be hoped that the Joint Slavery Trafficking Analysis Centre (JSTAC) – a recently created unit consisting of analysts from the National Crime Agency, police, Border Force, Immigration Enforcement, HMRC and the Gangmasters and Labour Abuse Authority – will help improve the intelligence picture. JSTAC, together with the proposed revision of the NRM referral form and digitalisation of the NRM (see next section), has the potential to help improve the quality and accessibility of data and intelligence on modern slavery. Without such improvements, calibrating the success of these criminal justice measures, and the effectiveness of the wider anti-slavery response, will not be possible.

Adult support entitlements

Support for adult victims of modern slavery is a devolved matter. Access to specialist support for adult victims of trafficking across the UK is largely tied to whether they have been identified as a potential victim through the NRM (see later), although services in Scotland and Northern Ireland currently have greater flexibility as to the time frame in which they can support an individual before and after a referral into the NRM. The MSA and the respective Acts in Scotland and Northern Ireland each contain provisions regarding adult support; however, the MSA is significantly weaker in this regard than its counterparts.

Both the Scotland and Northern Ireland Acts place a legal duty on ministers to provide support and assistance to victims, explicitly stating the minimum types of support to be provided (the list is non-exhaustive), reflecting the support standards set out in the Trafficking Convention and European Union (EU) Trafficking Directive. They also state that support should be provided in the period between a reasonable grounds and conclusive determination that the person is a victim, as well as prior to the reasonable grounds determination (ie if a referral about the individual is about to be made) and after the conclusive determination is made, for as long as deemed necessary. The Northern Ireland Act goes further still by stating that support can continue to be provided to persons who are conclusively determined *not* to be victims if continued support is deemed necessary, and to eligible victims even if they leave Northern Ireland.[13]

Both the Scotland and Northern Ireland Acts also include the key principles and safeguards for support provision listed in the Trafficking Convention and EU Trafficking Directive, that is, that support must be provided on an informed and consensual basis, and that support provision should not be dependent on an individual's willingness to act as a witness in criminal proceedings. Northern Ireland goes further still, stating that consideration should be given to the special needs and particular vulnerabilities of victims, and that support must be offered from a person who is of the same gender.

The adult support provisions within the Northern Ireland and Scotland Acts commenced in January 2015 and May 2016, respectively. The commencement of these provisions did not result in any considerable change in practice; the Acts effectively enshrined the support system already in place. However, following a consultation on the Human Trafficking and Exploitation Strategy in Scotland, the Scottish government announced[14] that the support period for victims was to be extended from 45 days to 90 days, the first country in the UK to do so.

The MSA does not explicitly place a duty on the state to provide support and assistance to victims, or set out victims' support entitlements. Rather, the arrangements for identifying and supporting victims are to be set out in guidance issued by the Secretary of State, under section 49 ('Guidance about identifying and supporting victims'), which may be revised from 'time to time'. Therefore, unlike those in Scotland and Northern Ireland, victims in England and Wales cannot look to the MSA to claim rights to support. The reason given by the UK government for not including support provisions in the Bill was that the NRM, the system through which victims of modern slavery are formally recognised and provided access to specialist support, was not fit for purpose and therefore should not be set out in inflexible legislation. A review of the NRM[15] undertaken by a senior civil servant in the Home Office supported this position. However, critics argued that this was a disingenuous argument: the minimum standards of victim protection and support, and safeguards regarding the provision of this support (such as not tying support to the victims' willingness to participate in criminal proceedings against their trafficker), could be included in the legislation regardless of whether the administrative details of the NRM decision-making process were also set out in law. The government's argument, however, satisfied the majority of parliamentarians and, as such, no victim support standards were included. However, the government did concede to including a clause (section 50) that enabled the Secretary of State to introduce statutory regulations on victim identification and assistance at a later date.

At the time of writing, the statutory guidance under section 49 has not yet been published. The drafting process was commenced in 2015 but was subsequently postponed until the pilot of the reformed NRM had come to an end and the evaluation of it had been published. This has now happened, and in October 2017, the Home Office announced a number of reforms to the NRM decision-making process and support package for victims.[16] These include creating:

- a single, expert unit in the Home Office to handle all NRM cases, replacing the current case management units in the National Crime Agency and UK Visas and Immigration;
- an independent panel of experts to review all negative decisions, adding significantly to the scrutiny that such cases currently receive; and
- a new digital system to support the NRM process.

The reforms to support include granting potential victims a three-day period of support within a safe house prior to referral into the NRM, extending the period of support post-conclusive grounds decisions. The proposed reforms, particularly those regarding the enhanced support for victims, are welcome but still do not go far enough in most commentators' views.

Of particular concern is the UK government's reluctance to commit to granting confirmed modern slavery victims leave to remain in the UK, often required by non-British nationals to remain in the UK and to continue accessing support and services to aid their recovery and rehabilitation. A Work and Pensions Committee inquiry into modern slavery in 2017 recommended that:

> all confirmed victims of modern slavery be given at least one year's leave to remain with the same recourse to benefits and services as asylum seekers are granted. This would allow time for victims to receive advice and support, and give them time to plan their next steps.[17]

This recommendation was roundly rejected by the government, which argued that 'having a blanket policy of granting discretionary leave to all victims risks incentivising individuals to make false trafficking claims in an attempt to fraudulently obtain leave to remain or delay removal'.[18] While this 'pull factor' argument was swiftly repudiated by the Committee, both during and after the inquiry, it is one that the government returns to repeatedly, and is in keeping with the wider anti-immigration rhetoric that it espouses (see Chapter Six).

Although the package of NRM reforms include an extension of the support period post-conclusive grounds from 14 days to 45 days, it does not include any measures to help simplify the immigration system for modern slavery victims, or introduce any concessions to make it easier for victims to access welfare benefits and support post-NRM. Without the stability that comes with having a regularised immigration status, victims will find long-term recovery and rehabilitation difficult. As such, this package of NRM support reforms may have only limited effect. At the time of writing, a Private Member's Bill sponsored by Lord McColl is attempting to address some of these limitations.

Child guardianship and the presumption of age

The appointment of independent child guardians for unaccompanied and trafficked children is internationally recognised best practice (FRA 2015) and included within both the Trafficking Convention (Article 10(4)) and EU Trafficking Directive (Article 14(2)). The purpose of a guardian is act as a trusted adult for the child, to support them and make decisions related to their care based on their best interests, and to advocate for long-term solutions. All three UK Acts make provision for a guardian-type role; however, there are again significant differences between them (see Table 4.3).

In the first instance, all three laws have decided upon different names for the role of guardian: in Scotland, they have legislated for 'Independent Child Trafficking Guardians'; in Northern Ireland, it is 'Independent Guardians'; and in England and Wales, it is 'Independent Child Trafficking Advocates'. Terminology aside, there are real differences in the scope, function and intention of the role across each of the nations. Currently, each jurisdiction has a different interpretation on eligibility for guardianship, for example, who is entitled to have a guardian, how the guardian is appointed and when and for how long a guardian will be able to represent the child. At a time when we know that traffickers systematically move children across the UK and do not limit themselves to within national borders, there is an urgent need to ensure that a trafficked child's access to a skilled and trained guardian does not become a postcode lottery. There is currently no single monitoring mechanism that is responsible for oversight of policy on guardianship for trafficked children in all jurisdictions. The UK has international reporting obligations under the United Nations (UN) Convention on the Rights of the Child, as well as the Trafficking Convention. It is essential that there is policy coherence on guardianship across the UK to enable consistency in reporting in order to ensure coherent protections for children no matter where in the UK they come to the attention of the authorities.

At the time of writing, none of the systems of guardianship have yet commenced. In September 2014, a pilot Child Trafficking Advocate scheme was launched and tested over 12 months across 23 local authority areas in England. The evaluation of the 2014/15 trial of Independent Child Trafficking Advocates was completed in September 2015 and the evaluation findings were published in

Table 4.3: Types of guardian role: UK jurisdictions

	MSA	Northern Ireland Act	Scotland Act
	England/Wales	*Northern Ireland*	*Scotland*
Child guardianship/ advocates	Section 48 – Independent Child Trafficking Advocates	Section 21– Independent Guardian	Section 11 – Independent Child Trafficking Guardians

December 2015.[19] Government ministers responded to the evaluation report, stating that it was not satisfied with the pilot model following evaluation and intended to consult further. It announced in June 2016 that it was intending to restart the process with three 'early-adopter' sites in Hampshire and the Isle of Wight, Wales, and Greater Manchester, to be established in November 2016 and running until March 2019.

Calls have been made, including by the Independent Anti-Slavery Commissioner,[20] for the scheme to be continuously monitored and evaluated, and rolled out beyond these early-adopter sites as soon as possible, preferably before March 2019. In a welcome move in October 2017, the UK government committed to rolling out the Independent Child Trafficking Advocates scheme nationally, although a time frame for this was not given as part of this announcement. Given the internationally recognised benefits of child guardianship, their roll-out should be expedited.

Northern Ireland

The Northern Ireland legislation is the most comprehensive and detailed of all three laws and the most explicit on the functions and duties of the Independent Guardian. However, there are a number of key decisions to be made prior to commencement and further regulations must be laid before the Northern Ireland Assembly before implementation. Section 21 of the Act places a duty on the Health and Social Care Board to make arrangements to enable an Independent Guardian to be appointed to assist, represent and support a child. The arrangements must be made with a charity that will provide for the appointment of a person as an Independent Guardian. Section 21(11), as amended by section 101(3) of the Justice Act (Northern Ireland) 2015, provides that charities already registered under the Charities Act (Northern Ireland) 2008, charities waiting to be called forward to register under that Act and charities registered in England, Wales or Scotland are eligible to be considered by the Health and Social Care Board to provide an Independent Guardianship service in Northern Ireland. The procurement exercise for the Independent Guardianship service started in May 2017 with the publication of a Prior Information Notice. If all goes as planned, it is expected that the first Independent Guardians will have started work by the end of 2017. The procurement and management of the service is being managed by the Health and Social Care Board.

Scotland

In Scotland, the Independent Child Trafficking Guardians are to be appointed for a child:

- whom a relevant authority has reasonable grounds to believe is or may be a victim of human trafficking;
- whom a relevant authority has reasonable grounds to believe is vulnerable to *becoming a victim* of human trafficking; and
- for whom no one in the UK has parental rights or responsibilities (this is an important and marked difference to the proposals in England and Wales).

Unlike the MSA or Northern Ireland Act, the Scottish child trafficking guardian model excludes British children or others where there exists someone with parental responsibility in the UK. The rationale during the Bill debates was that Scotland already has alternative systems of protection for children in Scotland that would apply in these circumstances. However, the case is not at all clear what would happen if a child from abroad was trafficked in a family group where a member of the family was complicit in the trafficking and the child was separated from the family. This will need to be tested robustly during future consultations to ensure that no child falls through the gaps or where a lack of clarity among professionals leads to a child not getting a guardian from the earliest possible moment.

Scotland has an advantage over the rest of the UK in that it already has a well-regarded and well-tested model of guardianship run by the Aberlour Child Care Trust and the Scottish Refugee Council[21] in operation. The existing Scottish Guardianship Service works with children and young people who arrive in Scotland unaccompanied and separated from their families. The current service supports unaccompanied asylum-seeking and trafficked children and young people, and has provided an extensive evidence base for all those across the UK looking to see how a model of guardianship could best support trafficked children. The Scottish government has not yet said how the proposed model of Independent Child Trafficking Guardians will interface with the Scottish Guardianship Service or whether a new service will be put out for tender through the government's procurement processes.

One element that is almost certain to be inconsistent across the three laws is the age at which the guardian/advocate can remain with the young person. Northern Ireland has it written into statute that a guardian is available for children up to 21 years of age in some circumstances. In Scotland, it will ultimately be a matter for the regulations to determine this upper age limit; however, current social work practice in Scotland is to allow children to access local authority care up to 26 years of age, and the current Scottish Guardianship Service already includes young people over 18. In England and Wales, this upper age limit is not specified in the MSA, but will be a matter for regulations.

It is also not clear in any of the three laws whether a guardian can be appointed in circumstances where a young person has already been determined to be 18 years or older but who has challenged this assessment in a court process. These young people need particular attention as their vulnerability is increased when they are, potentially incorrectly, placed into the adult system. There needs to be policy coherence with the principle of 'benefit of the doubt' on age, which is now embedded into law, and greater clarity for the role of guardian/advocate.

Non-criminalisation of victims

The principle of non-punishment/prosecution of victims can be found in the Trafficking Convention and EU Trafficking Directive.[22] All three laws make provision for the non-prosecution of victims who may have committed a criminal offence as a result of exploitation. However, there are differences in the way each jurisdiction has approached these situations (see Table 4.4).

Table 4.4: Types of statutory defence: UK jurisdictions

MSA	Northern Ireland Act	Scotland Act
England/Wales	*Northern Ireland*	*Scotland*
Section 45 and schedule 4: Defence for slavery or trafficking victims who commit an offence	Section 22: Defence for slavery and trafficking victims compelled to commit an offence	No statutory defence provision in the Act, but the non-punishment provision is embedded within section 8: Lord Advocate's Instructions on prosecution of victims of offences

The non-punishment provision exists in all three Acts. The MSA and the Northern Ireland Act include a statutory defence, whereas in Scotland, the Act allows the principles of the non-punishment provision and its practical interpretation to be detailed in the Lord Advocate's Instructions.

MSA and Northern Ireland Act: statutory defence

The statutory defence in the MSA (section 45) states:

> Section 45 (4) A person is not guilty of an offence if –
> (a) the person is under the age of 18 when the person does the act which constitutes the offence,
> (b) the person does that act as a *direct consequence* of the person being, or having been, a victim of slavery or a victim of relevant exploitation, and
> (c) a reasonable person in the same situation as the person and having the person's relevant characteristics would do that act.

There is concern over the interpretation of the term 'direct consequence', which is central to the defence. The Act does not define the term 'direct consequence' used in section 45(4)(b) and there is no further explanatory note. The Northern Ireland Act likewise includes the phrase 'direct consequence' and similarly fails to further explain this term. Concerns regarding potential difficulties of interpretation were raised as part of the Haughey MSA review, published in July 2016, which also questioned whether the statutory defence is consistent with Article 8 of the Trafficking Directive. The MSA review recommended that:

> In respect of s45 of the Modern Slavery Act, which provides for a defence for slavery or trafficking victims who commit an offence, consideration should be given to clarifying and/or enhancing the term 'direct consequence', and to clarifying the process by which s45 is raised and applied. (Recommendation 25)

The statutory defence in the MSA and in the Northern Ireland Act both contain a 'reasonable person test', that is, whether a reasonable person in the same situation as the person charged with the offence and having the person's relevant characteristics would have no realistic alternative to undertaking the criminal act. 'Relevant characteristics' refer to age, sex and any physical or mental illness or disability. In Northern Ireland, this test only applies to adult cases, but in the MSA, this test must also be applied to children, that is, those under 18. Throughout the Modern Slavery Bill, numerous contributors raised concerns about the inclusion of this reasonable person test, particularly in regard to children.

Under international law, namely, the UN Trafficking Protocol, the Trafficking Convention and the EU Trafficking Directive, all legally binding in the UK, the presence of any of 'the means' – including compulsion – are irrelevant when defining a child as a victim of trafficking. However, the reasonable person test requires a juror to decide whether a reasonable child with relevant characteristics would have acted in the same way and, as such, inadvertently retains the need for a child defendant and victim to prove compulsion in their actions in order to access the protection of the statutory defence.

Legal professionals have also questioned whether this test is workable in practice, for both children and adults. As the Immigration Law Practitioners Association (ILPA) explained[23]:

> This part of the test is an attempt to import an objective element, that of the 'reasonable person', but with a subjective twist – the reasonable person must have the same characteristics as the victim in question.... It would require a member of the jury to attempt to imagine what s/he would have done, if s/he had exactly the same personal circumstances and background as the person in question, and were placed in the same situation. The purported objective test is thus a hybrid: it is so subjective (by importing the need for the 'reasonable person' to be, in effect, the same person as the victim, and in the same situation) that it is unable to achieve the intended objectivity. A judge would have real difficulty in directing any jury as to the correct approach as a result.

The use of the statutory defence will need to be carefully monitored to ascertain whether the inclusion of the 'reasonable person test' forms a barrier to victims accessing protection from unnecessary punishment and prosecution.

Scotland Act: Lord Advocate's Instructions

Section 8 of the Scotland Act allows the principles of the non-punishment and its practical interpretation to be detailed in the Lord Advocate's Instructions, which, in turn, provide an easily understood set of guidelines for lawyers and non-lawyers. The Preamble to the Lord Advocate's Instructions illustrates the evolving nature of criminality, and explains that the statutory defence may be invoked in offences committed as part of the process of trafficking or as a consequence of trafficking. Paragraph 4 of the Preamble states that:

The list of offences which victims of human trafficking or exploitation may commit is constantly evolving. The most common types of offences which victims commit in *the process* of trafficking or exploitation include immigration offences and possession of false identity documents. The offences which victims commonly commit as *a consequence* of the trafficking or exploitation include the production or being concerned in the sale and supply of controlled drugs, shoplifting, theft by housebreaking, benefit fraud and offences linked to commercial sexual exploitation. Prosecutors should also be alert to the fact that victims of human trafficking or exploitation may themselves commit human trafficking or exploitation offences in relation to other individuals. (Emphases added)

On the principles of the non-punishment provision, the Lord Advocate's Instructions leave little room for doubt:

7. If there is sufficient evidence that a child aged 17 or under has committed an offence and there is credible and reliable information to support the fact that the child;
(a) is a victim of human trafficking or exploitation and
(b) the offending took place in the course of or as a consequence of being the victim of human trafficking or exploitation,
then there is a *strong presumption* against prosecution of that child for that offence.

8. If there is sufficient evidence that a person aged 18 or over has committed an offence and there is credible and reliable information to support the fact that the person;
(a) is a victim of human trafficking or exploitation
(b) has been compelled to carry out the offence and
(c) the compulsion is directly attributable to being the victim of human trafficking or exploitation,
then there is a *strong presumption* against prosecution of that person for that offence.

In addition, the Lord Advocate's Instructions require that in all cases where the suspect has been identified as a victim of human trafficking and exploitation, they must be reported to the National Lead Prosecutor for Human Trafficking and Exploitation for a final decision to be made. This practice could prove significant for monitoring and enhancing understanding of criminal practices and, if successful, should be adopted in England, Wales and Northern Ireland. The central gathering of case data by the National Lead Prosecutor when the defence is raised would greatly assist in building a UK-wide picture on the use of this defence.

Implementation and use of the non-punishment provision

Following the passage of the three Acts, all three prosecuting agencies across the UK – the CPS in England and Wales, the COPFS in Scotland and the PPS in Northern Ireland – produced revised guidance on non-prosecution.[24] The College of Policing Authorised Professional Practice (APP) on modern slavery also includes reference to the statutory defence under section 45 of the MSA, although it is very limited in the details, offering little by way of guidance for police if they suspect a perpetrator may be a victim of trafficking.

In 2015, UNICEFUK (United Nations Childrens' Education Fund UK) published research[25] on the use of the statutory defence in cases involving children. The research reported that there were 'serious shortcomings in the implementation of the non-punishment principle', stating that, in some cases, defence lawyers who had potentially represented victims of trafficking were unaware of the statutory defence. In other instances, the defence lawyer was aware of the statutory defence and had raised it but found that neither the custody sergeant nor CPS lawyers knew about this new provision (a detailed analysis of cases in respect of cannabis farming is provided in Chapter Eight). Cases were also reported where the statutory defence had been raised and the CPS alerted that a potential victim of trafficking was involved but the CPS refused to review the case due to the absence of a positive conclusive grounds decision, which is in contradiction of their own guidance.

It is not yet possible to easily quantify the number of cases (adults or children) in which the statutory defence has been raised, and what the subsequent outcome has been, because such information is not routinely collected or collated. It goes without saying that without such central data collection, it will not be possible for the UK to monitor the effectiveness of the statutory defence.

The Lord Advocate's Instructions provided for by section 8 of the Scottish Act provide the clearest example of the principles and guidance for a statutory defence. The wording is unambiguous and can easily be used in policy and training for people without legal training.

There is also a strong element of oversight and accountability built into the Lord Advocate's Instructions that is currently missing in the other jurisdictions. It seems clear that England, Wales and Northern Ireland ought to adopt the practice set out in the Lord Advocate's Instructions to require that in cases where the suspect has been identified as a victim of human trafficking and exploitation, the case must be reported to the National Lead Prosecutor for Modern Slavery/Human Trafficking and Exploitation.

Conclusion

Since the introduction of the legislation in 2015, the MSA has received the most frequent and prominent accolades of the three laws, by actors nationally and internationally. While it may be true that the Scotland and Northern Ireland Acts are not as broad in scope as the MSA, due to the reserved powers of the UK Parliament, closer inspection of comparable provisions across the three Acts shows that the MSA is, in a number of areas, weaker than its counterparts. This is particularly true in the area of victim protection; unlike its counterparts in Scotland and Northern Ireland, the MSA does not explicitly place a duty on ministers to provide support to victims in England and Wales, or set out the protection and support that they are entitled to. Through the drafting of these laws, the devolved governments in Scotland and Northern Ireland have shown themselves to be the most progressive and victim-focused. In the areas of child guardianship and in the interpretation of the non-punishment principle, it is Scotland that is leading the way.

The introduction of the MSA and the respective Acts in Scotland and Northern Ireland has undoubtedly been, on balance, a positive and welcome step in the development of the UK's response to modern slavery. Their introduction has served to raise public and political awareness of modern slavery and acted as the catalyst for a number of policy reviews, some resulting in positive policy changes. There has also been renewed political commitment to tackling this issue and the creation of numerous strategic and operational groups and bodies to drive the agenda forward. With the creation of roles such as the Independent Anti-Slavery Commissioner, the hope is that modern slavery eradication will remain high on the political agenda.

However, while the introduction of the Acts has led to a flurry of activity at the national and strategic levels, the impact at the local level, particularly in terms of the experiences of victims, has been limited to date. Many of the Acts' key provisions, such as the Statutory Guidance on victim identification and assistance (section 49 of the MSA), are yet to be implemented. In some cases, where provisions have commenced, there has been a failure at the national level to communicate this adequately to implementing partners, for instance, with the statutory defence (section 45 of the MSA).

Moreover, it is still not yet possible to comprehensively monitor the impact of the legislation due to significant gaps in data collection, a gap highlighted in the most recent report from the Group of Experts on Action against Trafficking in Human Beings (GRETA). The lack of a UK-wide modern slavery data strategy and the absence of a monitoring matrix to measure the implementation and impact of the legislation are significant weaknesses in the UK's response, a point that has also been highlighted in the recent report from the National Audit Office (NAO 2017). This criticism is, for the most part, aimed at the UK government as the Northern Ireland and Scottish governments have recently made welcome progress in this regard. For instance, the Scotland Human Trafficking and Exploitation Strategy, published in May 2017, now includes quantitative progress indicators to monitor the implementation of each element of the strategy, and makes clear the authority responsible for collecting data for each of the indicators. The inclusion of these indicators clarifies lines of responsibility, encourages buy-in and increases the accountability of the responsible authorities. If the UK government is to credibly claim that it is the 'world leader' in addressing modern slavery, then the inclusion of a monitoring framework, similar to that in Scotland, should also be included in next Modern Slavery Strategy. As is stands, the claim of being world-leading, especially in the light of the damning NAO report, looks very flimsy.

Acknowledgement
This chapter is based in significant part on the Anti-Trafficking Monitoring Group's report entitled 'Class Acts? Examining modern slavery legislation across the UK', published in October 2016. Available at: www.antislavery. org/atmg

Notes
[1] See: www.thesundaytimes.co.uk/sto/comment/regulars/guestcolumn/ article1304361.ece

[2] See: www.jennymarra.com/human-trafficking-bill/4579313773. MSPs are Members of the Scottish Parliament.

3   See: www.legislation.gov.uk/ukpga/2015/30/contents/enacted

4   See: www.legislation.gov.uk/nia/2015/2/contents/enacted

5   See: www.legislation.gov.uk/asp/2015/12/contents

6   See: www.gov.uk/government/uploads/system/uploads/attachment_data/ file/448200/Consultation_Government_Response__final__2_pdf.pdf

7   See: www.gov.uk/government/speeches/defeating-modern-slavery-theresa-may-article

8   Section 113 of the Anti-Social Behaviour and Policing Act 2014.

9   For instance, see updated Crown Prosecution Service (CPS) guidance on 'Human trafficking, smuggling and slavery'. Available at: www.cps.gov. uk/legal/h_to_k/human_trafficking_and_smuggling/#a05

10 See: www.gov.uk/government/news/home-secretary-strengthens-police-response-to-modern-slavery

11 Within the annual report, it was announced that the 'The Prime Minister's Modern Slavery Taskforce has taken on the majority of functions of the IDMG and the Home Secretary will assume the IDMG's role of acting as the national rapporteur for the UK'.

12 See: www.gov.uk/government/publications/modern-slavery-act-2015-review-one-year-on

13 The reasoning behind this can be found in the explanatory notes: 'Subsection (9) provides a further discretionary power which would ensure that the Department is able to continue to provide support to an individual beyond the point where a Conclusive Determination is made, where that is considered necessary'.

14 See: www.glasgowlive.co.uk/news/glasgow-news/scottish-government-doubles-support-human-13187625

15 See: http://webarchive.nationalarchives.gov.uk/20141202113228/https:// nrm.homeoffice.gov.uk/documents/2014/11/nrm-final-report.pdf

16 See: www.gov.uk/government/news/modern-slavery-taskforce-agrees-new-measures-to-support-victims

17 See: https://publications.parliament.uk/pa/cm201617/cmselect/ cmworpen/803/80308.htm#_idTextAnchor063

18 See: https://publications.parliament.uk/pa/cm201719/cmselect/ cmworpen/672/67202.htm

[19] See: www.gov.uk/government/uploads/system/uploads/attachment_data/file/486138/icta-horr86.pdf

[20] See: www.antislaverycommissioner.co.uk/media/1104/iasc-letter-on-independent-child-trafficking-advocates-to-karen-bradley-mp.pdf

[21] See: www.aberlour.org.uk/services/scottish-guardianship-service/

[22] Article 26 of the Trafficking Convention and Article 8 of the EU Trafficking Directive.

[23] Immigration Law Practitioners' Association, briefing for the Modern Slavery Bill, House of Commons, second reading, 8 July 2014.

[24] For England, see: www.cps.gov.uk/legal/h_to_k/human_trafficking_and_smuggling/#a20. For Scotland, see: https://eur-lex.europa.eu/LexUriServ/LexUriServ.do?uri=OJ:L:2011:101:0001:0011:EN:PDF. Northern Ireland's guidance is not publicly available.

[25] See: https://downloads.unicef.org.uk/wp-content/uploads/2017/05/Unicef-UK-Briefing_Victim-Not-Criminal_2017.pdf

References

ATMG (Anti-Trafficking Monitoring Group) (2013) *In the dock*, London: Anti-Trafficking Monitoring Group.

ATMG (2017) *Class Acts?*, London: Anti-Trafficking Monitoring Group.

CoE (Council of Europe) (2005) *Convention on action against trafficking in human beings*, Strasbourg: Council of Europe.

FRA (European Union Fundamental Rights Agency) (2015) *Guardianship for children deprived of parental care: A handbook to reinforce guardianship systems to cater for the specific needs of child victims of trafficking*, Brussels: European Union Fundamental Rights Agency.

HMICFRS (Her Majesty's Inspectorate of Constabulary and Fire and Rescue Services) (2017) *Stolen freedom*, London: Her Majesty's Inspectorate of Constabulary and Fire and Rescue Services.

Home Office (2016) *The Modern Slavery Act review*, London: Home Office.

Home Office (2017) *Annual report on modern slavery*, London: Home Office.

NAO (National Audit Office) (2017) *Reducing modern slavery*, London: National Audit Office.

FIVE

Child trafficking in the UK

Chloe Setter

Introduction

Child trafficking has been noted to have a 'lower profile' than that of adult trafficking (Annison 2013a). However, numbers of recorded child victims are more than a third of the total of those identified in the UK by relevant authorities. Trafficked children have 'particular vulnerabilities', as recognised by the European Union (EU) Anti-Trafficking Directive, and this chapter will explore those specific needs and examine the UK's response to children who have been exploited. It will look at whether the National Referral Mechanism (NRM) works effectively for children and it will assess how current policy/practice impacts on this affected group.

Definitions and offences

The United Nations Convention on the Rights of the Child defines a child as being an individual who is under the age of 18. According to the internationally accepted definition of human trafficking, child trafficking means the 'recruitment, transportation, transfer, harbouring or receipt of persons … for the purpose of exploitation'. It defines exploitation as, 'at a minimum, the exploitation of the prostitution of others or other forms of sexual exploitation, forced labour or services, slavery or practices similar to slavery, servitude or the removal of organs' (Article 3 of the [Palermo] 'Protocol to prevent, suppress and punish trafficking in persons especially women and children', supplementing the United Nations Convention against Transnational Organized Crime, adopted by General Assembly resolution 55/25 of 15 November 2000; see UNODC 2003).

A more expanded explanation of exploitation can be found in the EU Anti-Trafficking Directive (Preamble, para 11, Directive 2011/36/EU of the European Parliament and of the Council of 5 April 2011 on preventing and combating trafficking in human beings and protecting its victims, and replacing Council Framework Decision 2002/629/ JHA):

> In order to tackle recent developments in the phenomenon of trafficking in human beings, this Directive adopts a broader concept of what should be considered trafficking in human beings than under Framework Decision 2002/629/ JHA and therefore includes additional forms of exploitation. Within the context of this Directive, forced begging should be understood as a form of forced labour or services as defined in the 1930 ILO Convention No 29 concerning Forced or Compulsory Labour. Therefore, the exploitation of begging, including the use of a trafficked dependent person for begging, falls within the scope of the definition of trafficking in human beings only when all the elements of forced labour or services occur. In the light of the relevant case-law, the validity of any possible consent to perform such labour or services should be evaluated on a case-by-case basis. However, when a child is concerned, no possible consent should ever be considered valid. The expression 'exploitation of criminal activities' should be understood as the exploitation of a person to commit, inter alia, pick-pocketing, shop-lifting, drug trafficking and other similar activities which are subject to penalties and imply financial gain. The definition also covers trafficking in human beings for the purpose of the removal of organs, which constitutes a serious violation of human dignity and physical integrity, as well as, for instance, other behaviour such as illegal adoption or forced marriage in so far as they fulfil the constitutive elements of trafficking in human beings.

In the UK legislation, there are some discrepancies about how the criminal offences of trafficking are drafted between the three jurisdictions (for a fuller discussion, see Chapter Four). The drafting of the offence of human trafficking is broadly the same in the Modern Slavery Act (MSA) and the Human Trafficking and Exploitation (Criminal Justice and Support for Victims) Act (Northern Ireland) but significantly different in the Scottish Human Trafficking and Exploitation Act (Beddoe and Brotherton 2016). Across all of the legislations, there is no specific offence relating to children. A problematic area for children is found in the drafting of the MSA's human trafficking offence, which states that individuals, both adults and children, cannot consent to the 'travel' element of the offence. Yet, the Palermo Protocol, the Anti-Trafficking Convention and the EU Anti-Trafficking Directive all make it clear that children cannot consent to any of the acts of trafficking, or the exploitation itself. This lack of clarity is a concern with regards to how practitioners understand and use the law.

Trafficking itself is a broad and complex phenomenon. It is commonly now referred to in parts of the UK (in particular, England and Wales) as 'modern slavery', yet this term actually encompasses the broader suite of trafficking, slavery, servitude and forced or compulsory labour. Child trafficking affects a wide group of young people (see Cooper et al 2017). Many children are trafficked across international borders and smuggled into the UK, often as unaccompanied children, yet some arrive legally on prearranged visas. Not all unaccompanied children are victims of trafficking, although being unaccompanied significantly increases their vulnerability to exploitation. Many trafficked children are not unaccompanied – they may arrive with (real or putative) family or guardians – and they may not always claim asylum. Victims may be EU citizens and not subject (at least at present) to immigration control. A large proportion are also British nationals trafficked internally around the UK. Children can also be trafficked out of the UK for exploitation in other countries. It is not uncommon for children to be moved frequently around towns, cities, countries and even continents for the purpose of exploitation. This complex picture gives rise to many myths and misunderstandings about what trafficking is and how it manifests in the UK, meaning that many children are not identified as potential victims quickly or even at all.

The current picture

Child victims of trafficking represent about a third (34%) of all known victims in the UK. In 2016, from NRM data, there were 1,278 children suspected as being victims of trafficking, an increase of 30% from 2015 (NCA 2017). There is a statutory duty on local authorities, under section 52 of the MSA, to notify the Secretary of State, through the NRM, where there are 'reasonable grounds' to believe that an individual may be a victim of modern slavery or trafficking. Potential child victims of modern slavery must currently be referred 'as soon as practicable to the NRM by a first responder and assessed by a competent authority (a trained decision-maker) within the UK' (DfE 2017: 5).[1]

Potential child victims recorded in the NRM come from a wide range of countries, 85 being referenced in 2017. The data are broken down into exploitation types, with the following categories: domestic servitude; forced labour; sexual exploitation (non–UK nationals); sexual exploitation (UK nationals); organ harvesting; and unknown exploitation. These are, however, broad categories that do not reflect the complex and nuanced nature of exploitation. It is arguable that they are not the correct categories to represent the situations of modern slavery seen in the UK. For example, it is widely accepted that forced criminality – that is, children forced to commit crimes, such as drug running, drug cultivation, theft and so on – represents the majority of the 'forced labour' category referrals for children, yet there is no separate category for this. Domestic servitude could be argued to be a form of forced labour, and there is not a specific category for the forced begging of children. It is unclear why only sexual exploitation is separated into UK nationals and non-UK nationals for children (this is not the case for adults). The Home Office (2017) has published a 'typology' of modern slavery offences, which found there to be 17 known types of offences of modern slavery, highlighting the complexity of the cases manifesting in the UK.

The reality of child trafficking is far more complicated than the arbitrary categorisation established in the NRM. In many cases, children are exploited in more than one way, which is simply not reflected in the NRM statistics. There may, indeed, be a primary exploitation type; however, this might only be the case at the point of referral. As the case unfolds, it could become clear that the child has experienced other forms of exploitation, yet the NRM does not currently have the structure to reflect this complexity, which leaves us with a narrow and somewhat inaccurate picture of child modern slavery in the UK.

The NRM shows how many referrals come from each part of the UK, with England referring the lion's share of child cases (1,961) in 2017, followed by Scotland (63), Wales (84) and Northern Ireland (610). In terms of population, it is to be expected that England would refer proportionately more cases. However, the relatively low numbers in the other countries is concerning. The UK government's own scientific analysis led it to conclude in 2014 that there were up to 13,000 people living in modern slavery across the UK (Home Office 2014b) and the National Crime Agency (NCA) raised this estimation to likely be in the 'tens of thousands'.[2] Given that children represent, on average, a third of all victims, approximately 4,000 of these 13,000 victims (or perhaps as many as 10,000 at least if the higher NCA total estimate is taken) would be children. Given that only 2,118 children were referred as potential victims in 2017, it is not clear whether children's cases are not being identified or, rather, not being referred into the NRM. Unlike adults, children do not have to give consent to be referred into the NRM (Home Office 2017), and so it stands to reason that children should be strongly represented in recorded potential cases of modern slavery.

Issues with data

It is important to look at who is making children's referrals into the NRM: Home Office Immigration Enforcement referred 23 children in 2017; UK Border Force referred 91; and UK Visas and Immigration made 583 referrals. The NCA referred two children, yet local police forces made 559 referrals for children. Local authorities referred 722 children's cases (double the number in 2016) and non-governmental organisations (NGOs) accredited as 'first responders'[3] in the NRM referred 138 children. It is interesting to note that NGOs referred a far greater number of adults than children. This is likely to be because the Salvation Army runs the support contract for adult victims of trafficking, whereas the care of children is the responsibility of individual local authorities. It is also for this reason that the collection of data around child victims of trafficking is complex and the data themselves are incomplete.

As child protection is devolved in the UK, there is inconsistency in law, policy and practice across Scotland, England, Wales and Northern Ireland. In addition, the care of children is tasked at a local authority level and there is therefore much room for variation, despite national policy in each country. There are currently 418 principal (unitary, upper and second tier) councils in the UK, including 27 county councils, 201 district councils and 125 unitary councils (LGIU 2017). Considering the number of councils, it is surprising that local authorities are responsible for so few referrals into the NRM. A crude average calculation of the number of referrals of children against the number of councils in the UK would reveal only a handful of children from each area being referred as suspected victims. The NRM reveals which local authorities have referred adults and children, and it makes for a mixed picture.[4]

Some areas (Birmingham, Coventry City, Hampshire, Tower Hamlets and Surrey) referred proportionately higher numbers of children in 2016, whereas many others struggled to refer any at all (Aylesbury Vale, Bolton, Cumbria, Edinburgh City, Gloucester, Lancashire, Leeds City, Leicester, Lewes, London Enfield, London Westminster, Norfolk, Nottinghamshire, Rotherham and Somerset).

Many others only referred one case or a small number. The NRM concerns children of all nationalities, including British nationals who may be being abused in sexual exploitation or 'county lines' drug running.[5] Given the geographical variation in these low-referring areas, as well as the fact that some are highly populated urban areas with diverse populations, the lack of referrals is deeply worrying.

Local authorities are bound by a duty to record modern slavery concerns:

> Local authorities should ensure that they have processes in place to monitor their policies and performance relating to both unaccompanied children and child victims of modern slavery, including trafficking, and should record modern slavery concerns on the child's care plan. They should ensure that responsible managers look beyond this guidance to understand the risks and issues facing unaccompanied children and child victims of modern slavery and to review best practice in planning for the care of these children. (DfE 2017: 7)

However, research beyond the NRM data recording has also shown that local authorities are inconsistent in their recording of child trafficking. Every Child Protected Against Trafficking UK (ECPAT UK), in partnership with the NGO Missing People, analysed data obtained by Freedom of Information (FOI) requests concerning the numbers of unaccompanied and trafficked children in the care of local authorities across the UK, as well as examining instances of missing episodes. It stated that the research 'identified a worrying lack of consistency in the way in which local authorities identify and record risk of trafficking and exploitation' (Simon et al 2016: 22). It highlighted the London area response, for example: 'Responses from London authorities showed considerable variance between boroughs. Despite London being a key destination for human traffickers, 10 of 33 London authorities reported no trafficked children and a further 4 could provide no information' (Simon et al 2016: 22).

Of 217 local authorities contacted with FOI requests, 80% provided no information on the number of trafficked children in their care. Many councils cited an exemption to the Freedom of Information Act that allows public bodies not to respond to requests where the cost of responding would 'exceed the appropriate limit' as it would involve examining the individual case files of all children cared for. The most common reason given for declining to respond was, however, not having a searchable data-field for trafficking on case management systems. Several local authorities acknowledged this failing during the course of the research and committed to improving data-recording practices in relation to child trafficking.

Separately, there have been estimates of the number of children affected by sexual exploitation. An inquiry by the Office of the Children's Commissioner for England (2012) found that at least 16,500 children were identified as being at risk of child sexual exploitation during one year and 2,409 children were confirmed as victims of sexual exploitation in gangs and groups during the 14-month period from August 2010 to October 2011. This data seriously challenges government estimates. There appears to be a disconnect between data on child sexual exploitation and child trafficking, or modern slavery, data. ECPAT's *Heading back to harm* report (Simon et al 2016: 24) found that:

> although 42% of the respondents stated that British children were, in their experience, 'rarely' or 'never' recorded as trafficked. It appears that many British victims of child sexual exploitation (CSE) are not being referred to the NRM and being identified as victims of trafficking. This may be due to a lack of understanding of the definition of trafficking, with many practitioners thinking it affects only those who cross international borders.

It is clear that the data available on child trafficking provide only a partial picture of the true scale of child exploitation in the UK. Data often remain locally, in silos, and do not seem to always reach the national level (ie the NRM). Local authorities use different case-management systems, many of which do not currently allow them to easily search case files in order to obtain information about modern slavery. This is concerning as it means that Local Safeguarding Children Boards (LSCBs) and local authority leaders may be unaware of the scale of trafficking locally. From a national perspective, it means that child trafficking data are massively incomplete and the data that we do have are likely to be a vast underestimate of the real extent of child exploitation occurring in the UK.

It is important to note that the NRM only records children who have actually been identified as potential victims of modern slavery by a designated 'first responder'. First responders include: police forces; the NCA; the UK Border Force; Home Office Visas and Immigration; the Gangmasters Licensing and Abuse Authority; local authorities;

health and social care trusts (Northern Ireland); the Salvation Army; Migrant Help; the Medaille Trust; Kalayaan; Barnardo's; Unseen; the TARA (Trafficking Awareness Raising Alliance) Project (Scotland); NSPCC; BAWSO; New Pathways; and the Refugee Council – many of which actually work only with adult victims.

Many referred may not receive a positive 'reasonable grounds' or 'conclusive grounds' decision by (at the time of writing) one of the two competent authorities (the Home Office or the NCA). In 2016, there were only 635 conclusive decisions out of the 3,805 adult and children's cases referred (these data do not distinguish between adults and children). The NRM does not currently have a system of appeal for negative decisions. At present, the only way to challenge a decision is by way of legal challenge, which is potentially cumbersome, time-consuming and expensive. However, successful challenges are not reflected in the NRM data. A recent announcement by Home Secretary Amber Rudd has proposed that an independent panel of experts will review negative decisions, but details have yet to be revealed.

There are also many other children who may not have been referred into the NRM for various reasons. First, they may still be in a situation of exploitation and are not visible to authorities or NGOs. Second, they may be visible but those in contact with them have not recognised the indicators or risk. Third, they are suspected as being a potential victim but the 'first responder' is not aware of the duty to refer into the NRM and so does not make a referral. Fourth, the 'first responder' is aware but chooses not to make a referral.

Identification of child victims

There are well-documented concerns about the identification of children as being at risk of or being victims of modern slavery, namely, due to low awareness among practitioners and much criticism of the NRM, particularly with regard to child victims. In its second-round evaluation of the UK, the Council of Europe's Group of Experts on Action against Trafficking in Human Beings (GRETA) found that 'child trafficking remains underreported' (GRETA 2016: 23). In one report, the Anti-Trafficking Monitoring Group (ATMG)[6] stated:

> We have found evidence of poor decision-making, a worrying lack of child-specific knowledge and child safeguarding, an inappropriate focus on immigration, low awareness of the NRM, a lack of training and a lack of a

formal recovery and reflection period for children. (Setter and Finch 2014)

Concerns were also raised about potential discrimination or racism in cases involving non-EU nationals. The ATMG found that in an analysis of cases in 2012, 80% of EU/European Economic Area (EEA) nationals received a positive decision, compared with 20% of third-country nationals. It concluded that there is 'valid concern that the immigration status of a trafficking victim inappropriately influences NRM decisions and that hence the decision-making is unfair and discriminatory' (Annison 2013b).

Early criticism such as this informed the Home Office's internal review of the NRM in 2014. It found that social workers may not have specific awareness of trafficking and that local authorities may not see the benefit of referring children into the NRM (Home Office 2014a). Additionally, it highlighted that Directors of Children's Services 'rarely had any intelligence to help them plan interventions with other agencies in relation to trafficking' (Home Office 2014a). A pilot revised NRM followed shortly after, which was evaluated in 2017 but did not make specific recommendations for children's cases. Research has shown that social workers, who play a key role in the lives of children affected by modern slavery, often lack experience and training. The recent US State Department's *Trafficking in persons* report for the UK recommended making trafficking training 'mandatory for all social workers and care providers working with trafficking victims, especially those working with children' (Ellis et al 2017), yet this has not been realised and many social workers have never received any training on modern slavery. Some areas of the UK that previously had specialist teams for unaccompanied children had disbanded those and many social workers had not received any training or resources to understand how to identify at-risk children (Finch 2017). The report *Heading back to harm* (Simon et al 2016) showed that the professionals surveyed believed that training for professionals in contact with trafficked, unaccompanied and separated children was the most effective intervention to prevent children going missing from care and being re-trafficked.

In 2017, the charity ECPAT UK launched a public campaign to push for better multi-agency working on child trafficking, as well as improved support for those identified. It highlighted that although children who were victims of modern slavery would qualify for care through existing statutory provision, they were not receiving specialist support. It argued that a positive NRM decision should translate into guaranteed specialist care, which should be funded by central government to enable local authorities to give this support, which included:

- multi-agency decision-making about trafficking identification;
- the immediate appointment of an independent legal guardian or advocate;
- access to specialist accommodation placements (such as specialist foster care);
- quick and guaranteed access to specialist psychotherapy/counselling;
- publicly funded lawyers who are trained in trafficking issues and law relating to children;
- a grant of leave that would ensure a durable solution (for those with immigration concerns);
- improved access to compensation;
- guaranteed non-prosecution for crimes that were a direct result of any exploitation[7];
- a multi-agency assessment of re-trafficking risk and a subsequent safety plan; and
- automatic special measures in all courts.

The need for multi-agency working in child protection cases is well established. High-profile child sexual exploitation scandals in the UK, such as those in Rochdale, Rotherham and Oxford, have shown the critical need for multi-agency working in cases of abuse, both in terms of responding to actual exploitation and in prevention-based work (Jay 2014). There have been several serious case reviews on the issue of child sexual exploitation, all of which have particularly recommended better communication and information sharing between agencies involved in children's cases.[8] However, the NRM remains a centralised system in which those making decisions about whether a child is a victim of modern slavery never come into contact with the child, relying solely on paperwork.

The government announced a raft of changes to the NRM in October 2017, following much criticism by NGOs and the media about the response to victims in England and Wales, in particular.[9] This included the creation of an 'expert unit' in the Home Office that will handle all NRM referrals and make all decisions about whether somebody is a victim of modern slavery. In addition, there will be an 'independent panel of experts' to review negative conclusive decisions and the rolling out of a digitised system for the NRM to improve data collection and analysis. Charities have consistently urged the government to embed the NRM into existing multi-agency child protection arrangements, such as Multi-Agency Safeguarding Hubs, at a local or regional level in order to improve identification, joined-up intelligence and coordinated support. However, despite evidence by both the government's own internal review and criticism from charities working with children, calls for a separate system for children were not heeded in the latest announcements, and the latest announced changes have yet to be implemented.

Legal guardianship and issues with support

There remains much concern about the level of support that those identified child victims of modern slavery receive across the UK, even after a positive 'reasonable' or 'conclusive' grounds decision (Franklin and Doyle 2012). This is clearly seen in relation to the issue of guardianship for children. Article 16.3 of the EU Anti-Trafficking Directive decrees that: 'Member States shall take the necessary measures to ensure that, where appropriate, a guardian is appointed to unaccompanied child victims of trafficking in human beings'. This is also recommended by the UN Committee on the Rights of the Child (1982) for all separated children. However, the picture across the UK on guardianship is mixed.

Northern Ireland made provision in its Human Trafficking and Exploitation Act 2015 for an 'independent guardian' for all separated children and all trafficked children. This service is still being established but the guardians will be individuals employed by an independent charity with five years' post-qualification experience as a social worker. In Scotland, a non-statutory 'guardianship' system has been in place since 2010 for unaccompanied migrant children, which includes those from that cohort who may have been trafficked. Scotland also made provision in its own Human Trafficking and Exploitation Act 2015 for a statutory service for children who are victims of trafficking and those for whom there is no one with parental responsibility. There has also been a delay in the setting up of this statutory service and, currently, the non-statutory Scottish Guardianship Service, run by the charity Aberlour, continues to deliver the service for unaccompanied migrant children, pending the statutory regulations coming into force.

In England and Wales, the MSA contains an enabling section for 'Independent Child Trafficking Advocates'. This does not make any provision for the wider group of separated or unaccompanied children, but focuses instead on those who are suspected of being victims of modern slavery. It followed a year-long trial of advocates by the charity Barnardos in 23 local authority areas in England. In July 2016, the Home Office asked interested parties to bid to provide Independent Child Trafficking Advocates in 'early-adopter' sites for a maximum of two years from November 2016. These areas were selected as Hampshire and the Isle of Wight, Greater Manchester, and Wales. Despite commitments from two consecutive ministers with responsibility for modern slavery, there has been criticism of the decision to delay a national roll-out.[10]

The most recent announcement from the Home Office in October 2017 on the issue stated: 'The government will also roll out nationally the provision of Independent Child Trafficking Advocates, who will provide specialist support and act in the best interests of trafficked children. The service is currently running in Wales, Hampshire and Greater Manchester'. This announcement did not add any further details on the anticipated national roll-out and, in particular, there was no time frame attached to the announcement. However, the Home Office put out an invitation to tender for qualitative research on the early-adopter sites. In England and Wales, there have been long-standing calls for an advocacy or guardianship system to apply to all separated children, not just those identified as trafficked, with cross-party support from MPs.[11] In particular, charities working with unaccompanied children have highlighted that separated children also suffer from a lack of parental responsibility and will also likely have complex needs. Additionally, because trafficking is difficult to identify quickly, a system only for those formally identified will mean that many are not referred to a guardian/advocate immediately; the early months are a critical period for keeping the child safe.

The UN Children's Fund (UNICEF) and The Children's Society completed a cost–benefit appraisal of a guardianship system for unaccompanied children, finding that for every £1 spent on a service over three years, as much as £1.25 could be saved (UNICEF UK and The Children's Society 2014). This increased to £2.39 once the financial benefits for separated children who reach adulthood (the age of 18) were factored in. The research found overall potential benefits of £107 million and savings of £62 million over the first three years after a service was introduced. The service is estimated to cost £6,237 per child per year, with a total cost of the service of £45 million for the first three years after introduction. However, despite the repeated calls and evidence, there has been little movement on this front from the government in Westminster regarding the wider cohort of separated children.

Aside from its shortcomings in establishing a guardianship system, there are other areas in which the UK is falling behind in its obligations in the EU Anti-Trafficking Directive. The EU Anti-Trafficking Directive highlights that children are 'more vulnerable than adults' and that 'assistance and support measures for child victims should focus on their physical and psycho-social recovery and on a durable solution for the person in question'. It puts the onus on the state to enable this to happen: 'Member States shall take the necessary measures with a view to finding a durable solution based on an individual assessment of the best interests of the child'. However, a durable solution has yet to be realised in the UK. A durable solution has been defined as a plan that is a:

> sustainable solution that will ensure that an unaccompanied or separated child is able to develop into adulthood in an environment which will meet his or her needs as well as fulfil his or her rights as defined by the Convention on the Rights of the Child and will not put the child at risk of persecution or harm. (UNHCR and UNICEF 2014: 22)

There is currently no 'best interests' determination[12] process in place in any part of the UK in order to find an individual durable solution for each trafficked child.

There has been criticism of the immigration approach to those children who have been trafficked from outside of the EU. The current approach sees children usually granted limited leave to remain until the age of 17.5 or 18. Yet, it has been argued that this undermines the ability of the child, or those supporting the child, to find an individual durable solution for that child and prevents local authorities from making long-term plans for the child, which can facilitate a clear pathway to adulthood (UNHCR and UNICEF 2014). Ultimately, this short-term approach can leave the child vulnerable to further risk of exploitation. It also leaves children feeling in limbo and with great uncertainty about their futures. This can exacerbate mental health issues and is a major contributing factor to why children run away from care (Simon et al 2016).

Further issues arise if the child is engaged with criminality, which may actually be an indicator of their exploitation or be the purpose for their exploitation. Many trafficked children are first encountered by authorities in situations of criminality, such as a police raid on a cannabis factory or arrest for pickpocketing (see Chapter Eight). Others are first found in immigration raids, for example, in a nail bar or restaurant. In these instances, they are often seen first and foremost as criminals, or, indeed, illegal immigrants. Their potential status as a victim of trafficking is frequently overlooked (Finch 2017; HMICFRS 2017) and it may be some time before this is raised or they are referred into the NRM. This means that they may not receive the appropriate protection and puts them at risk of going missing and further exploitation.

Article 8 of the EU Anti-Trafficking Directive states that member states shall, in accordance with the basic principles of their legal system, take necessary measures to ensure that competent national authorities are entitled not to prosecute or impose penalties on victims of trafficking in human beings for their involvement in criminal activities that they have been compelled to commit as a direct consequence of being trafficked. All parts of the UK have non-prosecution guidance, but this is implemented differently in policy across the UK (see Chapter Three). Additionally, England and Wales' MSA and Northern Ireland's Human Trafficking and Exploitation Act provide a statutory defence of trafficking in law, while Scotland's legislation instead provides for the Lord Advocate to publish instructions on the non-prosecution of victims. Despite advancements in policy and law, charities continue to report trafficked children and young people being criminalised (Finch 2017), which can have a serious and long-lasting impact on the child's immediate well-being and future prospects (Simon et al 2016). These children are particularly vulnerable.

Children at risk of going missing

Children in the care system and unaccompanied migrant children are particularly vulnerable to trafficking (USSD 2017). The issue of children who may have been trafficked going missing from the UK care system, with many ending up in exploitation, has existed for many years, with high numbers being reported by both West Sussex Council and Hillingdon, where Gatwick and Heathrow airports are situated, respectively.[13] Child victims of trafficking have long been known to be at a high risk of going missing (CEOP 2010). The European police agency, Europol, warned that there are as many as 10,000[14] 'missing' or unaccounted-for unaccompanied children in the EU, many of whom it warned were vulnerable to trafficking and exploitation. This number may have increased as a result of continuing refugee migration from the Middle East and North Africa.

Research has found a worrying number of children who are at risk of trafficking going missing from the UK care system. In 2016, the *Heading back to harm* (Simon et al 2016) report revealed that, from September 2014 to September 2015, 28% of trafficked children (167 children) in care and 13% of unaccompanied children (593 children) in care went missing at least once. Of these, 207 missing trafficked or unaccompanied children had not been found. The research highlighted that trafficked and unaccompanied children go missing for longer periods than other missing children. It also reported that around a third of trafficked and unaccompanied children are missing for more than a week. This contrasts strikingly with previous research showing that just 2% of missing children are away for more than a week (NCA Missing Persons Bureau 2016). Fewer trafficked children appear to have gone missing in Scotland but the Scottish government has set up a Missing Persons Working Group to look further into the issue (Finch 2017).

There has been little analysis of the type of accommodation into which children who may have been trafficked are placed and possible links with going missing or re-trafficking. Generally, children are placed in supported lodgings, semi-supported lodgings, residential care homes, foster care, emergency housing, bedsits and, despite a policy ban, bed-and-breakfast accommodation. A recent official report found that although the majority of victims of child sexual exploitation lived at home with their families, those in care were disproportionately represented. It also found that victims were more likely to be exploited if they were living in care homes than if they were in foster families (Office of the Children's Commissioner for England 2012).

GRETA has criticised a lack of safe accommodation for children who are suspected or known to have been trafficked. It also said: 'There are no agreed standards for accommodating child victims of trafficking who are often provided general assistance which does not cater for their special needs' (GRETA 2016: 49). These special needs may vary but studies have found high rates of mental health issues among trafficked children. For example, one study found that a quarter of children who had been trafficked had post-traumatic stress disorder (PTSD) symptoms and one in eight had tried to harm or kill themselves (Kiss et al 2015).

It has been argued that specialist foster care – in which experienced foster carers receive additional support, training and finance, and are fully supported by childcare professionals[15] – is a good option for children who may have been trafficked. A pilot (Shuker 2013) of specialist foster care in 2012 found it to have beneficial results for children, yet this was discontinued due to the cost of running the service. In 2016/17, the Department for Education commissioned the Refugee Council and ECPAT UK to deliver introductory training to around 1,000 foster carers accommodating unaccompanied and trafficked children. The department has stated that it intends to commission further training to meet the high demand; however, this training alone would not be enough to constitute specialist foster care. The Northern Ireland Commissioner for Children and Young People has said that she would prefer separated children to be placed in specialist foster care but no such provision is presently available (Finch 2017).

There are few specialist options across the UK for children who have been trafficked, despite their particular need for specialist support and the high risk of them going missing. One service, the Baca Project in the East Midlands, provides specialist support for unaccompanied children aged 16 and over. It claims that 40% of its service users were trafficked young people. Its services include high-level safeguarding and 24/7 supervision if required. Another service on the south coast of England, run by Love 146, piloted a safe accommodation service in 2014. It offered long-term support to child victims in a 'holistically supportive' environment with trained staff.

Assessing age

A particularly difficult area of practice involving children who may have been trafficked is that of assessing age. This may also exacerbate the factors prompting children to run away from care (Simon et al 2016). Many children who present in the UK from abroad will not have any identity documents. This may be for various reasons, such as that the trafficker has taken them, they may be fake documents provided by smugglers or traffickers, or they may have never had any to begin with. Determining age accurately is crucial as it can affect the level of support received and impact on any protection claim. Yet, there is no scientifically proven way to accurately assess age. The Home Office often conducts an initial 'assessment' based solely on appearance and demeanour if a young person is claiming asylum (Coram Children's Legal Centre 2017); however, this approach is criticised as being flawed. Even if the Home Office is treating the person as an adult, when a referral is made to a local authority, the authority must do its own assessment and treat the young person as a child while it does so. Many age determinations are challenged by way of judicial review, which are both costly to the local authority and hugely damaging to the young people involved. For example, the London Borough of Croydon paid out nearly £1.2 million in costs for wrong decisions about children's ages in 2013.[16] The sensitivity around age assessments was demonstrated with published photographs in the media of the arrival of children from Calais under the 'Dubs agreement', which caused several MPs and commentators to claim that those arriving did not physically appear to look like children, despite criticism from NGOs about the risk to the individual young people of publishing the photographs.[17]

In 2015, 789 children were recorded as having had their ages disputed; however, this does not represent the total number in the UK as it only reflects Home Office disputes (Coram Children's Legal Centre 2017). The English and Welsh, Scottish, and Northern Irish legislations all provide for a 'presumption of age' clause, which essentially gives the individual the benefit of the doubt if age is in question so that they can continue to be supported as a child until any formal assessment is concluded. Statutory guidance in England and Wales states:

> Where an age assessment is required, local authorities must adhere to standards established within case law. Age assessments should only be carried out where there is reason to doubt that the individual is the age they claim. Age assessments should not be a routine part of a local authority's assessment of unaccompanied and trafficked children. (DfE 2017: 13)

Despite this and similar guidance in Scotland, concerns have been raised over the lack of training of those conducting assessments, the misapplication of the presumption and the quality of age assessments.

There has not been an age dispute challenged by judicial review in Northern Ireland for five years, so it is seen to be less of an issue there, possibly because the number of social workers conducting assessments is small and so they may be more accurately applying the legislation and policy (Finch 2017), although this needs confirming.

Conclusion

Ultimately, child trafficking presents a major challenge for those working in the UK to understand, recognise, prevent and respond to. Approaches are often focused on children who have already been exploited and there is far less work done to prevent the exploitation in the first place. The set-up of the independent advocates in England and Wales is a case in point, where only those who have been identified as trafficked benefit from support but other separated children who are particularly vulnerable to exploitation are not provided with preventative support.

Projects funded by the Home Office's new Modern Slavery Innovation Fund are making attempts to better understand the root causes of why children are trafficked to the UK from other countries and their experiences *en route* to the UK.[18] However, this is limited to children coming from several high-profile countries and may not have the depth and longevity to sufficiently scope what is such a wide and complex problem. There continues to be a need to join up the workings across government departments in order to tackle root causes, such as gender inequality, poverty, conflict, lack of opportunities, economic and social policy, and ineffective child protection systems, and also to explore the UK's role in tackling the abuse of children in company supply chains. Internationally, nationally and locally, there must be improved communication and joined-up multi-agency working in order to assess and manage risk, and to protect young victims.

In cases of domestic trafficking, the political and media focus continues to be on child sexual exploitation, particularly the model where groups of adult men exploit teenage girls in a 'loverboy'[19] scenario. There has been some success in the prosecution of such cases following the shocking revelations of inaction by authorities in Rochdale and Rotherham but the wider picture on convictions involving child trafficking and modern slavery is improving very slowly. A total of only 81 modern slavery prosecutions were recorded in 2016 (HM Government 2017) but it is not known how many cases involved those under 18.

There is a move towards better understanding the 'county lines' model of trafficking, whereby children are used to move drugs for gangs. Yet, as with child sexual exploitation and cannabis farming, the victims commonly face 'blame' for their role in the criminality, with many being wrongly arrested and imprisoned. This already requires shifting attitudes towards children with gang involvements and presents a large challenge to authorities who are failing to see children as victims of trafficking or implementing the non-prosecution principle (Berlowitz et al 2012).

The ramifications of what impact Brexit might have on child protection and the ability to bring perpetrators to justice are yet to be fully known, but experts are warning that the loss of cross-border measures could severely hamper the UK's ability to deal with international cases of child abuse and trafficking.[20] This issue is tentatively explored elsewhere in the book (see Chapters One and Ten).

It is clear that there is still much progress to be made if the UK truly wants to get anywhere near keeping its promise to 'defeat modern slavery'. Children are, without doubt, particularly vulnerable to trafficking and abuse. Without significant shifts in attitudes, increased resources locally and a more holistic, global approach, they will continue to be put at risk, with the traffickers always one step ahead (HRC 1982).

Notes

1 Yet more of the provisions of the NRM are undergoing review at the time of writing.

2 See *The Guardian*, 10 August 2017. Available at: www.theguardian.com/world/2017/aug/10/modern-slavery-uk-nca-human-trafficking-prostitution

3 First responders are agencies authorised to refer potential cases of modern slavery into the NRM.

4 The Local Government Association is currently (January 2018) issuing guidance for local authorities that may help to make the picture more consistent and accurate.

5 '*County lines*' is a national issue involving the use of mobile phone '*lines*' by groups to extend their drug-dealing business into new locations outside of their home areas.

6 The ATMG is a coalition established in 2009 to monitor the UK's implementation of European anti-trafficking legislation. The group examines all types of human trafficking, including internal trafficking and the trafficking of British nationals.

7 This is allegedly covered by the statutory defence included in clause 42 of the MSA; however, as Burland also shows in Chapter Eight, it is frequently being disregarded by criminal justice agencies.

8 See Somerset Serious Case Review (published November 2017) (available at: http://sscb.safeguardingsomerset.org.uk/working-with-children/serious-case-reviews/) and Oxfordshire Serious Case Review (published February 2015) (available at: www.oscb.org.uk/wp-content/uploads/SCR-into-CSE-in-Oxfordshire-FINAL-FOR-WEBSITE.pdf).

9 See: www.independent.co.uk/news/uk/home-news/slavery-policy-child-victims-national-referral-mechanism-government-overhaul-exploitation-a7998656.html

10 See: https://hansard.parliament.uk/Commons/2016-06-28/debates/ E20D6E81-D841-4DD4-9F57-0FCBC7E3085F/IndependentAdvocates ForTraffickedChildren

11 See: https://hansard.parliament.uk/Commons/2016-04-19/debates/ 16041924000001/UnaccompaniedChildren

12 A 'best interests' determination describes the formal process with strict procedural safeguards designed to determine the child's best interests for particularly important decisions affecting the child. It should facilitate adequate child participation without discrimination, involve decision-makers with relevant areas of expertise and balance all relevant factors in order to assess the best option (UNHCR and UNICEF 2014).

13 See: http://news.bbc.co.uk/1/hi/uk/7773736.stm

14 See: www.theguardian.com/world/2016/jan/30/fears-for-missing-child-refugees

15 See: www.barnardos.org.uk/fosteringandadoption/fostering/types_of_foster_care.htm

16 See: www.theguardian.com/world/2013/may/17/council-asylum-seeker-children-classed-adults

17 See: https://you.38degrees.org.uk/petitions/stop-the-sun-identifying-calais-children

18 See: www.gov.uk/government/news/home-secretary-pledges-11-million-for-groups-fighting-modern-slavery

19 See: www.mydangerousloverboy.com/

20 See: www.antislavery.org/wp-content/uploads/2017/07/ATMG-Brexit-paper.pdf

References

Annison, R. (2013a) *Hidden in plain sight: Three years on: Updated analysis of UK measures to protect trafficked persons*, London: Anti-Trafficking Monitoring Group.

Annison, R. (2013b) *In the dock: Examining the UK's criminal justice response to human trafficking*, London: Anti-Trafficking Monitoring Group.

Beddoe, C. and Brotherton, V. (2016) *Class Acts: Examining modern slavery legislation in the UK*, London: Anti-Trafficking Monitoring Group.

Berelowitz, S., Firmin, C., Edwards, G. and Gulyurtlu, S. (2012) *'I thought I was the only one in the world', The Office of the Children's Commissioner's inquiry into child sexual exploitation in gangs and groups*, London: Office of the Children's Commissioner for England.

CEOP (Child Exploitation and Online Protection) (2010) *Threat assessment of child exploitation and sexual abuse*, London: CEOP.

Cooper, C., Hesketh, O., Ellis, N. and Fair, A. (2017) *A typology of modern slavery offences in the UK*, London: Home Office. Available at: www.gov.uk/government/uploads/system/uploads/attachment_data/file/652652/typology-modern-slavery-offences-horr93.pdf

Coram Children's Legal Centre (2017) *Seeking support*, London: Coram Children's Legal Centre.

DfE (Department for Education) (2017) *Care of unaccompanied migrant children and child victims of modern slavery: Statutory guidance for local authorities*, London: Department for Education.

Ellis, N., Cooper, C. and Roe, S. (2017) *An evaluation of the National Referral Mechanism pilot*, London: Home Office. Available at: www.gov.uk/government/uploads/system/uploads/attachment_data/file/653703/evaluation-national-referral-mechanism-pilot-horr94.pdf

Finch, N. (2017) *Lighting the way: Steps that lawyers, legal guardians and child trafficking advocates in the UK can take to better identify and protect children who may have been trafficked*, London: ECPAT UK. Available at: www.ecpat.org.uk/Handlers/Download.ashx?IDMF=1dcfdd01-44fd-4b0f-90c3-ccbc36649a80

Franklin, A. and Doyle, L. (2012) *Still at risk? A review of support for trafficked children*, London: Refugee Council and The Children's Society.

GRETA (Group of Experts on Action Against Trafficking in Human Beings) (2016) *Report concerning the implementation of the Council of Europe Convention on Action against Trafficking in Human Beings by the United Kingdom*, Strasbourg: GRETA and Council of Europe. Available at: https://rm.coe.int/CoERMPublicCommonSearchServices/DisplayDCTMContent?documentId=09000016806abcdc

HM Government (2017) '2017 UK annual report on modern slavery'. Available at: www.gov.uk/government/uploads/system/uploads/attachment_data/file/652366/2017_uk_annual_report_on_modern_slavery.pdf

HMICFRS (Her Majesty's Inspectorate of Constabulary and Fire and Rescue Services) (2017) *Stolen freedom: The policing response to modern slavery and human trafficking*, London: Her Majesty's Inspectorate of Constabulary and Fire and Rescue Services. Available at: www.justiceinspectorates.gov.uk/hmicfrs/wp-content/uploads/stolen-freedom-the-policing-response-to-modern-slavery-and-human-trafficking.pdf

Home Office (2014a) 'Review of the National Referral Mechanism for victims of human trafficking'. Available at: http://webarchive.nationalarchives.gov.uk/20141202113228/https:/nrm.homeoffice.gov.uk/documents/2014/11/nrm-final-report.pdf

Home Office (2014b) 'Modern slavery: an application of multiple systems estimation'. Available at: www.gov.uk/government/publications/modern-slavery-an-application-of-multiple-systems-estimation

Home Office (2017) 'National referral mechanism guidance: adult (England and Wales)'. Available at: www.gov.uk/government/publications/human-trafficking-victims-referral-and-assessment-forms/guidance-on-the-national-referral-mechanism-for-potential-adult-victims-of-modern-slavery-england-and-wales

HRC (United Nations Human Rights Committee) (1982) 'CCPR general comment no. 6: Article 6 (right to life)', 30 April. Available at: www.refworld.org/docid/45388400a.html (accessed 16 November 2017).

Jay, A. (2014) *Independent inquiry into child sexual exploitation in Rotherham, 1997–2013*, London: TSO.

Kiss, L., Yun, K., Pocock, N. et al (2015) 'Exploitation, violence, and suicide risk among child and adolescent survivors of human trafficking in the Greater Mekong subregion'. *JAMA Pediatrics*, 169(9): e152278.

LGIU (Local Government Information Unit) (2017) *How many councils are there?* Available at: www.lgiu.org.uk/local-government-facts-and-figures/#how-many-councils-are-there (accessed November 2017).

NCA (National Crime Agency) (2017) *National Referral Mechanism statistics 2016 end of year summary*, London: National Crime Agency.

NCA Missing Persons Bureau (2016) *Missing persons data report 2015–16*, London: National Crime Agency. Available at: http://nationalcrimeagency.gov.uk/publications/876-missing-persons-data-report-2015-2016-1/file

Office of the Children's Commissioner for England (2012) 'Accelerated report, briefing for the Rt Hon Michael Gove MP, Secretary of State for Education, on the emerging findings of the Office of the Children's Commissioner's inquiry into child sexual exploitation in gangs and groups, with a special focus on children in care', July.

Setter, C. and Finch, N. (2014) *Proposal for a revised National Referral Mechanism (NRM) for children*, London: Anti-Trafficking Monitoring Group.

Shuker, L. (2013) *Evaluation of Barnardo's Safe Accommodation Project for sexually exploited and trafficked young people*, Luton: University of Bedfordshire, Institute of Applied Social Research. Available at: www.beds.ac.uk/__data/assets/pdf_file/0007/281374/Barnardo27s-SA-Project-Evaluation-Full-Report.pdf

Simon, A., Setter, C. and Holmes, L. (2016) *Heading back to harm: A study on trafficked and unaccompanied children going missing from care in the UK*, London: ECPAT UK.

UN Committee on the Rights of the Child (1982) Report on separated children, referenced at: www.ohchr.org/en/hrbodies/crc/Pages/CRCIndex.aspx

UNHCR (United Nations High Commissioner for Refugees) and UNICEF (United Nations Children's Education Fund) (2014) *Safe & sound: What states can do to ensure respect for the best interests of unaccompanied and separated children in Europe*, London: UN High Commissioner for refugees. Available at: www.refworld.org/docid/5423da264.html (accessed 16 November 2017).

UNICEF (United Nations Children's Education Fund) UK and The Children's Society (2014) *Protecting children through guardianship: The costs and benefits of guardianship for unaccompanied and separated migrant children*, London: UNICEF UK.

UNODC (United Nations Office on Drugs and Crime) (2003) *Protocol on trafficking in persons*, New York, NY: United Nations Office on Drugs and Crime. Available at: www.unodc.org/unodc/en/organized-crime/intro/UNTOC.html

USSD (US State Department) (2017) *Trafficking in persons report 2017*, Washington, DC: United States State Department. Available at: www.antislaverycommissioner.co.uk/media/1143/trafficking-in-persons-report-2017.pdf

SIX

Human trafficking: addressing the symptom, not the cause

Kate Roberts

The current policy context

When 'Reema'[1] arrived at Kalayaan (a charity that supports migrant domestic workers in the UK), she was scared and anxious. She had slipped out of her employer's house at dawn with only a small plastic bag containing her few belongings. She had managed to find her passport from the hiding place where her employer normally kept it locked away. This had given her the courage to escape into a city without any money, where she knew no one, had nowhere to go and could not understand a word that anyone was saying.

Reema had learned of Kalayaan through Facebook and understood that she could get help from the organisation. However, once she met with staff and had her options within the UK explained to her, her hopes were dashed. Reema had entered the UK on the Overseas Domestic Worker (ODW) visa. Introduced in 1998 in response to shocking evidence of abuse of migrant domestic workers in the UK, the original ODW visa provided protection in law for migrant domestic workers who entered the UK on this visa. The visa recognised them as workers, enabling them to access corresponding protections in employment law, and permitted them to change employers (as long as they remained in one full-time job as a domestic worker in a private household without recourse to public funds). This meant that mistreated workers could leave and look for another job. This basic right to withdraw their labour meant that they could challenge mistreatment or abuse as both they and their employers knew that they could ultimately leave and find alternative work if they wanted to.

However, in 2012, the terms of this visa were changed, limiting the holder to six months in the UK with no option to renew and no change of employer, no matter the circumstances. If a worker left their job, they breached the immigration rules. Migrant domestic workers, who usually work in isolation in private homes where their working conditions are hidden and unregulated, experience extremely unequal power relations with their employers. The changes to the visa length and requirement to stay with the same employer dramatically worsened this imbalance of power, making it almost impossible in practice for workers to challenge any mistreatment or abuse.

The original visa recognised ODWs as workers with rights that they could exercise in practice, which did much to prevent abuse. In contrast, the measures implemented in the context of the Modern Slavery Act (MSA) do nothing to prevent exploitation. A worker has to be identified as having been trafficked or a victim of modern slavery before the system will offer any help. This chapter will use the situation of people on the ODW visa to examine the limited options that are available to trafficked people in general in the UK through the National Referral Mechanism (NRM) for identifying victims of trafficking. It will critique these by examining what the NRM and associated support means in practice for trafficked people, the gaps in support that leave people vulnerable to further exploitation and also the missed opportunities of a polarised approach that lacks any measures to stop an exploited person's situation from deteriorating. The situation facing children who are trafficked is discussed in Chapter Five.

This chapter will discuss how campaigning and amendments to the MSA, together with a government-commissioned review, resulted in workers being able to change employers within the six-month duration of their visa. In addition, those formally confirmed as trafficked are now permitted to apply for a two-year-long visa to work as a domestic worker in a private home without recourse to public funds. However, as this chapter argues, these measures fall short of the rights contained within the original visa, which not only worked to support domestic workers to escape abuse, but also went a long way towards preventing exploitative work and provided a pathway for those who had left exploitative work to move on with their lives.

This chapter will argue that the UK needs to move beyond the 'rescue and release' law enforcement-based approach that it has taken to date. This has focused on 'rescuing' victims, referring them into the NRM and focusing on prosecutions, rather than the recovery needs of the individuals who were trafficked. Instead, if the UK is really serious about decreasing trafficking and modern slavery, we need to examine and address the factors that make people vulnerable to exploitation, including the deliberate creation of a 'hostile' environment for immigration, which has proven to those without papers that contact with the authorities will result in arrest and detention rather than identification as a victim of crime. This is something that traffickers know and use as a method of control. Instead, we need to address the causes of trafficking and make sure that people are able to access support before their situation deteriorates to equate to modern slavery, no matter their immigration status, the state of their mental health or the existence of any criminal record. Finally, we need to look at the support that we provide to trafficked people and the purpose of this. We have to make sure that our response meets the needs of the individual people who are in the identification system, that it supports justice and compensation, and that it empowers trafficked people to move on with their lives, with different pathways and opportunities available according to need. This chapter uses the example of migrant domestic workers, such as Reema, who enter the UK on the ODW visa to illustrate the shortcomings of the UK's wider approach to trafficking and modern slavery, and the negative effect of the conflict between its approach to immigration and its stated aims on modern slavery. This chapter argues that we must end the hostile environment for immigration and circumstances that allow people to become vulnerable as a result of immigration insecurity if we are serious about addressing slavery in the UK.

The ODW visa in practice

Having listened to Reema disclose details of her situation, pay and conditions of work, staff at Kalayaan identified her as potentially trafficked. This was of no interest to Reema, who saw herself as a worker (albeit one in exploitative work) rather than a victim of trafficking. Entering into the NRM for identifying victims of trafficking,[2] the UK's victim identification and support system, would mean that she could not work while a decision as to if she was trafficked was being made. Reema explained again and again that her family were dependent on her salary and, above all, she needed to make regular remittances. She could not engage in a system that, in 'rescuing' her, would prevent her from working and earning money. After a tearful day, she left the centre having refused all help or to give consent for an NRM referral. She had decided to return to her employers, where she worked more than 16 hours a day with no day off and no holiday for £26 a week.

Reema's experience is one example of the limitations of the UK's response to trafficking and modern slavery. Despite plenty of high-level rhetoric, in practice, the UK government does almost nothing to support those who are vulnerable to trafficking and modern slavery to prevent their abuse or to rebuild their lives following identification as trafficked or a victim of modern slavery. Instead, they are 'rescued', given limited support while they go through an identification process and soon afterwards 'released' (see, eg, Bordell 2017). All government-funded support in the UK is channelled through the NRM for identifying victims of trafficking, which is contracted out through services run or subcontracted out by the Salvation Army.[3] The NRM is an identification system offering some support in the form of accommodation, casework support and access to services, including legal aid and medical services, to those who are waiting for an identification decision. There are currently no minimum standards of support, or support catering for specialist high needs.[4] There is no legal aid for advice to inform consent for a referral into the NRM and support ends abruptly once a trafficking decision is made. The UK has no national records as to what happens to individuals who have been through the NRM, but anecdotal evidence and individual cases show that some people who have been through the NRM either become destitute or re-enter exploitation to avoid destitution.[5]

Migrant domestic workers, the UK's ODW visa, restrictions and exploitation

Tens of thousands of ODW visas are issued each year to workers accompanying their employers to the UK to work in their private households. In 2015, 17,000 ODW visas were issued,[6] a reflection of the UK's encouragement of the employers of domestic workers to come to the UK. As Lord Reay put it during a House of Lords debate on ODWs on 28 November 1990:

> Looking at our national interest, if wealthy investors, skilled workers and others with the potential to benefit our economy were unable to be accompanied by their domestic staff they might not come here at all but take their money and skills to other countries only too keen to welcome them.[7]

The introduction of the ODW visa in 1998[8] was a progressive piece of legislation brought about by years of campaigning by migrant domestic workers themselves, together with their supporters. Before this time, domestic workers entered the UK informally either as visitors with the (incorrect) implication that they were accompanying their employer to the UK on holiday, or under a concession, with a stamp in their passport saying that they were to work with their named employer (Kalayaan 2011: 14). This meant that they were not recognised as workers, could not enforce UK employment law and were treated as undocumented and subject to immigration removal when they escaped abuse. Treatment commonly reported by domestic workers included psychological as well as physical abuse. This includes being spat at, called animal names, being prevented from having a mobile phone or contact with their own families or friends, and having no space of their own, forcing them to sleep on the floor of the children's room, the lounge or in the kitchen. As workers brought to the UK are dependent on their employer for accommodation, work and information about the UK, and a private household is both an unregulated and hidden workplace with significant power imbalances between the employer and worker, there is much potential for mistreatment.

The original ODW visa, which entailed the right to leave an employer without jeopardising one's immigration status, went some way to redressing this imbalance, significantly empowering workers to challenge abuse, including in the courts, and allowing domestic workers to move on from abusive or exploitative employment and rebuild their lives through alternative, decent employment. The disastrous impact on domestic workers arising from the 2012 ODW visa, which removed this fundamental right, was raised time and time again during the passage of the MSA through Parliament, together with calls to reinstate the rights contained within the original visa.[9] The Joint Committee on Human Rights and the Public Bill Committee both recommended that the right to change employer be reinstated. Amendments to this effect were tabled in both Houses, and voted into the Bill in the House of Lords, only to be voted out again in the Commons.[10] The government conceded with an amendment that resulted in section 53 of the MSA. This allowed domestic workers to change employers during the six months on their visa.[11] The government also committed to an independent review of the visa, with the-then minister responsible, Karen Bradley, stating in a House of Commons debate on the Modern Slavery Bill on 17 March 2015: 'We have asked for this review to take place and we look forward to the recommendations. I cannot commit a future Government, but the intention is that whoever is in government ... will implement the review's recommendations'.[12]

The provision to change employer within the six-month period of their non-renewable visa was strongly criticised by domestic workers and supporting organisations as tokenism, it being clear that it is impractical, if not impossible, to find decent work as a domestic worker in a private household in one full-time role, a role that almost inevitably involves caring for a child or elderly person, and so involving significant relationship building and trust, with only a few months left on one's visa. The recommendations of the independent review, conducted by James Ewins QC, were seen as more positive.[13] The review recommended that extending an ODW visa beyond the initial six months should not be conditional on receiving a positive NRM decision as having been trafficked, but rather that all domestic workers should be able to change employer (but not work sector) and renew their visa for 12-month periods to total up to two years beyond the initial six months. It also recommended that workers who were conclusively identified as trafficked should have recourse to public funds to assist in their recovery from abuse and that each domestic worker in the UK over 42 days be obligated, as a condition of both their and their employer's visa, to attend an information session, without their employer and with their contract of employment and passport in their possession, in order to learn about their rights in law in the UK and to have a source of information and advice outside of their employer's household.

Extraordinarily, despite the minister's commitment, the recommendations made in the review were not implemented; instead, the Immigration Act 2016 allows for the grant of extensions to the visas of migrant domestic workers who entered the NRM and were conclusively found to have been trafficked. There were also commitments made to tighten the obligations of employers of ODWs and to introduce advice and information sessions. At the time of writing, almost three years after the implementation of the MSA, there are still no information sessions in place. Changes introduced in the Immigration Act 2016 mean that domestic workers who have been positively identified through the NRM as having been trafficked can apply for a two-year visa. However, this provision does not even attempt to prevent trafficking in the way that having the right to change employer and apply to renew a visa if in work did. It does not reinstate any negotiating power for migrant domestic workers, for it is only once their treatment has deteriorated to the extent that it equates to trafficking, modern slavery or forced labour that they are enabled to apply for this visa. Not only is this reactive and inhumane, but it also means that domestic workers alleging trafficking will be seen as having an ulterior motive, and so are likely to be seen as less credible, potentially undermining criminal prosecutions against their traffickers. Workers themselves continue to despair of their limited options:

"When you are in the NRM, you don't know what will happen. If I get a positive decision, I will only get two years of visa. Do you think with two years' work I will get back on my feet? So, I will have to try again. I will apply for work overseas and I am scared the same thing will happen. I will be trafficked. All those things which happened behind closed doors, will happen again." (Testimony from anonymous domestic worker speaking at Justice 4 Domestic Workers event, 22 July 2017, at Unite the Union)

Modern slavery responses: undermined by the hostile environment

The UK government's deliberate creation of an environment that is 'hostile' to 'illegal workers' is one example of how, while rightly declaring outrage at those who abuse and enslave others, the UK has created a space in which criminals can more easily exploit people with insecure immigration status. The treatment of migrant domestic workers who entered the UK on an ODW visa after April 2012 is one example of this. Kalayaan, an organisation that provides advice and support to migrant domestic workers, has published the levels of abuse reported to them by workers. These reports show that while the level of abuse of migrant domestic workers in the UK generally is unacceptably high, the abuse and exploitation of those who are tied to their employers is higher than of those who are not (Kalayaan 2015). Rather than taking a system that worked well to provide some protection for these workers against abuse[14] and building on this, for example, by introducing information sessions for migrant domestic workers to learn about their rights and report abuse, the hostile environment on immigration was created over misplaced concerns about having a system in place which meant that so-called 'low-skilled' migrants could have access to an immigration route through which they could eventually apply for settlement.[15]

While not all of those identified as potentially trafficked are migrants (in 2017, 677 of the 5,145 referrals into the NRM were of UK nationals),[16] as explained earlier, insecure immigration status is frequently used as a tool to exploit as victims believe they cannot go to authorities for help. People in the UK without documents are taught that rather than being listened to, the chances are that they will be removed as an immigration offender. Similarly, if the authorities have immigration enforcement targets, it is hard to see how these fit with building the trust often needed for victims to disclose their treatment, particularly given that many indicators of trafficking are also what may make victims appear not to be credible to those with an immigration enforcement remit, for example, not having possession of their passport or immigration documents, not knowing their employer's name, their own immigration status or the address where they worked, or appearing coached.

At the time of writing, all government-funded support for adult potential victims of trafficking is through the NRM. The NRM is primarily an identification system; however, all existing support has been shoehorned into the period of the identification process, which is supposed to last for 45 days, or six weeks.[17] The Home Office's own review of the NRM in 2014[18] recognised its shortcomings, outlining:

> a disjointed system where awareness of human trafficking was often low and of the NRM processes still lower, and describing the difficulties faced by support providers in moving people on from the victim care contract so soon following identification. There are many critics of decision-making, the quality and communication of decisions, and the ability to manage and share information effectively in the best interest of victims. (Para 2.1.5)

Recommendations from the 2014 Home Office review included increased awareness raising, an overhaul of the referral process, providing support based on an individual assessment of the need of the victim and the testing of decision-making through multidisciplinary decision-making panels. It also recommends a single case-management system and improved data collection. Disappointingly, despite the review's findings and recommendations, and the piloting of multi-disciplinary decision-making systems, the NRM remains unchanged at the time of writing.[19] Some welcome but limited reforms to the NRM[20] and to survivor support[21] were announced by the government on 17 October and 26 October 2017, respectively, but, as yet, the detail and timing of the implementation of these reforms remains unknown.[22]

Under the system in place at the time of writing, upon identification as a potential victim, adults need to consent to a referral into the NRM. They will be entitled to government-funded support only on receipt of a positive reasonable grounds, or first-stage, decision. This should take place five days after the receipt of a referral by the decision-making competent authority[23] and has a low decision-making threshold: 'suspect but cannot prove'. Following receipt of a positive reasonable grounds decision, the potential victim will receive temporary admission to the UK, so they should not be removed. This time is what is known as the 'recovery period'. As well as the offer of accommodation within a safe house, people should be supported to receive medical assistance and counselling, to report their abuse to the police, and to receive immigration advice and advice on other potential claims, such as a compensation claim against their trafficker. In practice, many of these services have long waiting lists and the limbo and uncertainty during this decision-making process makes the prospect of recovery and reflection remote. The final-stage, or conclusive grounds, decision should be made after 45 days but, in practice, the time period varies significantly. According to the National Audit Office (NAO 2017), the average time taken to make a conclusive grounds decision is 132 days. The decision is made on the threshold of 'on the balance of probabilities'. At this point, the person is given either a positive or negative decision as to whether (the system believes that) they have been trafficked. Neither leads to a care plan or comprehensive support to prevent further abuse.[24]

This is a blunt system that misses opportunities to prevent abuse and rebuild lives. The overwhelming focus on modern slavery and reaching this threshold has ignored the continuum of exploitation, and the fact that, as with migrant domestic workers, if someone who is being exploited has no realistic way to challenge mistreatment or the denial of their rights before these equate to trafficking or modern slavery, then it is likely that their exploitation will continue and conditions will deteriorate (see also Skrivankova 2010).

There is no system of support available for people who are being taken advantage of and exploited but whose treatment does not equate to trafficking. For anyone without immigration status in the UK, contact with the authorities holds a risk of detention and removal, even if they are reporting a crime.[25] Likewise, those who are criminalised by their abuse risk not being recognised as victims. This is particularly common for people who have committed immigration offences or whose exploitation involved being made to commit crimes, including benefit fraud or cannabis cultivation.[26] If a negative NRM decision is made, there is no referral system for appropriate preventative support on the basis that the individual must be a vulnerable adult to have been referred into the NRM by a first responder. Instead of being clear that a negative decision simply indicates that there was not enough evidence to make a positive decision at that time, it is instead seen to infer that they were not believed and potentially affects credibility on other matters, such as immigration or criminal prosecutions. There is no formal method to appeal a negative decision. The decision can be judicially reviewed or the accommodation provider or first responder can make a reconsideration request but without special dispensation funding for support will be lost during this time. This is likely to mean that even if the negative decision is overturned, the victim will be lost, having had no casework support, contact or accommodation.

Even a positive final-stage, or conclusive grounds, decision may have no tangible impact on a victim's life; it does not translate into ongoing support or the granting of immigration status. In England, Northern Ireland and Wales, following a positive trafficking decision, a victim is given two weeks to leave support and accommodation.[27] Although specialist ongoing support is provided by some individual NGOs using charitable funding, such as the Snowdrop project, this does not exist on a national basis and there is only capacity nationally to work with a small number of victims.

Given that there is currently no support before an NRM referral – in terms of food, government funding for an interpreter or legal aid, or a safe space to wash, eat or sleep – informed consent, which is necessary for an adult to be referred into the NRM, is challenging to achieve in practice. Those victims who are encouraged by their exploiters to fear the UK authorities are unlikely to self-identify or to be familiar with the term 'human trafficking'. When speaking to the first responder who is completing an NRM referral on their behalf, they are unlikely to fully understand what they are being asked and will not know what is relevant to disclose. Trauma and confusion may lead to inconsistencies in their story. In other cases, the taboos around their abuse may be too great. For these reasons, the announced commitment to the provision of a statutory place of safety for three days following the identification of a potential victim is particularly welcome. However, the nature of this provision is still unclear. To ensure informed consent, it will be vital that there is legal aid funding specialist advice during this time, as well as individual advocacy and a separation from immigration procedures, but this has not been confirmed.

What happens to trafficked people?

When the UK introduced the NRM in 2009, little attention was given to what happens to victims following identification. This was probably because, for many potential victims, particularly those with no immigration status or no recourse to public funds, any support was seen as an improvement on nothing. However, the ending of support, and of contact with trafficked people by their former care providers, so soon after a conclusive grounds decision means that, in 2017, there is still little information or data available nationally as to what becomes of the majority of people who have been through the NRM, although the voluntary sector is doing what it can to fill the gaps. The recently announced provision of government-funded support until 45 days (instead of 14 days) after positive identification as a victim is an improvement on the current situation but, on its own, will do little to give a picture as to what happens to survivors of trafficking in the longer term.[28] Eight years after the NRM was introduced in 2009, three years after the Home Office review[29] highlighted significant concerns in 2014 and almost three years after the MSA was enacted, we still have no accurate information as to what happens to victims.

Since January 2017, City Hearts, a charity subcontracted by the Salvation Army to provide safe-house support to individuals who are in the NRM, have attempted to keep in touch with people who leave their safe houses through an 'Integrated Support Programme' using their charitable funding.[30] They provide weekly drop-in sessions where individuals who have left their service can come in for general support or to relax and catch up. City Hearts proactively calls individuals on a fortnightly basis when they first leave their services. Other NGOs which provide services within the government-funded care contract, such as Hestia[31] and the Medaille Trust,[32] have also recently announced programmes offering some support for a period beyond the government-funded contract.

As well as providing an important source of continuity and practical help for individuals who would otherwise inevitably struggle with the cut-off of support, the ongoing provision of some services to trafficked people also begins to make it possible to track what happens to people after they have left the NRM. Although City Hearts' Integrated Support Programme is still young, the large proportion of take-up – with 97% of survivors to which it was offered requesting the service – shows that there is real demand.[33] City Hearts report that survivors' needs have included support with housing, benefits, medical needs and legal advice.[34] These are all needs that are basic to recovery and reintegration. While it is excellent that some organisations are offering this service, it also serves to highlight how many more survivors who have been housed in an area where ongoing support services are not available are likely to be falling into difficulties. It is also important that levels of support that are appropriate for different survivors' needs are available. A drop-in service alone is unlikely to be able to offer adequate support to the most high need survivors, who should be referred to one-to-one needs-based casework support. The Snowdrop Project, specialising in individualised long-term support to trafficked people outside of the NRM, recently revealed that 80% of people newly referred to their services experience legal issues, 75% are living in unstable accommodation and that, while all have some mental health needs, a significant minority have complex mental health needs.[35]

In 2016, the Human Trafficking Foundation published a report called *Day 46* (HTF 2016), which followed the situation of 30 women who had lost support following the closure of the former 'Poppy Project' due to financial insolvency. The women that the project supported were given two weeks' notice that their support, and, in some cases, accommodation, would end. Coincidentally, this is the same as the length of time that individuals in the UK who receive a positive conclusive grounds decision as having been trafficked have to exit the government-funded service. The report author spoke to 30 of the 73 survivors that the Poppy Project had been supporting six months after the closure of the service. Of the 43 not interviewed, 18 were not contactable and were completely unaccounted for. This may be because they had moved on with their lives or they may have fallen back into exploitation or become destitute. The report found that survivors who were contacted were clearly struggling. One described feeling like 'I have been thrown from the frying pan into the fire'; another said, 'I've been treated worse than an animal. I was given a positive trafficking decision and then not offered accommodation, even animals get shelter' (HTF 2016: 2).

The lack of data as to what happens to individuals who get a positive conclusive grounds decision through the NRM means that there is no national picture as to what happens to trafficked people or the outcomes of the NRM and associated government-funded support. According to the NAO (2017), the Home Office has forecast that it will spend around £90 million on the victim care contract for the period 2015/16 to 2019/20. The anecdotal evidence available is, unsurprisingly, worrying. There have been successful legal challenges, including Galdikas and Subatkis,[36] where individuals found by the UK authorities to have been trafficked, and who were cooperating with the police, were left destitute. A claim by a European Economic Area (EEA) national in 2016 led to Bristol City Council accepting that local authorities have a duty to provide welfare support to victims of trafficking under Article 3 and Article 4 of the European Convention on Human Rights, Article 12 of the Convention Against Trafficking and Article 11 of the EU Anti-Trafficking Directive. The case concerned a trafficked person who had received a positive conclusive grounds decision and yet was refused accommodation or any subsistence support. She resorted to selling sex as this was the only way she could find to survive.[37]

The NAO (2017) report is deeply critical of the lack of verifiable outcomes of the UK's anti-slavery efforts. The report highlights the lack of monitoring of activities, of levels or effectiveness of expenditure, and of accountability. It criticises the lack of data, the length of time taken to reach trafficking decisions, the cost of care, the lack of care standards and inspection, and the lack of any information on outcomes for victims who have left support.

An 'inexcusable' lack of support

The report of an inquiry into modern slavery by the Work and Pensions Select Committee, published in the spring of 2017, found an 'inexcusable' lack of support for victims of modern slavery.[38] The inquiry was initiated following a request from the Independent Anti-Slavery Commissioner, who raised concerns as to the lack of government-funded support available to victims following leaving the safe house.[39]

The Committee heard in evidence how the current system of government-funded support, focused only on the identification system for victims (the NRM) and not being connected to mainstream services, leaves many victims cut off soon after being identified as trafficked. They also received evidence as to how EU nationals who had been in forced labour and so could not evidence work were found not to have been exercising their treaty rights, could not pass the habitual residence test[40] and so were not eligible for benefits, consequently becoming destitute and, in some cases, receiving removal notices (ie the threat of deportation). The same victims are not being considered for residence permits as, being EU nationals, they are incorrectly not considered to have any immigration issues.[41]

The Committee found that few victims were coming forward due to a combination of low awareness and training, but also poor support available overall. They criticised the lack of data collection and the fact that even a positive conclusive grounds decision does not result in a grant of leave. They received evidence that, in practice, a positive conclusive grounds decision can mean nothing more than a 'piece of paper' to victims[42] as it does not confer a grant of leave or any entitlement to benefits and other support. The Committee heard that a victim can receive a positive conclusive grounds decision together with a letter about voluntary returns suggesting that they make arrangements to leave the UK. The Committee highlighted this contradiction between immigration control and anti-slavery measures, and recommended that all confirmed victims should be granted 'at least one year's leave to remain with a personal plan for their recovery, which should act as a social passport to support for at least the 12-month period of leave to remain'.[43]

The government's response to the Committee's recommendations was received on 30 November 2017.[44] It is a clear example of its determination not to address the vulnerabilities to exploitation and re-exploitation caused by immigration policies and the resulting insecurities. The response argues that:

> the decision about whether an individual is a victim of modern slavery and their immigration status are, and must remain, separate decisions. The Government does not accept that all confirmed victims of modern slavery should be given at least one year's leave to remain in the UK.[45]

The response goes on to state: 'The Government believes that having a blanket policy of granting discretionary leave to all victims risks incentivising individuals to make false trafficking claims in an attempt to fraudulently obtain leave to remain or delay removal'.[46]

This makes clear that, when it comes to it, immigration control, and how this is perceived, trumps trafficking. This approach does not attempt to consider how the UK's immigration policies could be adapted to meet the needs of trafficked people. Nor does it appreciate that rather than being a 'blanket policy', 12 months' leave to remain in the form of a residence permit issued to confirmed victims of trafficking is a minimum level of security from which someone who has been trafficked can begin to reflect, recover and possibly feel safe enough to disclose some of the more traumatic aspects of what has happened to them, and possibly seek justice. The suggestion that trafficked people will make 'false trafficking claims' appears unfounded. With the Home Office estimating that there are up to 13,000 victims in the UK[47] and, in contrast, there being only 5,145 referrals of potential victims into the NRM in 2017, the problem is one of victims not coming forward, or not consenting to a referral, rather than the making of 'false trafficking claims'. Nor does this approach show any confidence in the UK's own anti-trafficking systems. No trafficked person in the UK can make a trafficking 'claim' through the NRM; instead, they need to be identified as potentially trafficked and a referral into the NRM needs to be made on their behalf by a first responder.[48] They then need to have first- and second-stage decisions made by others as to whether they have been trafficked or are a victim of modern slavery. If there are concerns that the system is wrongly identifying people as trafficked who are not, the logical response is to improve the identification system, not to make it so unhelpful in practice that no one wants to be referred into it.

According to written evidence to the Committee from the-then responsible minister, Sarah Newton, dated February 2017, in 2015, only 12% of victims with a positive conclusive grounds decision received a residence permit.[49] This is a surprisingly small proportion of confirmed victims to receive a very basic and time-limited entitlement from which to begin to rebuild their lives. The Council of Europe Trafficking Convention (Article 14) explains that a grant of leave in the form of a renewable residence permit can be issued if the individual's stay is 'necessary owing to their personal situation', for 'pursuing compensation claims', as well as 'for the purpose of their co-operation with the competent authorities in investigation or criminal proceedings'. Paragraph 184 of the Explanatory Note to the Trafficking Convention explains that 'Personal situation' includes 'a range of situations, depending on whether it is the victim's safety, state of health, family situation or some other factor'. It is impossible to imagine a case where personal circumstances would not be ongoing at the point of the conclusive grounds decision if the phrase 'personal situation' were interpreted in this way.[50] Even in 'historic' cases where a victim is identified long after leaving the situation of exploitation, they should still be entitled to, and are likely to need, support, including a residence permit allowing recovery, as it is unlikely that, having not been identified before, they will ever have received support towards rehabilitation and recovery.[51] The surprisingly low number of residence permits issued and the government's response to the Work and Pensions Select Committee inquiry recommendations demonstrate how immigration control is prioritised over preventing trafficking, even when, in practice, the immigration asks are very small and would have a marginal effect on net immigration figures.[52]

Lord McColl tabled a Modern Slavery (Victim Support) Bill that, if passed, would do much to ensure the basic support and rights of people who have been identified as trafficked in the UK.[53] The Bill, which is awaiting committee stage at the time of writing, ensures that support is available to victims during the identification process, as well as for a minimum of 12 months following a positive conclusive grounds decision. During this time, trafficking survivors would have discretionary leave to remain in the UK, allowing them to work if they were ready and able to do so. Despite the sensible and moderate asks contained within this Bill, it has not been supported by the government.[54]

Offering trafficked people identified through the official system a minimum of 12 months in which to begin to reflect on and rebuild their lives is far less generous than the system in the US, in place since 2002. The 'T visa' in the US for victims of trafficking was introduced to allow for human trafficking investigations and prosecutions, and to offer protection to victims. Once a T non–immigrant visa is granted, a victim can apply for permanent residence after three years.[55] Only 1,062 T visas were granted to trafficking victims in 2015.[56] The relatively very low number of applicants for the T visa (given the fact that the US population is five times that of the UK), which has been in place for 15 years, further undermines suggestions that granting 12 months' leave to remain in the UK will create a pull factor.

Like the GRETA report published shortly afterwards, the 2015 US *Trafficking in persons* (TIP) report,[57] which examines every country's response to human trafficking, found the nature of support in the UK insufficient, noting that the:

> government did not provide sufficient care for victims following the 45-day reflection period. Authorities have acknowledged NRM support is not intended to provide rehabilitation, and noted many victims were still profoundly vulnerable after 45 days. NGOs reported cases of victims returning to prostitution or being re-trafficked due to lack of long-term support.[58]

There are now examples of developing excellent practice offering pathways to recovery where trafficked people are able to access them. As discussed earlier in the chapter, giving domestic workers the right to change employers did much to prevent abuse at no cost to the public purse. The Co-operative has partnered with City Hearts, the Snowdrop Project and other NGOs to run the 'Bright Future' programme.[59] This programme aims to offer a paid work placement, and, if appropriate, a job, in the Co-op food business to survivors of slavery. The premise for this programme is that decent work is key to recovery as it provides an opportunity for reintegration, purpose and a means to earn a decent living and provide for family or pay off debts, in short, allowing a trafficked person to address some of the vulnerabilities that may have led to their being trafficked in the first place. This makes complete sense. However, the Co-op, or any other employer, can only offer work placements and employment to individuals who have the right to work. Prior to the changes to the immigration rules in 2012, when the ODW visa became tied to one employer, Kalayaan used to put a lot of capacity into its 'job service', finding decent jobs for domestic workers who had 'run away' from abusive employers. This was one of the most popular services offered by the organisation; workers, whatever they had experienced, saw working and providing for their families as their top priority. However, following the changes to the immigration rules that prevented ODWs from changing employers without breaching the immigration rules, Kalayaan had to end the job service.

It is likely that a period of leave during which a victim can begin to rebuild their life following trafficking would also allow for a greater number of compensation claims and prosecutions against traffickers. With insecure immigration status leading to huge uncertainty and insecurity relating to practical needs such as housing and subsistence, it is very difficult for any former victim to proactively seek justice, for example, through the employment tribunals or in a civil court, or by giving evidence to the police against their former abuser.

In July 2016, when she became Prime Minister, Theresa May was clear that, despite the MSA, more needed to be done to address modern slavery. At the time, she wrote an article for the *Sunday Telegraph*, stating: 'Just because we have some legislation does not mean that the problem is solved'.[60]

There is clearly still very much to be done in the UK to address some of the contradictions and gaps in how we identify people who have been trafficked or enslaved, and in the support systems available. We need to be clear that preventing slavery must be a priority over immigration enforcement, and move the debate beyond the rescue rhetoric to address the causes of slavery by empowering victims, allowing them reasonable options. This includes additional legislation, such as that within Lord McColl's Bill, to ensure that victims have legal rights to rely on. These must ensure immigration options to allow for a chance to recover, to claim compensation and to make sure that individuals are not being returned to situations where they are likely to be re-exploited or even re-trafficked. Specialist, victim–centred support, from identification, with a range of options for rebuilding lives with no arbitrary cut-off point, would do much not only to prevent slavery, but also to stop the revolving door whereby individuals, deserted by the system, slip back into exploitation.

Notes

1   Not her real name.

2   See: www.nationalcrimeagency.gov.uk/about-us/what-we-do/specialist-capabilities/uk-human-trafficking-centre/national-referral-mechanism

3   In England and Wales. In Scotland, services are run by Trafficking Awareness Raising Alliance (TARA) and Migrant Help; in Northern Ireland, services are run by Migrant Help and Women's Aid.

4   In October 2017, the UK government committed that the Trafficking Survivor Care Standards produced by the Human Trafficking Foundation (HTF) will be included in the next care contract.

5   See, for example, cases listed in HTF (2017).

6   House of Commons Library, 'Calls to change Overseas Domestic Worker visa conditions', briefing paper 4786, May 2016.

7   See: http://hansard.millbanksystems.com/lords/1990/nov/28/overseas-domestic-workers

8   Introduced as a concession in 1998 and into the immigration rules in 2002.

9   See briefings throughout the passage of the Bill through Parliament, available at: www.kalayaan.org.uk/resources/briefings/

10 See: www.kalayaan.org.uk/wp-content/uploads/2014/09/Kalayaan-Briefing-for-Commons-MSB-17.3.15.pdf

11 See: www.legislation.gov.uk/ukpga/2015/30/section/53/enacted

12 See column 650, at: https://publications.parliament.uk/pa/cm201415/cmhansrd/cm150317/debtext/150317-0001.htm

13 See: www.gov.uk/government/uploads/system/uploads/attachment_data/file/486532/ODWV_Review_-_Final_Report__6_11_15_.pdf

14 Draft International Labour Organisation (ILO) 'Multilateral framework on labour migration non-binding principles and guidelines for a rights-based approach to labour migration', Geneva, 31 October–2 November 2005. Annex II, 'Examples of best practice, VI prevention of and protection against abusive migration practices', part 82, report of the Special Rapporteur on the human rights of migrants, Jorge Bustamante, Mission to the United Kingdom of Great Britain and Northern Ireland, United Nations, Human Rights Council, 16 March 2010.

15 'Calls to change overseas Domestic Worker visa conditions', Briefing Paper 4786, 13 May 2016, Melanie Gower, House of Commons Library, chapter 2.1.

16 National Crime Agency (NCA) 'National Referral Mechanism statistics – end of year summary 2016'. Available at: www.nationalcrimeagency. gov.uk/publications/national-referral-mechanism-statistics/2016-nrm-statistics/788-national-referral-mechanism-statistics-end-of-year-summary-2016/file

17 On 26 October, the Home Office announced increased 'move on support', including extending support following a positive conclusive grounds decision to 45 days following the decision, and nine days following a negative decision. They have not announced when these changes will be implemented. See: www.gov.uk/government/news/modern-slavery-victims-to-receive-longer-period-of-support

18 See: www.gov.uk/government/uploads/system/uploads/attachment_data/file/467434/Review_of_the_National_Referral_Mechanism_for_victims_of_human_trafficking.pdf

19 In June 2017, the 'recovery period' available within the NRM, in terms of government-funded support and accommodation available to victims, was increased to 90 days in Scotland.

20 See: www.gov.uk/government/news/modern-slavery-taskforce-agrees-new-measures-to-support-victims

21 See: www.gov.uk/government/news/modern-slavery-victims-to-receive-longer-period-of-support

22 The announcement that subsistence rates for possible victims who are in the NRM will be aligned with those for asylum seekers is worrying. These low rates (£37.75 a week at the time of writing) keep recipients at destitution levels and are likely to undermine recovery and rehabilitation.

23 The UK has two competent authorities: the NCA's Modern Slavery Human Trafficking Unit (MSHTU) and Home Office Visas and Immigration (UKVI). All referrals are initially sent to the MSHTU, who pass on cases where the individual is subject to immigration control to the UKVI.

24 In early 2018, the government also announced a reduction in support for victims of slavery. See: www.theguardian.com/global-development/2018/mar/02/cuts-support-slavery-victims-uk-pose-mega-risk-of-homelessness

25 See: www.independent.co.uk/news/uk/crime/london-rape-woman-arrest-immigration-police-metropolitan-victim-home-office-germany-a8081016.html

26 See, for example, 'Trafficked into detention', *Detention Action*, November 2017. Available at: http://detentionaction.org.uk/wordpress/wp-content/uploads/2017/11/Trafficked-Into-Detention-Briefing.pdf

27 As previously mentioned, the government have committed that this will be increased to 45 days but, as yet, there is no date for implementation.

28 Also announced was six months of weekly drop-in centres run by the Salvation Army and a commitment to a trial with six local authorities for move on support. As yet, there is no detail as to what this will entail, the timing for implementation or how the needs of survivors who need specialist casework support will be met.

29 See: www.gov.uk/government/uploads/system/uploads/attachment_data/file/467434/Review_of_the_National_Referral_Mechanism_for_victims_of_human_trafficking.pdf

30 City Hearts Integrated Support Programme, Interim Report, January–March 2017. Available at: http://city-hearts.co.uk/wp-content/uploads/2017/05/ISP-Interim-Report-J-M2017.pdf

31 See: www.hestia.org/news/hestia-launches-the-phoenix-project

32 See: www.medaille-trust.org.uk/what-we-do/victim-care

33 See note 32, p 2.

34 See note 32, p 4.

35 Evidence by Lara Bundock, Snowdrop Chief Executive Officer, to the All Party Parliamentary Group on Trafficking and Modern Slavery, 27 November 2017.

36 See: www.theguardian.com/global-development/2016/mar/30/we-are-hopeful-now-brothers-freed-from-slavery-seek-british-policy-change

37 See 'Ground-breaking case on local authority responsibilities for supporting victims of trafficking'. Available at: http://dpglaw.co.uk/ground-breaking-case-local-authority-responsibilities-supporting-victims-trafficking/

38 See: www.parliament.uk/business/committees/committees-a-z/commons-select/work-and-pensions-committee/news-parliament-2015/report-victims-modern-slavery-16-17/

39 See: www.antislaverycommissioner.co.uk/media/1107/stephen-crabb.pdf

[40] See para 33, at: https://publications.parliament.uk/pa/cm201617/cmselect/cmworpen/803/803.pdf

[41] See paras 26 and 27, at: https://publications.parliament.uk/pa/cm201617/cmselect/cmworpen/803/803.pdf

[42] See para 40, at: https://publications.parliament.uk/pa/cm201617/cmselect/cmworpen/803/803.pdf

[43] See: www.parliament.uk/business/committees/committees-a-z/commons-select/work-and-pensions-committee/news-parliament-2015/report-victims-modern-slavery-16-17/

[44] See: https://publications.parliament.uk/pa/cm201719/cmselect/cmworpen/672/67202.htm

[45] See: https://publications.parliament.uk/pa/cm201719/cmselect/cmworpen/672/67202.htm

[46] See note 45.

[47] See: www.gov.uk/government/uploads/system/uploads/attachment_data/file/655504/6.3920_HO_Modern_Slavery_Awareness_Booklet_web.pdf

[48] See: www.nationalcrimeagency.gov.uk/about-us/what-we-do/specialist-capabilities/uk-human-trafficking-centre/national-referral-mechanism

[49] See: www.parliament.uk/documents/commons-committees/work-and-pensions/Letter-from-Sarah-Newton-MP-to-Chair-re-modern-slavery-session-17-2-2017.pdf

[50] The *PK (Ghana)* judgment, handed down in February 2018, found that the guidance in place at the time was not compliant with the Council of Europe Convention for Action Against Trafficking in Human Beings.

[51] See arguments set out in a letter from Vicky Brotherton (Anti-Trafficking Monitoring Group) and Kate Roberts (HTF) to the Work and Pensions Select Committee, dated February 2017. Available at: www.parliament.uk/documents/commons-committees/work-and-pensions/Written_Evidence/Letter-to-Frank-Field-MP-re-Discretionary-Leave-Human-Trafficking-Foundation-Anti-Trafficking-Monitoring-Group.PDF

[52] During 2016, there were only 635 positive conclusive grounds decisions made under the NRM, See: www.nationalcrimeagency.gov.uk/publications/national-referral-mechanism-statistics/2016-nrm-statistics/788-national-referral-mechanism-statistics-end-of-year-summary-2016/file

[53] See: https://publications.parliament.uk/pa/bills/lbill/2017-2019/0004/18004.pdf

54 See: https://hansard.parliament.uk/lords/2017-09-08/debates/ C145B8B8-D46E-4F11-88C7-9C03081108C6/ModernSlavery (VictimSupport)Bill(HL)

55 See: www.uscis.gov/humanitarian/victims-human-trafficking-other-crimes/victims-human-trafficking-t-nonimmigrant-status/questions-and-answers-victims-human-trafficking-t-nonimmigrant-status

56 See p 52, at: www.justice.gov/archives/page/file/870826/download

57 See Table 31:34 of the '2015 report of the Interdepartmental Group on Modern Slavery'. Available at: www.gov.uk/government/uploads/system/ uploads/attachment_data/file/469968/IDMG_Report_Final.pdf

58 See: www.state.gov/documents/organization/245365.pdf

59 See Balch et al (2017) and: www.co-operative.coop/ethics/bright-future

60 See: www.gov.uk/government/speeches/defeating-modern-slavery-theresa-may-article

References

Balch, A., Craig, G., Roberts, K. and Woods, A. (2017) *Bright future: An initial evaluation*, Manchester: Cooperative Group.

Bordell, W. (2017) 'Expect more stories of slavery – and demand more victim support', blog post, *Huff Post*, 21 August. Available at: www. huffingtonpost.co.uk/will-bordell/stories-of-slavery_b_17790028. html

City Hearts (2017) *City Hearts Integrated Support Programme, interim report, January–March 2017*. Available at: http://city-hearts.co.uk/ wp-content/uploads/2017/05/ISP-Interim-Report-J-M2017.pdf

HTF (Human Trafficking Foundation) (2016) *Day 46. Is there life after the safe house for survivors of modern slavery?*, London: Human Trafficking Foundation.

HTF (2017) *Supporting adult survivors of slavery to facilitate recovery and reintegration and prevent re-exploitation*, London: Human Trafficking Foundation.

Kalayaan (2011) *Ending the abuse*, London: Kalayaan.

Kalayaan (2015) *Britain's forgotten slaves: Migrant domestic workers in the UK three years after the introduction of the tied visa*, London: Kalayaan.

NAO (National Audit Office) (2017) *Reducing modern slavery*, London: National Audit Office.

Skrivankova, K. (2010) *Between decent work and forced labour: Examining the continuum of exploitation*, York: Joseph Rowntree Foundation.

SEVEN

Still punishing the wrong people: the criminalisation of potential trafficked cannabis gardeners

Patrick Burland

Introduction

There is a long-standing recognition that the UK is a destination country for human trafficking for cannabis cultivation. This chapter examines the existing knowledge about human trafficking for cannabis cultivation in the UK, with a specific focus on how Vietnamese nationals are most commonly being exploited for this purpose. It then moves on to its main focus: the criminalisation of those potentially trafficked for cannabis cultivation. Trafficked persons who are exploited for the cultivation of cannabis in the UK are committing criminal offences under the Misuse of Drugs Act 1971. However, if we recognise people trafficked to grow cannabis as having been abused and exploited, and as victims of crime or human rights violations as a result of coercion and abuse, then punishing them should be seen as highly inappropriate. The criminalisation of trafficked persons is also counterproductive for efforts to prevent trafficking and prosecute traffickers.

The criminalisation of potential trafficked cannabis gardeners in the UK is highly inappropriate from a moral standpoint and, just as significantly, also contradicts the expectations of the 2005 Council of Europe Convention on Action against Trafficking in Human Beings (CAT) and policy and legislation on the non-punishment of trafficked persons in the UK. CAT Article 26 expects states to provide for the possibility of the non-punishment of trafficked persons, declaring:

> Each Party shall, in accordance with the basic principles of its legal system, provide for the possibility of not imposing penalties on victims for their involvement in unlawful activities, to the extent that they have been compelled to do so.

Over the last seven years, policy and legislation have been introduced to ensure that the UK acts in respect of this Article to prevent people from being punished for criminal acts committed as a direct consequence of their trafficking. In 2010, the Crown Office Procurator Fiscal Service (COPFS) published guidance on the non-punishment of trafficked persons in Scotland (COPFS 2010). In 2011 the Crown Prosecution Service (CPS 2011) in England and Wales produced policy on the non-punishment of trafficked persons. The Public Prosecution Service in Northern Ireland (PPSNI 2013) published policy on non-punishment in October 2013.

Section 45 of the Modern Slavery Act 2015 (MSA) established a statutory 'Defence for slavery or trafficking victims who commit an offence' in England and Wales. In Northern Ireland, section 22 of the parallel Human Trafficking and Exploitation (Criminal Justice and Support for Victims) Act (Northern Ireland) 2015, which received royal assent on 13 January 2015, introduced a statutory 'Defence for slavery and trafficking victims in relation to certain offences'. In Scotland, the Human Trafficking and Exploitation (Scotland) Act 2015, which received royal assent on 4 November 2015, did not produce a non-punishment provision. Instead, it required that the Lord Advocate in Scotland provide guidance on the non-punishment of trafficked persons (HTESA 2015 section 8).

The central thrust of this chapter is that despite policies on non-punishment by national prosecution services and the introduction of statutory legislation, potential trafficked cannabis gardeners are still being punished and on a worrying scale. Research underpinning this chapter has identified newspaper articles from the British media on 112 separate court cases between 1 April 2009[1] and August 2017 where a person or persons identified as potentially or actually trafficked were convicted for cannabis cultivation. In 35 of those cases, those convicted were informally identified as trafficked or enslaved by actors within the criminal justice system. This should be seen in the context of a total of 115 Vietnamese nationals who were conclusively identified by the UK government as having been trafficked for cannabis cultivation between 2009 and October 2016 (IASC 2017b: 8).

A 2017 briefing report by the United Nations Children's Fund (UNICEF 2017: 8) highlights that the statutory defence from punishment for trafficked persons in England and Wales provided through section 45 of the MSA has yet to be tested in court, but that it has been used at the investigation stage. This chapter examines cases where it is argued that the statutory defence *should* have been considered but was not. To date, there has not been any research that more widely examines the impact of the statutory defence on the responses to people trafficked for other forms of forced criminality. Therefore, it is not possible to compare the impact of policy and legislation on preventing people trafficked for other forms of forced criminality from being punished with those trafficked for cannabis cultivation.

We separately examine two types of cases where potentially trafficked cannabis gardeners have been convicted. The first group comprises people convicted without any apparent recognition that they were potentially trafficked. The second type of case involves people recognised as trafficked or enslaved by those in the criminal justice system who were still convicted and punished. Through examining these two types of cases, we highlight fundamental barriers in practice to preventing the punishment of people trafficked for cannabis cultivation. The first is an inability of actors within the criminal justice system to recognise indicators of trafficking and identify people as potential trafficked persons. The second barrier is an apparent lack of knowledge and understanding about the legislation and policy on non-punishment in cases where people have been informally identified. This chapter does not suggest wilful neglect in allowing the conviction of potential trafficked cannabis gardeners. Such a conclusion would require closer examination of the circumstances of the individual cases than was possible in this research. However, it does suggest a lack of training, knowledge and preparation for those involved in bringing these cases to sentence, notwithstanding around 10 years of evidence relating to this phenomenon.

Trafficking for cannabis production in the UK

The 2016 National Crime Agency (NCA) 'National strategic assessment of serious and organised crime' report acknowledges that people are trafficked for cannabis cultivation in the UK. It explains: 'There is a crossover between cannabis production and human trafficking, with many examples of victims of trafficking being kept as live-in gardeners on cannabis growing sites' (NCA 2016: 33). There is, in fact, a long-standing recognition of this trafficking trend in the UK. Since 2001, the US State Department (USSD) has annually published a 'Trafficking in persons report' (TIP) that reviews every country's response to human trafficking (USSD 2017). The first TIP report to make reference to human trafficking for cannabis cultivation in the UK was the 2007 report. It noted: 'Children, particularly from West Africa, are also trafficked to the U.K. for forced labour in cannabis factories'

(USSD 2007: 204). The problem of trafficking for cannabis cultivation in the UK has been discussed in every TIP report since 2009. Human trafficking for cannabis cultivation has only been mentioned in three other country profiles (Denmark, Ireland and Albania) in 16 years of the USSD TIP reports. Trafficking for cannabis cultivation in Denmark was only mentioned in the 2014 TIP report, in Ireland in the 2015 and 2016 reports, and in Albania in the 2017 report. On the basis of the findings of these reports, it would appear that the UK is unique in having a recognised long-term and sustained problem of trafficking for cannabis cultivation.

There are data on the number of people referred into the National Referral Mechanism (NRM) as potential trafficked cannabis gardeners in the UK.[2] A joint report by the UK Human Trafficking Centre (UKHTC) and the Serious Organised Crime Agency (SOCA) on human trafficking in the UK in 2012 highlighted that 69 people were referred into the NRM as potentially trafficked for cannabis cultivation. Of these, 56 (81%) were children (UKHTC 2013: 25). There was a 130% increase between 2011 and 2012 of the numbers reported as having potentially been trafficked for cannabis cultivation (UKHTC 2013: 17). An NCA strategic assessment report on the nature and scale of human trafficking in the UK in 2013 highlighted that 54 people were reported as having potentially been trafficked for cannabis cultivation in 2013; 29 of the 54 (54%) were children (NCA 2014: 30). The NCA strategic assessment on human trafficking in the UK in 2014 does not include a breakdown of the percentage of children reported as potentially trafficked for cannabis cultivation.

Vietnamese nationals

Vietnamese nationals have comprised a significant proportion of those identified as potentially trafficked for cannabis cultivation in the UK. This is highlighted in a number of TIP reports. The 2009 TIP report stated: 'It is estimated that hundreds of young children, mostly from Vietnam and China, are trafficked to the UK and subjected to debt bondage by Vietnamese organized crime gangs for forced work on cannabis farms' (USSD 2009: 295). The 2011 TIP report explained: 'Vietnamese and Chinese organized crime groups are involved in the forced labour of Vietnamese children on cannabis farms in the United Kingdom, where they were subject to debts of up to $32,000' (USSD 2011: 384).

Reports by the UKHTC, SOCA and the NCA have all provided data on Vietnamese nationals identified as potentially trafficked for cannabis cultivation. The joint report by the UKHTC and SOCA on human trafficking in the UK in 2012 noted that 66 of the 69 people (96%) reported as potentially trafficked for cannabis cultivation were Vietnamese (UKHTC 2013: 25). The NCA assessment report on human trafficking in the UK in 2013 highlighted that 46 of the 54 people (85%) reported as potentially trafficked for cannabis cultivation were Vietnamese (NCA 2014: 20). The 2014 NCA assessment report highlights that of the 65 referrals of potential trafficked persons claiming that they were exploited for cannabis cultivation, 47 (72%) were Vietnamese nationals (NCA 2015: 27). The percentage of Vietnamese nationals reported as potentially trafficked for cannabis cultivation fell in each of these years. However, Vietnam was still by far the most common country of origin. The second most common nationality in 2014 was Albanian, with only six reported potential cases (9%) (NCA 2015: 27).

The research

The research methodology used for this chapter was a content analysis of British newspaper articles. The methodology identified newspaper articles on cases of migrants convicted in the UK for the cultivation of cannabis who were potentially trafficked, using the keywords 'cannabis', 'prison' and 'immigrant', between 1 April 2009 and 9 August 2017. The newspaper articles were analysed for descriptions of experiences that met the three elements of the Palermo Protocol's definition of human trafficking; the act, means and purpose.[3] The newspaper articles were also analysed for trafficking indicators using the International Labour Organisation (ILO) 'Operational indicators of trafficking in human beings' (ILO 2009). The articles were additionally analysed for explicit reference to the defendants being described as trafficked or as slaves. Not all of the newspaper articles detailed the act, means and purpose. However, certain key details highlighted within each newspaper article suggested that the defendant had potentially been trafficked. The Home Office's own published guidance for officials responsible for formally identifying trafficked persons highlights that they may not need to identify a multitude of indicators and that one factor may be sufficient to recognise someone as a potential trafficked person:

> It is not the case that a set number of indicators will equate to a person being a victim. One or a combination of factors could suggest a person is a potential victim, so each case

should be considered on its own merits. (Home Office 2016: 25)

Through this methodology, newspaper articles were identified on 112 separate court cases where it was at least reasonably clear that the person or persons who were convicted for cannabis cultivation were potentially trafficked. Of the 112 cases identified as potential trafficking cases in this research, only three people were children at the time of their conviction. This is a consequence of the methodology using the keyword 'prison' in searching for potential trafficking cases.[4]

The limitations of this methodology are clear. For example, only cases that were reported in the media could be identified using the methodology. This means that the number of cases presented can be seen as a potentially small picture of the scale of potential trafficked persons criminalised for cannabis cultivation. It is also acknowledged that the newspaper articles provide a limited amount of information about the circumstances of those who were convicted, and of the court proceedings. An enhanced methodology would examine the court transcripts of these cases. This would provide more comprehensive, reliable data to analyse whether a person had been trafficked and the responses to them. Only the significant cost of accessing such a larger number of transcripts prevented this from being done.

Nonetheless, despite limitations with the methodology, the research has identified a serious issue. It does not need to be claimed that each person identified through this methodology would have been officially identified as trafficked or would have met the required criteria under the legislation to have avoided punishment. The methodology is able to highlight responses that raise significant questions about the ability of those within the criminal justice system to identify potential trafficked persons and their knowledge of policy and legislation on non-punishment, and thus raises questions about the frequent miscarriage of justice.

The 112 court cases discussed in the chapter where potential trafficked cannabis gardeners were convicted were heard at 54 different courts throughout the UK. This suggests a nationwide lack of knowledge about identifying trafficked persons and the policy and legislation on non-punishment within the UK's criminal justice systems.

Convictions of cannabis gardeners not identified as trafficked

Those within the criminal justice system should be familiar with the notion of human trafficking and its occurrence in the UK. It should be possible for them to recognise a person found inside a cannabis factory as someone who may have been trafficked. In 2013, the written judgment by the Lord Chief Justice of England and Wales, Lord Justice Moses, and Mrs Justice Thirwall on the case of *L, HVN, THN, and T -v- R*, a case concerning the criminalisation of a number of trafficked persons, stated that:

> Enough is now known about people who are trafficked into and within the United Kingdom for all those involved in the criminal justice process to recognise the need to consider at an early stage whether the defendant (child or adult) is in fact a victim of trafficking. (Lord Chief Justice of England and Wales and Mrs Justice Thirwall 2013)

However, it is shown here that people disclosing multiple strong trafficking indicators are being convicted for the cultivation of cannabis without any apparent recognition that they may have been trafficked. This is of enormous importance. To be treated in respect of policy and legislation on non-punishment requires an individual to be recognised as potentially trafficked. Jovanovic (2017: 62) argues that the main problem with applying the non-punishment provision is when 'authorities have failed to identify defendants as victims of human trafficking'.

Of the 112 cases that this research identified, there were 77 cases where people identified as potential trafficked persons do not appear to have been recognised as potential trafficked persons by the criminal justice system. The newspaper articles on these 77 cases make no reference to them being recognised as potentially trafficked or having been referred into the NRM.

Of the 77 newspaper articles, 37 include examples of both the act and means of trafficking that were discussed in court with regard to the experiences of the defendants. In none of the 112 articles on the court cases was it reported that the defendants had gained any significant personal financial benefit from working in the cannabis factories despite the enormous value of the cannabis. So, while 'exploitation' was not explicitly stated, people producing a high-value drug in dangerous and unpleasant environments while receiving no financial reward could be regarded as having been exploited. However, 17 of the 77 articles highlighted both examples of the act and means that were disclosed in court, as well as the explicit description of the defendants as having been 'exploited'. This means that in 70% of these cases, descriptions of experiences that could be identified as the act and means, or the act, means and purpose, were disclosed. There were newspaper articles on 13 cases in England and Wales in which descriptions of all three elements of the Palermo Protocol's definition of human trafficking – the act, means and purpose ('exploitation') – were discussed in court where the person who was convicted was not identified as potentially trafficked since the introduction of section 45 of the MSA. We now highlight some of the cases where it appears that people were not identified as potential trafficked persons to indicate the types of trafficking indicators not being recognised since the introduction of legislation on non-prosecution in the three legal jurisdictions of the UK.

In June 2015, a 47-year-old Vietnamese woman received a 30-month prison sentence for the cultivation of cannabis following a trial at Sheffield Crown Court. The court heard descriptions of the 'act'. The woman had been forced into prostitution to pay the €4,000 debt that she owed to those who had brought her into the UK. This debt can be identified as the 'means' for exploitation. The woman's solicitor told the court: 'She was given jobs to do – some less savoury than others. She was forced to work in a brothel but she is at an age where that did not prove very "profitable"' (Stigant 2015). The woman was then moved to a cannabis factory but managed to escape for 12 months before being recaptured. The woman's solicitor explained another means of exploitation in describing how she was told that 'unpleasant things would happen to her family back in Vietnam' if she did not cooperate (Stigant 2015). The solicitor explicitly expressed to the court that 'In many ways she has been exploited' (Stigant 2015). This trial happened after the MSA achieved royal assent but before section 45 came into force on 31 July 2015. However, as it appears that the woman was not recognised as a potential trafficked person, section 45 would not have prevented her punishment.

In December 2015, a Chinese man found inside a cannabis factory in Belfast received a 28-month prison sentence after being convicted of cannabis cultivation at Belfast Crown Court. The newspaper article on the case explains that a 'Snakeheads' gang brought the defendant into the UK when he was 17 years old. The defendant's solicitor told the court that his client had planned to work in the UK and send money back to his parents. The solicitor said that his client was 'deceived by the Snakeheads', 'who told him he would have to work to pay off a £30,000 debt to them' (McDonald 2015). The defendant worked in restaurants around the UK and the Republic of Ireland before he was brought to Belfast. The newspaper article explains that the defendant 'felt he was acting under a certain degree of duress, but he accepted he played a "gardener" role tending the plants "under the instruction of others'" (McDonald 2015).

A more recent case was heard at Newcastle Crown Court in February 2017, where a 22-year-old Vietnamese man received an eight-month prison sentence for the cultivation of cannabis. The solicitor described the act of transportation: 'he told the police he was taken to the address ... he was collected from the station and was taken straight to the property' (Kennedy 2017). The solicitor described the means of trafficking, stating: 'he was warned if he did leave, he would be beaten up' (Kennedy 2017). This was reiterated by the judge who heard the case, who acknowledged to the defendant: 'You were told not to answer the door to anyone and not to leave, under the threat of being found and assaulted' (Kennedy 2017). The defendant's solicitor explicitly explained that 'there was undoubted exploitation in this case'.

These cases are representative of the 70% of cases where the act and means, or the act, means and purpose, were highlighted in newspaper articles reporting on the convictions of people for cultivating cannabis who were not described as potential trafficked persons. The descriptions of the circumstances of the defendants working inside the cannabis factories in the aforementioned cases should have raised concerns and suspicions about whether the defendants were trafficked. However, the newspaper articles contain no reference to them being identified as potential trafficked persons. The apparent inability to recognise those experiences as trafficking indicators suggests a significant absence of understanding about human trafficking from some working in the criminal justice system, including CPS staff, barristers, solicitors and even judges.

Legislation and policy on non-punishment will be irrelevant if those within the criminal justice system are unable to identify potential trafficked persons. Those within national prosecution services and the criminal justice systems throughout the UK need adequate training to ensure the identification of trafficked persons for them to have the possibility of being treated in respect of policy and legislation. However, it is argued here that the identification of trafficked cannabis gardeners is undermined by the way in which a stereotypical victim of trafficking has been constructed through a victim discourse that has dominated the popular understanding of human trafficking.

Public and political responses to human trafficking have developed against the background of considerable hostility towards immigration and migrants. As Home Secretary, Theresa May promised to create a 'really hostile environment for illegal migration' (Kirkup and

Winnett 2012) in the UK. Those who want to see trafficked persons treated with compassion and provided support and assistance have, it was claimed, overemphasised the 'innocence' of victims and have focused on the most sensational examples that have then been falsely recognised as typical trafficking experiences. Srikantiah (2007) and Uy (2011) separately describe how a 'perfect victim' has been created, while Hoyle et al (2011) describe how the 'ideal victim' has been manufactured. This construction of the perfect, ideal or innocent victim can, in reality, exclude many trafficked persons from being identified. However, those exploited in cannabis factories, trafficked essentially for forced criminality, may be the furthest away from fulfilling the characteristics of the perfect stereotypical victim.

The victim discourse has also focused heavily on human trafficking as a problem affecting women and children. The emphasis on women and children was central within the development of responses to human trafficking. Davidson and Anderson (2006: 21) argue that women 'are lumped together with children as categories of persons requiring special protection, and constructed as the passive victims and objects of third parties within the migration process.' Ditmore (2005: 108) argues further that a consequence of the focus on women and children in human trafficking is that 'trafficked men are invisible and their situations continue to be less recognised and therefore more difficult to address'. A consequence of all of these elements of the victim discourse is that it will be highly difficult for men found inside cannabis factories to be identified and treated as trafficked persons.

The conceptualisation of human trafficking and trafficked persons that has emerged through a victim discourse needs to be challenged to ensure that people trafficked as cannabis gardeners, and all trafficked persons, can be identified. The presentation of human trafficking and trafficked persons by non-governmental organisations (NGOs), politicians and the media needs to be honest about the complexities and realities of the experiences of trafficked persons, and to reflect the variety of characteristics that they present.

The punishment of cannabis gardeners informally identified as trafficked or slaves

This research has found that potential trafficked cannabis gardeners are not just convicted as a consequence of not being identified as potential trafficked persons. We also identified newspaper articles on 35 cases where people were convicted following and despite their informal recognition as trafficked or enslaved in court. This included 28 cases where people were described as having been trafficked; 12 of these cases happened after the introduction of non-punishment legislation in the country where the case was heard. There were seven cases where people were described in court as having been slaves or in the situation of slavery when they were cultivating cannabis; two of these cases happened after the introduction of legislation.[5]

People identified as trafficked by the criminal justice system should be treated in respect of policy and guidance published by the national prosecution services on responding to those identified as potential trafficked persons and the legislation on non-punishment. However, two years after the legislation on non-punishment was introduced, research suggests that many are still not acting in respect of the legislation or policies on non-punishment. A UNICEF briefing on the punishment of trafficked children in the UK highlighted that 'Information obtained through interviews with defence lawyers and the police in England indicates some serious shortcomings in implementation of the non-punishment principle … evidence also shows that there are some defence lawyers who remain unaware of the statutory defence' (UNICEF 2017: 7). A report by Nadine Finch for Every Child Protected Against Trafficking UK (ECPAT UK) (Finch 2017: 63) also highlights concerns about the extent to which judges sitting in criminal courts understand the non-punishment provision. The cases discussed here demonstrate responses consistent with such concerns. They highlight practices that raise significant questions about a lack of recognition and understanding about the policy and legislation on non-punishment.

Actors within the criminal justice system need to be trained not only on identifying potential trafficked persons, but also on the rights of such persons with regard to being protected from punishment for crimes committed as a direct consequence of their trafficking situation. The Group of Experts on Action Against Trafficking in Human Beings (GRETA),[6] in its second evaluation of the UK's implementation of the CAT, recommended that UK authorities:

> strengthen their efforts to ensure compliance with the principle of non-punishment of victims of THB [trafficking in human beings] for their involvement in unlawful activities, to the extent that they were compelled to do so, including by promoting the existing guidance, and developing such guidance where there is none, amongst police staff, legal professionals, prosecutors and judges. (GRETA 2016: 71)

The UK's Independent Anti-Slavery Commissioner (IASC 2017a: 16), in partnership with the International Bar Association and the Judicial College, oversaw training on modern slavery to over 1,500 members of the judiciary in England and Wales between November 2016 and March 2017. However, it is not clear what this training provided with regards to the non-punishment of trafficked persons. This research has identified cases of people potentially trafficked for cannabis cultivation who have been convicted for cannabis cultivation since that training was offered.

In October 2015, a Vietnamese man recognised as potentially trafficked received a 14-month prison sentence for the cultivation of cannabis during a trial at Bradford Crown Court. The court heard that the defendant was deceived about the work that he would do in the UK and was locked inside the cannabis farm by those controlling him. The defendant showed the court the marks and bruises on his body that he said were the result of the beatings from those controlling him. The newspaper article on the case highlights that the defendant's barrister told the court that the Home Office were examining whether he was a victim of trafficking but it was explained that the CPS wanted to continue with criminal proceedings against him regardless of the decision (Loweth 2015).

This response contradicts CPS published guidance on responding to individuals receiving a formal trafficking decision following a referral into the NRM, which states that 'Prosecutors should take account of an NRM decision (reasonable grounds or conclusive grounds) regarding the status, or potential status, of the suspect as a victim of trafficking/slavery when considering the decision to prosecute' (CPS 2011: 31). In the aforementioned case, the CPS, by proceeding with the case regardless of the decision, was not taking into account the status of the defendant. The newspaper article suggests that the CPS would not have been moved in their decision even if the defendant received a positive conclusive grounds decision.

In October 2016, a man was sentenced to 10 months in prison following a trial at Shrewsbury Crown Court in which the judge said to the defendant: 'You came here looking for a new life and you found yourself in something approaching modern slavery' (*Shropshire Star* 2016). However, the judge then also emphasised the level of criminality of the cultivation of the cannabis, explaining: 'Nevertheless this was a big operation and you must have known it was illegal and it is right to describe this, if not as industrial, then as capable of producing cannabis on a significant scale' (*Shropshire Star* 2016). The comments from the judge reported in the press suggest that the judge had no knowledge of the non-punishment provision.

In April 2017, two men were each sentenced to 12 months in prison at Portsmouth Crown Court in a case that the Judge Recorder, Nicholas Atkinson QC, described as 'an example of modern day slavery' (Fishwick 2017). The newspaper article on the case reported that 'the men were forced to work at a house … to pay off debts to the traffickers' (Fishwick 2017). The newspaper reported that the prosecuting solicitor explained that 'it was not uncommon for people from South Asia to be trafficked into the UK and put into "bonded labour"' (Fishwick 2017). The newspaper article quoted the judge as telling the defendants: 'I'm satisfied that you were engaged in that by way of pressure, coercion and intimidation and you were clearly in a position whereby you've been exploited' (Fishwick 2017). However, the newspaper article also quoted the judge as having said to the defendants: 'I wish you both well and that this whole unfortunate involvement in this country will come to an end very shortly' (Fishwick 2017). In this remark, the judge can arguably be recognised as conveying sympathy and concern towards the two men who he has described as having been in 'modern slavery', to whom he gave custodial sentences. Within this case, the contradictory responses from the judge, conveying sympathy while offering punishment, suggest a lack of awareness from the judge about section 45 of the MSA. The conviction was patently avoidable.

A detailed description of the circumstances of a man recognised as trafficked who was convicted at a Crown Court in Wales in May 2016 for the cultivation of cannabis comes from a case study written and published by the solicitors who represented him. The man was referred to the Home Office as a potential trafficked person. The man, who did not speak any English, had paid USD20,000 to people in Vietnam to get him to the UK. Upon arrival, he was immediately taken to a house and told to look after the cannabis plants inside it in return for £50 a week plus food. He was threatened that if he left the house or let the plants die, he would be beaten up. When he was arrested, he did not have a passport and only had a small amount of money. It was emphasised that he had gone into debt to come to the UK and that he faced threats and coercion once he arrived. However, it was also highlighted that he had an economic motivation in migrating to the UK. The solicitor argued that his client should be placed in a lesser role because he performed a limited function under direction and was only engaged because he was being coerced and exploited. The case study notes that the 'court were sympathetic to the defendant's situation as a person who had been trafficked' (Michael J Reed Solicitors 2016). This is illustrated by the fact that the judge 'declined to confiscate the small amount of wages that he had received for looking after the cannabis plants' (Michael J Reed Solicitors 2016). Such a response is highly unusual, particularly since, in May 2016, the Immigration Act that created the offence of 'illegal working' gave the Home Office the power to seize wages from those found to have been working illegally in the UK. The judge allowed this man, who was punished for committing a criminal offence in the UK, to be given the wages that he had earned through his activities. The defendant pled guilty on a limited basis and received a 10-month prison sentence. However, due to time served on remand, he was not sent to prison. He was, however, detained in an immigration removal centre pending his removal from the UK.

This final case suggests a complete lack of understanding about section 45 from anyone involved within the criminal justice system. The defendant was clearly recognised as a potential trafficked person. However, the solicitor only argued for his client to be punished less severely because of his diminished responsibility rather than to argue that his client should not be punished. The judge's contradictory responses, responding with sympathy while punishing the man, also suggest a complete lack of awareness of the law.

Conclusion

The UK government and Prime Minister Theresa May have continually argued that the MSA is 'leading the world' in response to human trafficking (Home Office 2015: 3). However, this chapter has shown that the introduction of legislation on the non-punishment of trafficked persons has not been a panacea in preventing them from being punished. It has been shown here that people identified as trafficked and as slaves continue to be punished as if the legislation and policy on non-punishment were written with invisible ink. Potential trafficked cannabis gardeners in the UK continue to be punished by the criminal justice system as they were long before legislation and policy on non-punishment was introduced.

This chapter has not attempted to evaluate the statutory defence of non-punishment by examining what happens when it *has* been applied in cases of potential trafficked cannabis gardeners. Instead, what this chapter has done is more elementary but no less important. The chapter shows that in many cases involving potential trafficked cannabis gardeners, this statutory defence and the policy on non-punishment is not even coming into consideration because trafficked persons are not properly identified as trafficked or because the policy and legislation have not been applied. This chapter highlights an urgent need to ensure that all responders within the criminal justice system are able to identify potential trafficked persons and are aware of the requirements of policy and legislation to prevent them from being punished. A report by the Anti-Trafficking Monitoring Group (ATMG 2016: 7), a coalition of 11 organisations involved in anti-trafficking work in the UK, argued that 'the use of the defence needs to be monitored'. This chapter has found that the defence is not being used in cases where it could and should have been, strongly supporting the ATMG's call.

The UK government's response to human trafficking has been dominated by a law-enforcement approach. Theresa May has declared that the MSA 'delivered tough new penalties to put slave masters behind bars where they belong' (May 2016). However, failures to prevent the prosecution of trafficked persons harm the possibility of prosecuting traffickers. To date, nobody has been convicted of trafficking people for the purpose of cannabis cultivation in the UK. In *none* of the 112 cases identified in this research were those responsible for operating the cannabis factories or transporting, recruiting and controlling the cannabis gardeners convicted or even identified. In some of the cases, the judges expressed disappointment that those responsible for controlling the cannabis factories were not being made to face justice. In a case at Swansea Crown Court in February 2017, a woman and a man were sentenced to 13 months and 16 months in prison, respectively, for the cultivation of cannabis. The newspaper article reported that 'Passing sentence, Judge Walters said both defendants had been trafficked into Britain to act as "gardeners", cultivating the cannabis crop of behalf of others' (Evans 2017). In sentencing, the judge commented that it was a 'great pity' that those responsible for the cannabis factory had not been found (Evans 2017). The greater pity is that the judge saw it fit to send to prison two people that he had identified as trafficked, and that it is the people being trafficked for cannabis cultivation, and not the traffickers, who are being punished by the criminal justice system.

Notes

[1] The date that the UK agreed to begin upholding the requirements of the CAT.

[2] The NRM is the UK's mechanism for formally identifying trafficked persons and referring them to specialist support (see earlier chapters in this volume).

3   The act refers to 'how it is done', which includes the recruitment, transportation and transfer of persons. The means refers to 'what is done', which includes threats or use of force, coercion, abduction, deception, and an abuse of power or vulnerability. The purpose refers to 'why it is done', which means the form of exploitation (for a discussion of the Palermo Protocol, see Chapters Two and Six).

4   Using other search terms, such as 'young offender institution', might have identified further cases.

5   It is worth reiterating that the presumption against criminalisation pre-dated the actual legislative enactment of such a presumption.

6   GRETA is the Council of Europe-delegated body responsible for monitoring how countries are complying with the expectations of the CAT. See: www.coe.int/en/web/anti-human-trafficking/GRETA

References

ATMG (Anti-Trafficking Monitoring Group) (2016) 'Class Acts? Examining modern slavery legislation across the UK'. Available at: www.antislavery.org/wp-content/uploads/2017/01/atmg_class_acts_report_web_final.pdf (accessed 1 September 2017).

COPFS (Crown Office Procurator Fiscal Service) (2010) 'Guidance on human trafficking offences'. Available at: www.copfs.gov.uk/images/Documents/Prosecution_Policy_Guidance/Guidelines_and_Policy/Guidance%20on%20Human%20Trafficking%20Offences.pdf (accessed 1 September 2017).

CPS (Crown Prosecution Service) (2011) 'CPS policy for prosecuting cases of human trafficking'. Available at: www.cps.gov.uk/sites/default/files/documents/publications/policy_for_prosecuting_cases_of_human_trafficking.pdf (accessed 18 August 2018).

Davidson, J.O. and Anderson, B. (2006) 'The trouble with trafficking', in C. van den Anker and J. Doomernik (eds) *Trafficking and women's rights*, Hampshire and New York, NY: Palgrave Macmillan, pp 11–26.

Ditmore, M. (2005) 'Trafficking in lives: how ideology shapes policy', in K. Kempadoo (ed) *Trafficking and prostitution reconsidered. New perspectives on migration, sex work and human rights*, Boulder, CO: Paradigm Publishers, pp 107–26.

Evans, J. (2017) '£100,000 cannabis farm discovered in Swansea house by chance', *Wales Online*, 14 February. Available at: www.walesonline.co.uk/news/wales-news/100000-cannabis-farm-discovered-swansea-12662141 (accessed 1 September 2017).

Finch, N. (2017) *Lighting the way: Steps that lawyers, legal guardians and child trafficking advocates in the UK can take to better identify and protect children who may have been trafficked*, London: ECPAT UK. Available at: www.ecpat.org.uk/Handlers/Download.ashx?IDMF=1dcfdd01-44fd-4b0f-90c3-ccbc36649a80 (accessed 18 August 2018)

Fishwick, B. (2017) 'Raid uncovers £400,000 cannabis factory at Havant home tended by trafficking victims', *The Portsmouth News*, 7 April. Available at: www.portsmouth.co.uk/news/crime/raid-uncovers-400-000-cannabis-factory-at-havant-home-tendedby-trafficking-victims-1-7903483 (accessed 1 September 2017).

GRETA (Group of Experts on Action against Trafficking in Human Beings) (2016) 'Report concerning the implementation of the Council of Europe Convention on Action Against Trafficking in Human Beings by the United Kingdom, second evaluation report'. Available at: https://rm.coe.int/16806abcdc (accessed 1 September 2017).

Home Office (2015) 'Modern slavery and supply chains. Government response'. Available at: www.gov.uk/government/uploads/system/uploads/attachment_data/file/448200/Consultation_Government_Response__final__2_pdf.pdf (accessed 1 September 2017).

Home Office (2016) 'National Referral Mechanism: guidance for child first responders'. Available at: www.antislaverycommissioner.co.uk/media/1058/nrm_-_guidance_for_child_first_responders_v20_ext.pdf (accessed 1 September 2017).

Hoyle, C., Bosworth, M. and Dempsey, M. (2011) 'Labelling the victims of sex trafficking: exploring the borderland between rhetoric and reality', *Social and Legal Studies*, 20(3): 313–29.

IASC (Independent Anti-Slavery Commissioner) (2017a) '2016–2017 annual report'. Available at: www.antislaverycommissioner.co.uk/media/1164/iasc_annual-report-16-17-web.pdf (accessed 1 September 2017).

IASC (2017b) 'Combatting modern slavery experienced by Vietnamese nationals en route to, and within, the UK'. Available at: www.antislaverycommissioner.co.uk/media/1160/combating-modern-slavery-experienced-by-vietnamese-nationals-en-route-to-and-within-the-uk.pdf (accessed 1 September 2017).

ILO (International Labour Organisation) (2009) 'Operational indicators of trafficking in human beings'. Available at: www.ilo.org/wcmsp5/groups/public/---ed_norm/---declaration/documents/publication/wcms_105023.pdf (accessed 1 September 2017).

Jovanovic, M. (2017) 'The principle of non-punishment of victims of trafficking in human beings: a quest for rational and practical guidance', *Journal of Trafficking and Human Exploitation*, 1(1): 41–76.

Kennedy, R. (2017) 'Cannabis farmer was shipped from Vietnam to Newcastle then exploited and threatened by gangsters', *Chronicle Live*, 20 February. Available at: www.chroniclelive.co.uk/news/north-east-news/cannabis-farmer-shipped-vietnam-newcastle-12628561 (accessed 1 September 2017).

Kirkup, J. and Winnett, R. (2012) 'Theresa May interview: "We're going to give illegal migrants a really hostile reception"', *The Daily Telegraph*, 22 May. Available at: www.telegraph.co.uk/news/uknews/immigration/9291483/Theresa-May-interview-Were-going-togive-illegal-migrants-a-really-hostile-reception.html (accessed 1 September 2017).

Lord Chief Justice of England and Wales and Mrs Justice Thirwall (2013) 'Neutral citation number: [2013] EWCA Crim 991'. Available at: www.judiciary.gov.uk/wp-content/uploads/JCO/Documents/Judgments/l-hvn-thn-t-v-r-judgment.pdf (accessed 1 September 2017).

Loweth, J. (2015) 'Illegal immigrant beaten by drug gang-masters and locked in Bradford house to tend to massive cannabis farm', *Telegraph and Argus*, 8 October. Available at: www.thetelegraphandargus.co.uk/news/13810969.Illegal_immigrant_beaten_by_drug_gang_masters_and_locked_in_Bradford_house_to_tend_to_massive_cannabis_farm/ (accessed 1 September 2017).

May, T. (2016) 'My government will lead the way in defeating modern slavery', *The Daily Telegraph*, 30 July. Available at: www.telegraph.co.uk/news/2016/07/30/we-will-lead-the-way-in-defeating-modern-slavery/ (accessed 18 August 2018).

McDonald, A. (2015) 'Chinese national who grew cannabis to pay off gang debt is jailed'. *The Belfast Telegraph*, 23 December. Available at: www.belfasttelegraph.co.uk/news/northern-ireland/chinese-national-who-grew-cannabis-to-pay-off-gang-debt-is-jailed-34309140.html (accessed 1 September 2017).

Michael J Reed Solicitors (2016) 'Trafficked into the UK and forced to work in a cannabis farm', 10 May. Available at: web.archive.org/web/20170307234618/http://www.mjreedsolicitors.co.uk/news/cannabis-cases/trafficked-into-the-uk-and-forced-to-work-in-a-cannabis-farm/ (accessed 18 August 2018).

NCA (National Crime Agency) (2014) 'NCA strategic assessment. The nature and scale of human trafficking in 2013'. Available at: www.nationalcrimeagency.gov.uk/publications/399-nca-strategic-assessment-the-nature-and-scale-of-human-trafficking-in-2013/file

NCA (2015) 'NCA strategic assessment. The nature and scale of human trafficking in 2014'. Available at: www.nationalcrimeagency.gov.uk/publications/656-nca-strategic-assessment-the-nature-and-scale-of-human-trafficking-in-2014/file (accessed 1 September 2017).

NCA (2016) 'National strategic assessment of serious and organised crime 2016'. Available at: www.nationalcrimeagency.gov.uk/publications/731-national-strategic-assessment-of-serious-and-organised-crime-2016/file (accessed 1 September 2017).

PPSNI (Public Prosecution Service for Northern Ireland) (2013) *Policy for prosecuting cases of human trafficking*, Belfast: Public Prosecution Service. Available at: www.ppsni.gov.uk/Branches/PPSNI/PPSNI/Files/Documents/Publications/Policy%20for%20Prosecuting%20Cases%20of%20Human%20Trafficking.pdf (accessed 18 August 2018).

Shropshire Star (2016) 'Vietnamese man faces deportation after being jailed over Telford cannabis factory', 12 October. Available at: www.shropshirestar.com/news/crime/2016/10/12/vietnamese-man-faces-deportation-after-being-jailed-over-telford-cannabis-factory/ (accessed 1 September 2017).

Srikantiah, J. (2007) 'Perfect victims and real survivors: the iconic victim in domestic human trafficking law', *Boston University Law Review*, 87: 157–211.

Stigant, G. (2015) '£136k drug "gardeners" jailed', *The Sheffield Star*, 22 June. Available at: www.thestar.co.uk/news/crime/136k-doncaster-drug-gardeners-jailed-1-7318178 (accessed 1 September 2017).

UKHTC (UK Human Trafficking Centre) (2013) 'A strategic assessment on the nature and scale of human trafficking in 2012'. Available at: www.nationalcrimeagency.gov.uk/publications/15-ukhtc-strategic-assesssment-on-human-trafficking-in-2012/file (accessed 1 September 2017).

UNICEF (United Nations Children's Fund) (2017) 'Victim, not criminal. Trafficked children and the non-punishment principle in the UK'. Available at: www.unicef.org.uk/wp-content/uploads/2017/05/Unicef-UK-Briefing_Victim-Not-Criminal_2017.pdf (accessed 1 September 2017).

USSD (US State Department) (2007) 'Trafficking in persons report 2007'. Available at www.state.gov/documents/organization/82902.pdf (accessed 18 August 2018).

USSD (2009) 'Trafficking in persons report 2009'. Available at: www.state.gov/documents/organization/123357.pdf (accessed 1 September 2017).

USSD (2011) 'Trafficking in persons report 2011'. Available at: www.state.gov/j/tip/rls/tiprpt/2011/ (accessed 1 September 2017).

USSD (2017) 'Trafficking in persons report 2017'. Available at: www.state.gov/j/tip/rls/tiprpt/2017/index.htm (accessed 18 August 2018).

Uy, R. (2011) 'Blinded by red lights: why trafficking discourse should shift away from sex and the "perfect victim" paradigm', *Berkeley Journal of Gender, Law and Justice*, 26(1): 204–19.

EIGHT

Modern slavery and transparency in supply chains: the role of business

Colleen Theron

Introduction

This chapter, having briefly restated what is meant by the term 'modern slavery', will explore how business is implicated by it, and the salient requirements of the UK Modern Slavery Act (MSA) transparency in supply chain provision, in the context of growing mandatory reporting requirements for business to report transparently on their supply chain impacts. We also examine how business has responded to the MSA. It concludes with some practical steps that business can take to address the risk of modern slavery in its supply chains.

The liberalisation of trade, the growth in global value chains (GVCs) and the proliferation of multinational corporations (MNCs)[1] and their impact on the environment and human rights have recently led to a spotlight being shone on ethical trade and the protection of human rights. 'Modern slavery' has become a recognised global phenomenon, giving rise to questions on how the state and business should be tackling these issues.

Although ethical trade is still relatively in its infancy, corporate social responsibility (CSR) professionals, pressure groups, non–governmental organisations (NGOs) and international bodies such as the International Labour Organisation (ILO)[2] have spent years trying to manage the impacts of large-scale global business. While it may seem relatively straightforward to ensure certain factors such as decent work, decent wages and regular employment contracts throughout the supply chain, this has increasingly become no easy feat. Global business has expanded tenfold and MNCs are faced with assessing the benefits of supporting developing economies through supply contracts and ensuring that they are producing a responsibly sourced product.[3] As business has expanded, so have the mechanisms to conceal forced labour. The GVC theoretical framework has been deployed over the last two decades to analyse the drivers of labour exploitation in the global economy and the governance gaps that facilitate it.[4] Larger organisations have increasingly complex and ever-changing supply chains, making it almost impossible to stay on top of risk.[5] Another significant contribution to the exploitation by business of labour has been the significant growth by MNCs in outsourcing the number of workers employed directly. This outsourcing of the functions and responsibilities associated with employment increases the opportunity to exploit labour as it significantly dismantles employers' obligations to workers. (Phillips 2016). Phillips (2017: 436) also highlights that the consequence of GVCs has been the 'growth of a precarious and insecure and explosive workforce significantly made up in global production, performed by a workforce made up of informal, migrant, contract and female workers'.

Historically, the protection of human rights was the remit of government. However, with the growth of MNCs not governed by international laws, and in the absence of laws being enforced at a domestic level, this has led to a governance gap.[6] Ruhmkorf states that:

> the reason why the western transnational corporations operate with impunity is the existence of 'governance gaps.' In particular, the combination of the separate legal personality of companies and the territorial nature of law makes it difficult to translate the moral responsibility of western transnational companies into legal liability.[7]

International bodies such as the United Nations (UN)[8] have introduced best practice standards that sit outside of international law, and this work can be seen to have positioned a change in governmental thinking towards understanding that business needs not only support in these areas, but also a formalised strategy for managing risk. The presence of modern slavery in the operations and supply chains of many businesses is increasingly recognised as one of the major international challenges, with a need for an international response. One response to tackling the issue of the impact on human rights by business was the endorsement in 2008 by the UN of the 'Protect, Respect and Remedy' framework for business and human rights developed by Professor John Ruggie. In 2011, the UN Human Rights Council unanimously endorsed the UN Guiding Principles on Business and Human Rights, which operationalise the UN framework and define the key duties and responsibilities of states and business enterprises with regard to business-related human rights abuses.[9]

Another response to tackling the global issue of productive employment and decent work is the establishment of the Sustainable

Development Goals (SDGs). In 2015, 159 heads of state committed to the SDGs and to achieving sustainable development in three dimensions. Goal 8.7 seeks to:

> Take immediate and effective measures to eradicate forced labour, end modern slavery and human trafficking and secure the prohibition and elimination of the worst forms of child labour, including recruitment and use of child soldiers, and by 2025 end child labour in all its forms.[10]

Alliance 8.7[11] was created by the ILO to bring together a multi-stakeholder alliance, aiming to see a world free from forced labour, human trafficking and modern slavery. One example of a business embracing section 8.7 of the Alliance is Sky.

Governments around the world, including Australia, have committed to eliminating modern slavery domestically and internationally by introducing legislation. The Australian Parliament, in its report 'Hidden in plain sight',[12] claims that the UK government has taken a lead in the global effort to combat modern slavery, including its introduction of the MSA. While it is clear that governments have a significant role to play in tackling modern slavery, the role of business is key. The then UK Home Secretary, Amber Rudd, stressed 'the "vital role" of business in the fight against modern slavery and she sets out her belief that "business must not be knowingly or unknowingly complicit with modern slavery" or "be profiting, no matter how indirectly" from slavery' in the updated guidance for the MSA.[13]

Recognising the role of government in tackling the crimes of modern slavery and human trafficking, the US government publishes an annual 'Trafficking in persons report'. The 2017 report[14] notes that the anti-trafficking/modern slavery movement commenced in earnest with the adoption of the Palermo Protocol in 2000. The report also highlights the need for business to understand how to engage with survivors appropriately and responsibly as part of their efforts to advocate for social change.[15] Consumer pressure is also increasing, with customers now demanding more information from the businesses from which they buy.[16]

What is 'modern slavery'?

As noted elsewhere in this volume, there is no single international or legal definition of 'modern slavery'. It is used as an umbrella term covering a number of human rights abuses, of which human trafficking is one. This is key to understanding how the legislative framework seeks to address modern slavery and human trafficking both as criminal offences and in tackling the issues in supply chains. There are, however, internationally accepted definitions of 'human trafficking', 'forced labour' and 'child labour'. 'Slavery' is defined in the 1926 Convention to Suppress the Slave Trade and Slavery as 'the condition of a person over whom any or all the powers attaching to the right of ownership are exercised'.[17]

The definition of 'human trafficking' is found in the Palermo Protocol.[18] This defines 'human trafficking' as follows:

> Trafficking in persons shall mean the recruitment, transportation, transfer, harbouring or receipt of persons, by means of the threat or use of force or other forms of coercion, of abduction, of fraud, of deception, of the abuse of power or of a position of vulnerability or of the giving or receiving of payments or benefits to achieve the consent of a person having control over another person, for the purpose of exploitation. Exploitation shall include, at a minimum, the exploitation of the prostitution of others or other forms of sexual exploitation, forced labour or services, slavery or practices similar to slavery, servitude or the removal of organs.

According to the 1930 ILO Forced Labour Convention (No 29),[19] forced labour is 'work or service which is exacted from any person under the threat of a penalty and for which the person has not offered himself or herself voluntarily'.

There is also no single definition of 'modern slavery' in the MSA. It defines the offences of 'slavery, servitude and forced or compulsory labour' and 'human trafficking'.[20] The guidance provides definitions of these terms and recently updated guidance now includes the definition of 'child labour'.[21] The significant characteristic of all forms of modern slavery is that it involves depriving a person of their freedom. It might be the freedom to move jobs or to leave a country, or to have control over their own bodies.

Why is modern slavery relevant to business?

Various estimates have been made of the numbers of people in slavery worldwide, ranging recently from 40 million to 45 million (see Chapter Three). A 2017 ILO report calculates that of the 24.9 million victims of forced labour, 16 million are thought to be in the private economy, 4.8 million in forced sexual exploitation and 4.1 million in state-sponsored forced labour, including mandatory military conscription and agricultural work. Women and girls accounted for 71%, or 29 million, of all the victims in 2016.[22] The ILO acknowledges that there is no single source of reliable data available on modern slavery, and in order to determine these numbers, used a combined methodology in their report.[23] This lack of access to reliable data may also be the reason why the estimates of the number of slaves in the UK has changed over the past few years, with the National Crime Agency now estimating that these run to 'tens of thousands'.[24]

With the growth in the liberalisation of trade, it is highly likely that businesses will encounter slaves in their supply chains. Modern slavery is prevalent in virtually every sector across the globe. There is evidence that the risk affects almost every industry: timber, electronics, mining and metals, steel, automobiles, garments and textiles, shipping and transportation, and agriculture and seafood. According to the US Department of Labour,[25] 139 commodities and goods, ranging from electronics to flowers, are made using forced or child labour. In the past few years, investigations into commodities tainted by slavery have included prawns from Thailand,[26] debt bondage and forced labour[27] in the global electronics industry, and claims of the trafficking of migrant workers into the Scottish and Irish fishing industries.[28]

Incidents like the Rana Plaza[29] disaster in 2013, where a building collapsed killing 1,134 workers who were working in the garment industry, have focused the attention of the world on the dangers that global supply chains can pose for workers.[30] Media reports[31] also highlight the issue of child labour and debt bondage as a form of slavery in granite. Habitat and John Lewis, as a result of the report and pending further investigation, made decisions to remove black stone from sale. In 2015, a survey of UK companies actively managing labour standards in their supply chain revealed that 71% believed that there is a likelihood of modern slavery occurring at some stage in their supply chains (Lake et al 2015). This figure rose to 77% in the joint report published in 2016 by Hult International School and the Ethical Trading Initiative (ETI).[32]

The reality is that long, complex supply chains that rely on subcontractors impede traceability and, as the Hult report points out, make it challenging to verify services and goods bought and sold. The problem of modern slavery is also not limited to certain countries or sectors. It exists in formal and informal labour markets and both lawful and illicit industries. For example, Verisk Maplecroft reported that modern slavery constitutes 'high' or 'extreme' risk in 115 countries, with only four major Western countries rated as 'low'.[33]

Traffickers are able to target vulnerable workers anywhere to fill labour shortages along a supply chain. The electronics sector provides an example of where human trafficking can exist in almost all of the stages of the supply chain. It exists in the extractive stages when mining for raw material, in the component manufacturing stage (where separate pieces are produced or combined) and in the production stage (where goods are assembled and packaged in a factory).[34] The risks are more pronounced in industries that rely on low-skilled or unskilled labour. However, they are not confined to these areas. We are reminded that they can be present in the service industry, too. In a hotel, the sheets may be made with cotton harvested by forced/child labour, the housekeeper may be exploited in labour trafficking or the room itself used a brothel. One should also not ignore the involvement of legal and accountancy services and the financiers, where criminals have access to professional 'enablers' to facilitate their illegal business models.

Women and girls generally are especially vulnerable to human rights abuses linked to business practices. Oxfam reports that they are more likely to have unstable contracts, lower wages and less skilled jobs. As many women also undertake more domestic labour, in addition to paid employment, long hours and unfavourable working conditions have a greater negative impact on them.[35]

The financial rewards for those involved in the exploitation of individuals are a key driver of modern slavery in supply chains. A report by the Centre for Social Justice[36] highlights that 'clear, organised crime lies behind much of the modern-day slave trade, and it is enabled by modern technology, and modern means of travel'. In monetary terms, the annual illegal profits of forced labour (including sexual exploitation) in the European Union (EU) and developed economies is estimated by the ILO[37] to be USD150 billion. This figure is up from an estimate in 2015 by the Organized Crime Portfolio (OCP) of revenues from organised crime across the EU, worth £110 billion – the equivalent of 1% of EU gross domestic product.[38]

While there was no mention initially of including a transparency in supply chains (TISC) clause in the Modern Slavery Bill, as a result of pressure from NGOs and some businesses, the government decided to include a supply chain disclosure provision, seen as a bid to combat or at least recognise and tackle the scale of the problem in relation to business and to introduce a level playing field.[39] Section 54 (also known as the TISC clause) requires that businesses meeting the requirements of the Act have to publish an annual modern slavery and human trafficking statement (MSS).

The introduction of a requirement for business to disclose the steps that they are taking to tackle modern slavery in their supply chains arguably forms part of the growing mandatory reporting requirements being introduced globally. The extent to which these reporting provisions are influencing the practices of companies in relation to slavery is discussed later in the context of recent research.

Mandatory reporting trends: the global picture

There are increasingly moves by governments imposing disclosure requirements on business to encourage practices to help combat human rights abuses.[40] Corporate reporting about human rights and environmental issues is an increasingly important aspect of corporate transparency.[41] This is evidenced by the significant growth in sustainability reporting instruments globally. The 2016 'Carrots and sticks' report[42] states that the majority of reporting instruments, including the UK provision, are mandatory. It also indicates that the number of instruments identified that focus on the reporting of social information has doubled since 2013.[43] Information included in these instruments regards human rights, health and safety, working conditions and training. Table 8.1, taken from this report, shows the extent to which reporting instruments have increased since their previous report in 2013.

Governments are also demanding more information on the origin of products. For example, in the US, the growing body of federal and state regulations reflects the growing trend towards supply chain transparency.[44] Table 8.2 sets out examples of recent legislation in various Global North countries requiring mandatory disclosure on human rights or steps that companies are taking to manage the risk of modern slavery in their supply chains.

In February 2017, the Australian government initiated an enquiry into establishing a modern slavery Act. The Committee provided

Table 8.1: Trends in sustainability reporting instruments

		2006		2010		2013		2016	
Reporting instruments	Mandatory	35	58%	94	62%	130	72%	248	65%
	Voluntary	25	42%	57	38%	50	28%	135	35%
	Total	60		151		180		383	
Countries and regions		19		32		44		71 (64 with instruments)	

Table 8.2: Examples of legislation requiring companies to report on modern slavery issues

UK Companies Act 2006	Requires that all companies disclose on certain relevant environmental and social matters, with key performance indicators to the extent necessary for an understanding of the development, performance or position of the company's business.
The Companies Act 2006 (Strategic Report and Directors Report) 2013[a]	Directors have to prepare a strategic report. Listed companies have to report on human rights to the extent necessary for an understanding of the development, performance or position of the company's business. The Financial Reporting Council (FRC) has produced guidance on these requirements.[b]
European Non-Financial Reporting Directive (NFRD)	This[c] requires all member states to have transposed the objectives of the regulations by 2016. Applies to certain large entities with more than 500 employees. Undertakings subject to the NFRD to report on human rights and provide information on their policies.
UK Modern Slavery Act 2015	This[d] requires commercial organisations selling goods or services in the UK, with a turnover of £36 million or above, to publish an annual 'slavery and human trafficking statement', setting out the steps that it is taking to tackle modern slavery in their organisation and supply chains.
USA: California Transparency in Supply Chains Act 2010 (CTSA)	This only applies to retail sellers and manufacturers if they do business in the state of California and have annual worldwide gross receipts exceeding USD100,000.[e] Companies have to disclose on their websites efforts to eradicate slavery and human trafficking from their direct supply chain for tangible goods offered for sale.[f]
Federal Acquisition Regulation An Executive Order (13627) from 2012 signed by Barack Obama required the Federal Acquisition Regulation to be amended.	The amendments include regulations applicable to all contracts (such as the prohibition of using misleading practices for the recruitment of employees, using recruiters that do not comply with local labour laws, charging employees recruitment fees or providing housing that fails to meet host-country housing and safety standards) and regulations applicable to contracts where the portion performed outside the US exceeds USD500,000. Contractors must develop a *compliance plan* applicable to the portions of a contract performed outside the US, and submit a *certification* to the Contracting Officer on an annual basis stating that a compliance plan has been implemented.
French Vigilance Law No. 2017-399 of 27 March 2017 on the 'Duty of Care of Parent Companies and Ordering Companies'	This applies to France's largest companies – those registered in France with either: (a) more than 5,000 employees working for the company and its direct or indirect French-registered subsidiaries; or (b) more than 10,000 employees working for the company and its direct or indirect subsidiaries globally. Companies meeting these criteria must develop and enact annual 'vigilance plans' that detail the steps that they will take to detect risk and prevent serious violations with respect to human rights and fundamental freedoms.[g]

(continued)

Table 8.2: Examples of legislation requiring companies to report on modern slavery issues (continued)

Dutch 'Child Labour Due diligence law' ('Wet Zorgplicht Kinderarbeid')	This requires companies to examine whether child labour occurs in their production chain. If that is the case, they should develop a plan of action to combat child labour and draw up a declaration about their investigation and plan of action. That statement will be recorded in a public register by a yet to be designated public authority. The law will be effective from January 2020.[h]
US: Burma reporting requirement	Introduced in 2012 by the Office of Foreign Assets Control[i]: reporting requirements were placed on companies making new investments exceeding USD50,000. Information had to be included on due diligence procedures with respect to human rights/reporting rights.

Notes:

[a] See: www.legislation.gov.uk/ukdsi/2013/9780111540169/regulation/3

[b] See: www.frc.org.uk/getattachment/2168919d-398a-41f1-b493-0749cf6f63e8/ Guidance-on-the-Strategic-Report.pdf

[c] See: http://eur-lex.europa.eu/legal-content/EN/TXT/HTML/?uri=CELEX:32014L0095& from=EN

[d] See: www.legislation.gov.uk/ukpga/2015/30/section/54/enacted

[e] See: www.ardeainternational.com/downloads/anti-slavery-legislation-comparison-table- disclosure-supply-chains/

[f] See: https://oag.ca.gov/sites/all/files/agweb/pdfs/sb657/resource-guide.pdf

[g] See: https://business-humanrights.org/sites/default/files/documents/French%20 Corporate%20Duty%20of%20Vigilance%20Law%20FAQ.pdf

[h] See: www.business-humanrights.org/sites/default/files/documents/FAQChild%20 Labour%20Due%20Diligence%20Law.pdf

[i] See: www.treasury.gov/resource-center/sanctions/OFAC-Enforcement/Pages/20120711. aspx

in-principle support for developing a modern slavery Act, including mandatory supply chain reporting requirements for companies and business. In December 2017, the Committee published a report – 'Hidden in plain sight'[45] – setting out 49 recommendations with respect to introducing the proposed modern slavery Act.

In summary, within the UK, there are some key mandatory reporting requirements covering social and environmental impacts of which companies need to be aware. These are:

- The Companies Act 2006
- The Companies Act 2006 (Strategic Report and Directors Report) 2016
- The Companies, Partnerships and Group (Accounts and Financial Reporting) Regulations 2016/1245
- The MSA 2015.

In April 2017, the UK government enacted the Criminal Finances Act,[46] expanding the scope of the Proceeds of Crime Act 2002. The new Act allows UK prosecutors to use civil recovery measures against companies whose conduct 'constitutes the commission of a gross human rights abuse or violation' and where property has been obtained through this conduct.[47] While companies are required to comply with mandatory reporting requirements, many are adopting voluntary reporting frameworks to indicate what actions they are taking to address environmental and social issues (such as human rights and modern slavery).

Voluntary reporting frameworks: the UN Guiding Principles on Business and Human Rights

One key voluntary human rights reporting framework is the UN Guiding Principles on Business and Human Rights (UNGPs). These require that business has a duty to respect human rights and explain the responsibilities of business,[48] and emphasise the importance of transparency and communication, both for states and for companies (Principles 3 and 21). These requirements recognise that reporting is a key element for companies to address and mitigate human rights, including modern slavery impacts. The UNGPs also set out ways in which business should 'know and show' that they respect human rights, including:

- adopting a human rights policy[49];
- carrying out due diligence to identify, prevent, mitigate and account for how business addresses any human rights impacts associated with its activities or business relationships; and
- having processes to enable remediation of any impacts where appropriate.

While the UNGPs are not legally binding, they are internationally recognised as the key global normative framework for business and human rights. They also emphasise that the interaction between governments and business can be mutually reinforcing.[50]

The UN Guiding Principles Reporting Framework

In 2015, the UN Guiding Principles Reporting Framework[51] (the 'Framework') was published. This has been developed through the Human Rights Reporting and Assurance Frameworks Initiative

(RAFI), which is co-facilitated by Shift[52] (a not-for-profit working globally with business and governments to embed the Guiding Principles into practice) and Mazars[53] (an accounting firm). The aim of the Framework is to help companies report on their human rights performance in line with the UNGPs, drive improved accountability in relation to human rights and provide an indispensable contribution to the collective effort to embed the UNGPs in practice.[54]

Drivers for transparency

There are various factors driving company responses to addressing the risk of modern slavery. These include regulatory developments and managing reputational risk. The Hult report indicates that 97% of companies cited reputational risk resulting from public exposure of worker abuse found in the supply chain or company operations as the biggest driver for company action on modern slavery.[55] Business to Business (B2B) enterprises are also under growing pressure from their business customers to provide assurance on what they are doing to address modern slavery.[56] There is also evidence of organisations sitting below the threshold wishing to comply in order to demonstrate their ethical standards.

Customers are showing a greater level of interest in responsible sourcing issues, as well as increased investor interest. The Hult report also says that 25% of respondents see investor interest as a key driver,[57] suggesting that it is becoming critical for the credibility and legitimacy of business in the eyes of all its stakeholders to address modern slavery issues. This is translating into investing in corporate leadership.

In addition to the drivers just highlighted, the Chartered Institute of Procurement & Supply (CIPS)[58] set out a table (see Table 8.3) to help business understand the drivers to addressing modern slavery. The growing risk of legal liability, as evidenced by the cases in the next section, is also impacting on companies' responses.

Table 8.3: Business drivers to address modern slavery

Risks	Benefits
• Reputational damage	• Increased consumer confidence
• Loss of market share	• Improved employee morale
• Legal sanctions	• Exceed legal requirements

The risk of legal liability as a driver for good practice: recent court cases

The first reported conviction of a UK-based business for a human trafficking offence since the inception of the MSA was in January 2016. Mohammed Rafiq, the owner of the UK bed-making business Kozee Sleep, was convicted of conspiracy to traffic. Rafiq's conviction followed that of two Hungarian gangmasters who were found guilty of supplying the UK factories run by Kozee Sleep and its subsidiary Layzee Sleep with slave labour. The gangmasters promised Hungarian nationals good wages and housing if they travelled to the UK. Instead, the workers were detained in overcrowded, squalid conditions, without freedom to travel and forced to work 10 to 16 hours a day, often for up to seven days a week and for less than £2 a day. The court concluded[59] that Rafiq had knowingly employed these trafficked men and 'went along with their exploitation as a slave workforce'.

Earlier in 2017, two brothers were jailed for six years on account of modern slavery. The brothers recruited 18 vulnerable men from Poland to work at a Sports Direct warehouse in Derbyshire. The pair controlled their victims' bank accounts and kept most of their wages, totalling £35,000 between 2015 and 2016, Nottingham Crown Court heard. They were both sentenced to six years in prison for modern slavery.[60] In another case involving the trafficking of Lithuanian men to catch chickens for the 'Happy Eggs' brand, a landmark settlement of more than £1 million in compensation and legal costs was reached. The deal was the first settlement of a civil claim against a British company in relation to modern slavery.[61] These cases should provide a cautionary tale for global business. Kozee Sleep was a significant supplier to two key high-street brands, John Lewis and Next, and the 'Happy Eggs' brand is prevalent in many prominent supermarket supply chains. There have also been a series of lawsuits[62] launched in California by residents against Nestlé, Mars and Hershey, claiming that businesses linked to slave labour have deceived consumers through inadequate public disclosures, demonstrating that consumers are willing to take corporate accountability into their own hands.[63]

We now look in detail at aspects of the MSA, an example of a transparency reporting measure introduced in a bid to combat business practices that either directly or indirectly encourage modern slavery. The process of the establishment of the MSA is itself discussed in detail in the Introduction and in Chapter Two.

Key aspects of the MSA relevant to business

After lobbying by NGOs and latterly by some larger businesses, it was proposed by government that the TISC clause should be inserted (much like the CTSA provisions) to get businesses to disclose what steps they were taking to tackle modern slavery and human trafficking in their organisations and supply chains. Following a consultation on the TISC clause (in July 2015), the UK government introduced a turnover threshold of £36 million or above, surprisingly low in some commentators' views. Section 54 introduced the TISC clause, which is relevant to business. The mandatory aspects of the reporting requirement are quite limited, although its policy objective is quite broad.[64]

Who will the legislation apply to?

Commercial organisations carrying on all or part of a business in the UK and that supply goods or services with a global turnover equal to or more than £36 million will be subject to the disclosure requirement.[65] A 'commercial organisation' includes a corporate body (wherever incorporated) or a partnership (wherever formed) that carries on a business, or part of a business, in any part of the UK. As the reporting requirement is not limited in its application to entities incorporated in the UK, it has the potential to have extraterritorial effect.[66] It includes charities but excludes public organisations.[67] The Act does not restrict the requirements to listed or large companies, nor is the TISC clause limited by sector or product. This is unlike the CTSA, which is limited to retail and manufacturing businesses.[68] There is no single definition in the Act of 'business', which may be a concern.

Key elements of the MSS

The legislation does not prescribe what exactly needs to be covered in the statement. Section 54(5) highlights that the statement should aim to include[69] information that will cover the business structure and supply chains. The other aspects that the organisation should provide information on are its policies on slavery and human rights, existing due diligence processes in relation to human trafficking and slavery in its business and supply chains, and the effectiveness of the steps that it has taken (including key performance indicators). It should also include information on the areas of risk and how it is managing risks. The statement should refer to the training made available and provided to staff.

The guidance to the Act provides further information on the types of activities that could be included in each heading under Annex E. Updated guidance suggests that the reason why the information is helpful should also be included.[70] However, as it currently stands, a statement asserting that *no* steps have been taken suffices for the purposes of meeting the requirements of the law. The guidance suggests that the MSS must be easily accessible and published where it can be readily seen. This might seem unproblematic, but in some big companies, questions on where to include the MSS on their home page are not uncommon. The guidance also suggests that there should be some signposting where subsidiary companies are featured as links to the home page of a big company. If a business does not have a website, it must provide a copy of the statement to anyone who requests one in writing within 30 days.

In addition to the requirement for a director (or equivalent) to sign the statement, the legislation requires that the MSS be approved by a board of directors (or equivalent) and signed off by those responsible for the business, for example, a senior director (or equivalent).[71] The requirement for board approval and a signature from a director was seen as a key factor by some organisations lobbying for the TISC provisions.[72] The inclusion of this provision was seen as a critical means of elevating the issue of modern slavery risk beyond the marketing department and into the boardroom. The requirement also introduces fiduciary duties for directors that fail to ensure that they have exercised their duty of care sufficiently.

Enforcement: what are the implications if business does not comply?

The duties to report under the Act are enforceable by the Secretary of State (SoS). If a commercial organisation subject to the reporting requirements fails to publish an MSS, the SoS may apply to the court for an injunction compelling the organisation to comply. Failure to comply may result in an unlimited fine. The application in Scotland is for specific performance. There is, however, no personal liability for directors, unlike the disclosure provisions in the Companies Act 2006, where directors can be held liable for negligence in the event of providing false or misleading information. Directors who fail to take steps to complete a strategic report under the amendments to the Companies Act can also be guilty of an offence. Neither of these enforcement options exists under the provisions of the Act.

What guidance is available to business to complete the MSS and develop its processes?

The UK government guidance was updated in 2017.[73] This update has not made any changes to the law, but purports to drive best practice. The key features[74] of the updated guidance are that it:

- encourages organisations with turnovers less than £36 million to also produce a transparency statement;
- uses stronger language to encourage businesses to include information in relation to all six of the categories set out in section 54(5) of the MSA;
- removes the now superfluous guidance as to when a business will need to produce its first transparency statement;
- adds 'best practice' guidance in relation to approving and publishing transparency statements; and
- defines child labour.

Largely in response to the weakness of government guidance, civil society has also published guidance,[75] the latest being a set of mini-briefings[76] for companies and investors. CORE has published another set of short briefing notes on MSA reporting requirements.[77]

Determining relevant supply chains under the MSA

There is no distinction in the Act between upstream and downstream supply chains, and while it was anticipated that the obligations would only go upstream, that is in respect of goods and services being supplied to the organisation,[78] this has not been the case as more B2B organisations are requesting information from their value chains. There is also no legally binding requirement on an organisation to conduct due diligence in its supply chains. The guidance indicates that 'supply chain' has its everyday meaning and should not be confined to first-tier suppliers.[79]

The impact of the TISC provisions and the corporate response to these issues

While the limitations of the TISC provisions have been well documented, it is claimed by some that the Act is a landmark piece of legislation.[80] The Hult report[81] states that the Act has been a 'game changer' and has already had a significant impact on companies.

It states that the engagement of Chief Executive Officers (CEOs) with modern slavery has doubled, and the responsibility for 'ethical' trade has escalated. It also notes that communication between companies and their suppliers has increased by 58%, and companies are collaborating 50% more with peers, NGOs and multi-stakeholder initiatives. Additionally, 50% more companies are seeking external advice and expertise since the Act's passage.[82] Those more sceptical about its impact point to the lack of enforcement against companies that have failed to disclose MSSs,[83] and practice generally suggests that 'the game' has yet to be changed markedly. LeBaron and Ruhmkorf (2017) argue that the Act fails to establish new public labour standards or enforcement mechanisms. They reached this conclusion by carrying out an analysis of the policies and procedures of 25 FTSE 100 companies to determine their approaches to bribery and forced labour in response to the UK Bribery Act[84] and the MSA. They found that bribery is afforded a much more prominent role in company CSR and sustainability reporting.

Under the Act's reporting provisions, all companies falling within the threshold will have to have published their statements by September 2017. It is understood that the Act affects more than 20,000 companies, although the UK government has not released a list of companies expected to comply. The number of businesses publishing their statements is actually less than 15%. The Business and Human Rights Resource Centre (BHRRC)[85] maintains a public track record of companies' statements under the MSA. The updated registry holds, to date, over 6,000 statements from companies in 27 headquarters in 31 countries. The website Tiscreport.org[86] contains an open data registry repository for companies to file MSSs.

The BHRRC published an analysis[87] of MSSs, concentrating on the performance of the FTSE 100 companies as a litmus test of business action to combat slavery, given their resources and experience, followed by an updated report covering the first year of the FTSE 100 reports.[88] The initial analysis revealed patchy compliance. They found that a small number of leading companies produced rigorous statements but there was no company that received their top score out of 10 scoring tiers (with 1 being the highest tier and 10 the lowest). Only 15 (56%) of the company statements that they examined fully complied with the minimum requirements of the Act. The recent report shows that only 33% of MSSs on the Modern Slavery Registry explicitly say that the statement has been approved by the board or equivalent body, that is, 67% of published statements do not meet the Act's legal requirements.

While the initial report recognises that a number of companies are revising their practices and procedures to drive change, it notes that there is still a long way for companies to progress. It highlights the decisive role that company leaders can play in setting the culture of the company to tackle the eradication of slavery and it is recognised that the Act is driving some change. The more recent report states that there is a 'welcome cluster of leading companies taking robust action, like Marks & Spencer, Sainsbury and Unilever', while the majority show a 'lacklustre response to the Act at best'.[89] Given the potential reputational impacts across all sectors of failing to comply with the Act's requirements, ensuring that statements are transparent and underpinned by robust policies and procedures calls for more than a 'box-ticking' exercise for organisations.

CORE has also released a report[90] examining the MSSs of companies in the products and services industry. They found that almost two thirds of statements do not make reference to specific risks of slavery and human trafficking in the relevant raw material supply chain or specific sector.

Act into action: the MSA in practice

In 2016, CLT envirolaw (now Ardea International) explored how businesses were responding to the Act and implementing its requirements. The research was based on a series of survey questions across a network of events. Research groups were taken from the following events:

- General Council Members attending the Retail Week Conference for General Councils in London (100 respondents).
- The Advisory Board of Lawyers for Lexis In-house Advisors (eight respondents).
- The Sustainable Working Group held by the Association of Events Organisers (eight respondents).
- Attendees of the Annual Conference on Electrical & Electronic Equipment and the Environment (40 respondents).

Participants were all asked the same set of questions. While over three out of four respondents were aware of the Act, there were still 14% who had not heard of it or were unsure of its existence. A total of 85% of respondents firmly stated that they were aware of the Act; however, only one in four felt that they had sufficient awareness of what the Act required. This indicated not only a lack of awareness-raising in relation to the Act, but also a lack of detail around its implementation and the necessary support that businesses require to effectively challenge slavery.

While the Act does not set out what specific due-diligence systems businesses should have in place, one thing that is non-negotiable is the requirement for companies to produce an MSS. In spite of this, 61% of companies either did not have a statement in place or were unable to clarify whether or not a statement was in place. Seemingly, 46% of respondents who were aware of the Act were yet to produce a statement. This meant that almost 50% of companies sampled were failing to adhere to the Act (see Figure 8.1). In this research, it was noted that some companies may not have completed their reporting cycle yet and were thus not required to produce a statement as of the date of the research, which could affect the percentage of companies reported to be failing to adhere to the Act.

It is a commonly known fact that while there is a level of internal risk, this increases throughout each tier of the supply chain. As a result of this, many organisations are working to improve the traceability of products so that ethical trade programmes can begin to leverage practices on a more global scale (see Figure 8.2). Unfortunately, the lack of implementation internally by businesses was reflected in their limited commitments to supply chain management, with three out of four companies not following their commitments to the Act through to the lower tiers of their supply chain. A total of 47% were unaware or unable to clarify whether supply chain engagement occurred.

Figure 8.1: Ardea study: companies producing modern slavery statements

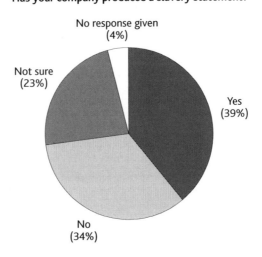

Has your company produced a slavery statement?

No response given
(4%)

Not sure
(23%)

Yes
(39%)

No
(34%)

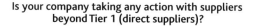

Figure 8.2: Ardea study: companies taking action against suppliers

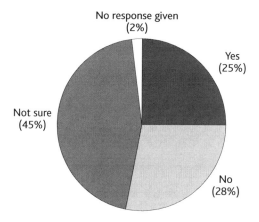

Is your company taking any action with suppliers
beyond Tier 1 (direct suppliers)?

No response given
(2%)

Yes
(25%)

Not sure
(45%)

No
(28%)

Ergon Associates[91] confirm the failings of companies to report on due diligence, although in their second report on what companies are reporting on, they noted that more companies were describing their structure, operations, supply chains and modern slavery policies in more detail. Altius[92] also reported that supplier compliance is hard to manage and that the training of suppliers is seen as key.

How have companies reacted otherwise to the MSA?

Companies and organisations have responded to the Act's requirements in different ways. This chapter primarily examines the reaction of business to the Act and does not discuss the impact of modern slavery in supply chains more broadly, although the one will arguably have an impact on the other. It is worth noting in this context that criticism is still levied at companies' failure to address labour exploitation through their CSR programmes, certification schemes and efforts, but that governments like the UK and the US are giving these programmes credibility by mandating reporting on these programmes.[93]

Research reveals that companies face a number of barriers and challenges in addressing modern slavery. Issues that have been highlighted in the Hult report[94] are: supply chain complexity; bringing their own operations into the scope of the Act (which includes logistics, warehousing, information technology [IT], procurement and catering); the lack of sufficient resources to conduct due diligence and to support supplier improvements; and concern about what should be shared publicly. These issues are exacerbated by the practical problem that companies often struggle with the inability to map out their supply chains.[95] This may be because they are not linear links, but multidimensional webs of relationships beyond the control or even contact of MNCs.

Box 8.1: Case study: the impact of the MSA on the UK jewellery sector

In December 2017, Ardea International (2017) published a report: *All that glitters is not gold: Shining a light on the supply chain disclosure in the jewellery sector: Has the Modern Slavery Act had an impact?*. Investigation into the impact of the MSA on companies' practices in the UK led to the initial interest in investigating the jewellery sector's approach to managing the risk of modern slavery in their supply chains and how they are reporting on this given the fact that the billion-pound jewellery industry is still 'tainted' by hidden and explicit cases of human rights abuses and modern slavery.

The primary objectives of the study were to:

1. Examine the companies' MSSs to see if they met the legal requirements of the Act and the steps being taken to address modern slavery issues. It also examined their statements to understand to what extent the reporting requirements of the Act have had an impact on their approach to identifying and managing the risk of modern slavery in their supply chains.
2. Examine any related CSR/human rights information relevant to understanding how they are tackling modern slavery in their supply chains.
3. Examine the role of third-party certification systems and industry regulatory systems (the Responsible Jewellery Council [RJC] and the Kimberley Process) to understand their impact on addressing modern slavery in supply chains.
4. Provide a resource to both the jewellery sector and to other business to better understand the impact of disclosure legislation and practices, and the role of industry certification bodies on company systems to address modern slavery issues in the supply chain.

The study focused on eight of the major jewellers in the UK: Signet Group (and the companies under its control), Tiffany & Co, Goldsmiths, Links of London, F. Hinds, Beaverbrooks, Boodles and Cartier. Half of the companies investigated failed to publish an MSS on their website homepage, and only three fully met the Act's disclosure requirements. Two (Beaverbrooks and Links of London) have since published statements on their homepages. These statistics do not include the subsidiaries of the Signet Group. The details of the subsidiaries and the key companies investigated are tabulated in the report to help benchmark the findings.[96] It was also found that there was very limited disclosure of the steps that these companies were taking to tackle modern slavery issues in both their statements and their related CSR reports.

The CORE coalition also published a report[97] that examined the MSSs of a number of the key jewellers covered in the Ardea report, confirming many of its findings. In particular, they found that none of the companies covered in their report provided substantive information in their statements on their supply chains, and the risks of slavery in relation to gold mining are not mentioned even though the risk of gold mining is mentioned in their other reports. The Ardea findings on the low percentage of companies adhering to the disclosure requirements of the Act are corroborated by recent research by BHRRC and CORE, which found that across the industry, only 14% of statements released under the MSA are fully compliant with section 54.

Ardea's report examined the role of third-party certification systems and industry regulatory systems (the RJC and the Kimberley Process) to understand their impact in addressing modern slavery in supply chains. The RJC[98] has over 1,000 members and has created a certification scheme. Compliance with the RJC code of practice means that RJC members are certified to show evidence of good practice in supply chains and must follow their provisions on different issues. The Kimberley Process[99] is an industry regulation scheme, an initiative of governments, industry and civil society, to ensure that conflict minerals do not enter the global diamond industry. However, loopholes and limitations in the certification schemes and industry regulation mean that potential human rights abuses can be covered up. While the Ardea study found that many improvements have been made to create more transparency in the industry's supply chain, companies still fail to produce an MSS.

The failure by the majority of companies involved in the Ardea report to comply with the requirements of the Act raises a number of questions about the Act's effectiveness, particularly in requiring companies to report on the steps that they are taking to address modern slavery. Is the failure by many companies to comply with the Act's requirements a result of the lack of enforcement or penalties, or a failure by consumers to raise these issues in buying decisions? Or, is it because for many companies, the publication of an MSS reflects the start of a reporting cycle? If the report is used as a benchmark, it will be useful to follow progress in the next reporting cycles and whether some of these questions are addressed.

Media and NGO scrutiny

The Act's critics suggest that it is not going far enough in tackling modern slavery.[100] While there has been criticism of the Act's TISC provisions, it is certainly enhancing the drive for greater transparency in business and sits alongside the recently implemented EU NFRD that requires certain large entities to report on human rights issues.[101]

The Home Office guidance requires that organisations should review and improve their statements on an annual basis. It is recognised that many businesses are still working out how to respond to the Act's requirements. However, as noted earlier, the lack of information provided by companies on their assessments of risk and due-diligence processes is starting to be scrutinised by the media, specialist consultancies and NGOs, which could open up greater NGO or civil action in this area.

An example of the benchmarking that has started to take place is the work of a not-for-profit organisation, Know the Chain, based in California. It has been benchmarking company disclosures[102] of those subject to the CTSA. It also provides some resources and guides for companies in certain sectors on how to improve their practices (see the recommendations in the next section).

Conclusions

The MSA and other similar reporting legislation are beginning to drive action for companies, albeit in a faltering way. It is noteworthy that there are several commonalties that exist in the growing mandatory reporting requirements, including the requirement to disclose the organisation's approach to human rights, with the aim of improving transparency and accountability.[103] This trend is set to continue. The challenge for business is acknowledging the issue and determining how they will respond to the complex and hidden nature of modern slavery. It is concerning that there still appears to be a large body of companies that have not published MSSs. It is also striking that those statements that have been examined in relation to how they are reporting on risks do not cover this in detail. As CORE states: 'acknowledging and understanding the potential risks of modern slavery is crucial: if businesses do not identify the risks, they cannot begin to take effective action to address these risks'.[104] The fact that the FTSE 100 companies are showing some improvement (as reported in the BHRRC report) is encouraging; however, it is concerning that half of those companies do not meet the Act's requirements and the majority do not provide details on the complexity of their supply chains and the risks that they have identified.[105] CORE argues that the failure to hold companies to account for their performance will render the Act redundant and continue to allow modern slavery to thrive. It is also apparent from the Ardea findings that for business to properly identify and remove the risk of modern slavery from their operations and supply chains, they must do more to ensure that their supply chains are properly mapped and audited. They must also go beyond the requirements of industry bodies such as the RJC and the Kimberley Process.[106] The cases being brought against companies and individuals for the crime of modern-day slavery provide a cautionary tale for business. Sports Direct's shares fell by 11% in the wake of allegations of how workers are treated.[107]

On the face of it, the Act only applies to larger companies that meet the threshold, but to be able to understand the risk in their supply chains, companies are having to carry out due diligence across their supply chains. Increasingly, it is common for companies to require that suppliers confirm that they comply with the Act and confirm that those below them comply with the Act. This may leave many smaller companies with little choice but to be proactive in order to maintain their relationships with larger organisations.

The role of procurement managers and ethical sourcing managers is likely to increase in relation to ensuring that products or services are procured ethically.[108] It is also critical to recognise that the global corporate supply chain can be a force for good. It can provide significant benefits to end users and assist with an influx of capital to help economic progress. Business also needs to be supported by governments that respect the rule of law and help enforce laws where injustices are uncovered, but the realities of this 'ideal' are significant. The challenge of tackling modern slavery cannot be addressed without collaboration from all sectors. This approach is echoed by the UK Independent Anti-Slavery Commissioner's approach (set out in his last annual report)[109] to promoting the requirement for business to engage with the Act and the benefits of supply chain legislation. Some recommended actions appear to be imperative to take this issue forward.

There are a number of ways that business can respond to addressing the risk of modern slavery to comply with the Act's requirements. These set out a good framework for business to consider what it needs to do. They are also aligned to the best practice principles for developing a robust framework to address human rights by the UNGPs.

The key things that business should consider doing are:

- Ensure that top management is supportive of tackling modern slavery in the organisation and supply chains.
- Understand how these obligations fit within any wider mandatory or voluntary reporting undertaken by the business.
- Put policies in place.
- Establish robust due-diligence processes.[110]
- Map the supply and value chain of the business.
- Understand what information it needs from its supply chain and how it will engage with supply chains.
- Take corrective action.[111]
- Assess what training is required.

CORE recently published a report setting out examples of best practice.[112] It is recognised that organisations cannot do all seven suggested points at the same time. The first step that an organisation should take is get buy-in from executive management and then determine the priorities for action. It might be that the company has to undertake a gap analysis or benchmarking exercise to determine what it needs to do and prioritise its efforts.[113]

Box 8.2: Some practical questions companies should ask

- Does your organisation have a turnover equal to or more than £36 million?
- Does your organisation have a human rights policy? If so, does it contain a reference to human trafficking, forced labour and/or slavery?
- Has your organisation taken steps to embed the policies and develop processes?
- Has your organisation mapped its supply chain and identified areas of risk?
- Has your organisation considered developing a code of conduct and particularly a supplier code of conduct? Or, does an existing code need to be revised in light of potential developments?

Notes

1   See Hang Anh Dinh, at: www.academia.edu/6745528/The_roles_of_MNCs_in_relation_to_child_labour_issue_in_developing_countries?auto=download

2   See: www.ilo.org/global/lang--en/index.htm

3   See Ardea International (2017). See also: www.ardeainternational.com/
    guides/modern-slavery-act-act-action/

4   See Crane, LeBaron, Allain and Behbahani, 'Governance gaps in
    eradicating forced labor: from global to domestic supply chains'. Available
    at: https://glc.yale.edu/sites/default/files/pdf/crane_et_al._governance_
    gaps_working_paper_march_2017.pdf

5   See FM Global, 'The new supply chain challenge: risk management in a
    global economy'. Available at: file:///Users/colleen.theron/Downloads/
    p0667_Chainsupply.pdf

6   See: www.chathamhouse.org/publication/business-and-human-rights-
    bridging-governance-gap. See also: www.opendemocracy.net/beyond
    slavery/gscpd/genevieve-lebaron-and-joel-quirk/genevieve-lebaron-and-
    joel-quirk-intro

7   Available at: www.e-elgar.com/shop/corporate-social-responsibility-
    private-law-and-global-supply-chains (accessed 5 January 2018).

8   See: www.un.org/en/index.html

9   See: www.ohchr.org/Documents/Issues/Business/Intro_Guiding_
    PrinciplesBusinessHR.pdf

10 See: https://sustainabledevelopment.un.org/sdg8

11 See: www.ilo.org/wcmsp5/groups/public/@dgreports/@dcomm/
    documents/genericdocument/wcms_421047.pdf

12 Parliament of the Commonwealth of Australia, Joint Standing Committee
    on Foreign Affairs, Defence and Trade, 'Hidden in plain sight – an inquiry
    into establishing a modern slavery Act in Australia'. Available at: http://
    parlinfo.aph.gov.au/parlInfo/download/committees/reportjnt/024102/
    toc_pdf/HiddeninPlainSight.pdf;fileType=application%2Fpdf

13 See p 6, at: www.gov.uk/government/uploads/system/uploads/
    attachment_data/file/649906/Transparency_in_Supply_Chains_A_
    Practical_Guide_2017.pdf

14 See: www.state.gov/j/tip/rls/tiprpt/2017/

15 See note 14, p 38.

16 See: www.ft.com/content/8712d586-c118-3c52-ab81-0ab7c5c932de

17 See: http://treaties.fco.gov.uk/docs/pdf/1956/TS0024.pdf

18 See: www.ohchr.org/EN/ProfessionalInterest/Pages/ProtocolTrafficking
    InPersons.aspx

19 See: www.ilo.org/global/topics/forced-labour/definition/lang--en/index. htm

20 See: www.legislation.gov.uk/ukpga/2015/30/section/1/enacted

21 See: www.gov.uk/government/uploads/system/uploads/attachment_data/ file/649906/Transparency_in_Supply_Chains_A_Practical_Guide_2017. pdf

22 See: www.ilo.org/wcmsp5/groups/public/---dgreports/---dcomm/ documents/publication/wcms_575479.pdf

23 See note 22. For a critical analysis on data analysis for statistics on modern slavery, see: www.opendemocracy.net/5050/anne-gallagher/global-slavery-index-seduction-and-obfuscation

24 See: www.theguardian.com/world/2017/aug/10/modern-slavery-uk-nca-human-trafficking-prostitution

25 See: www.dol.gov/ilab/reports/child-labor/list-of-goods/

26 See: www.theguardian.com/global-development/2014/jun/10/ supermarket-prawns-thailand-produced-slave-labour

27 See Verite, 'Forced labour in the production of electronic goods in Malaysia'. Available at: www.verite.org/wp-content/uploads/2016/11/ VeriteForcedLaborMalaysianElectronics2014.pdf

28 See: www.theguardian.com/global-development/2015/nov/02/revealed-trafficked-migrant-workers-abused-in-irish-fishing-industry

29 See: https://en.wikipedia.org/wiki/2013_Savar_building_collapse

30 See: www.opendemocracy.net/beyondslavery/ilc/neil-howard-genevieve-lebaron/making-supply-chains-work-for-workers-2016-international

31 See: www.theguardian.com/global-development/2017/sep/03/john-lewis-habitat-withdraw-granite-worktops-slavery-concerns

32 See: www.ethicaltrade.org/resources/corporate-leadership-modern-slavery

33 See: https://maplecroft.com/portfolio/new-analysis/2016/08/12/ modern-slavery-rife-58-countries-china-india-among-25-economies-posing-extreme-supply-chain-risks-global-index/

34 See: www.forbes.com/sites/stevebanker/2015/07/27/the-risk-of-human-trafficking-in-the-supply-chain/#a30ada317ed3

35 See 'Business and human rights: an Oxfam perspective on the UN guiding principles'. Available at: www.oxfam.org/sites/www.oxfam.org/files/tb-

business-human-rights-oxfam-perspective-un-guiding-principles-130613-en.pdf

36 See: www.centreforsocialjustice.org.uk/library/modern-response-modern-slavery

37 See: www.ilo.org/global/about-the-ilo/newsroom/news/WCMS_243201/lang--en/index.htm

38 See note 37, p 30.

39 See: www.gov.uk/government/uploads/system/uploads/attachment_data/file/448200/Consultation_Government_Response__final__2_pdf.pdf

40 See: www.cliffordchance.com/briefings/2017/02/hardly_soft_law_themodernslaveryact2015an.html

41 See: www.ardeainternational.com/training-education/publications/environmental-human-rights-corporate-reporting-law/

42 See: www.carrotsandsticks.net/wp-content/uploads/2016/05/Carrots-Sticks-2016.pdf

43 See note 42, p 19.

44 See: https://industries.ul.com/blog/what-companies-need-to-know-about-the-u-s-business-supply-chain-transparency-act

45 See: www.aph.gov.au/Parliamentary_Business/Committees/Joint/Foreign_Affairs_Defence_and_Trade/ModernSlavery/Final_report

46 See: www.legislation.gov.uk/ukpga/2017/22/introduction/enacted

47 See section 13, at: www.legislation.gov.uk/ukpga/2017/22/section/13/enacted

48 See: www.ardeainternational.com/guides/business-briefing-united-nations-guiding-principles-business-human-rights-ungps/

49 For a template to create a human rights policy, see: www.ardeainternational.com/guides/human-rights-policy/

50 See: www.oxfam.org/sites/www.oxfam.org/files/tb-business-human-rights-oxfam-perspective-un-guiding-principles-130613-en.pdf

51 See: www.ungpreporting.org/consult-the-reporting-framework/download-the-reporting-

52 See: www.shiftproject.org

53 See: www.mazars.co.uk/

[54] See the summary document of the RAFI Framework, p 3, at: www. ungpreporting.org/consult-the-reporting-framework/download-the-reporting-framework/

[55] See note 34, p 23.

[56] See note 34, p 23.

[57] See p 25, at: www.ashridge.org.uk/getmedia/bea3966b-0657-402f-81eb-c203b95759ad/Corporate-Leadership-on-Modern-Slavery-Full-Report-and-Case-Studies-2016.pdf

[58] See: www.cips.org/Documents/About%20CIPS/Ethics/CIPS_Modern Slavery_Broch_WEB.pdf

[59] See: www.lexology.com/library/detail.aspx?g=e28fea5f-032d-428b-974f-8484c4ba0ef8

[60] See: http://blog.cps.gov.uk/2017/01/brothers-who-brought-vulnerable-people-to-uk-to-exploit-them-jailed.html

[61] See: www.ardeainternational.com/can-business-afford-ignore-link-environment-modern-slavery-first-landmark-civil-case-uk-modern-slavery/

[62] See: www.theguardian.com/sustainable-business/2015/dec/14/modern-slavery-act-explained-business-responsibility-supply-chain

[63] See: www.ardeainternational.com/barber-v-nestle/

[64] See note 63.

[65] See the compliance flowchart of Ardea International, at: www.ardea international.com/guides/modern-slavery-act/

[66] See note 65.

[67] There are currently attempts in Parliament to include public bodies.

[68] See: www.ardeainternational.com/guides/anti-slavery-legislation-comparison-table-disclosure-supply-chains/

[69] The updated guidance has replaced the word 'may' with the words 'should aim to include'.

[70] See: www.gov.uk/government/uploads/system/uploads/attachment_data/file/649906/Transparency_in_Supply_Chains_A_Practical_Guide_2017.pdf

[71] See: www.legislation.gov.uk/ukpga/2015/30/section/54/enacted. Also see CORE guidance: http://corporate-responsibility.org/wp-content/uploads/2017/06/Core_RecommendedcontentFINAL-1.pdf

[72] See the Finance Against Trafficking response to the Bill review, at: www.ardcainternational.com/downloads/finance-trafficking-response-modern-slavery-bill-evidence-review/

[73] See: www.gov.uk/government/publications/transparency-in-supply-chains-a-practical-guide

[74] See: www.herbertsmithfreehills.com/latest-thinking/uk-government-issues-updated-guidance-on-modern-slavery-act-reporting

[75] See: http://corporate-responsibility.org/wp-content/uploads/2016/03/CSO_TISC_guidance_final_digitalversion_16.03.16.pdf

[76] See: http://corporate-responsibility.org/mini-briefings-modern-slavery/

[77] See note 76.

[78] See: www.allenovery.com/SiteCollectionDocuments/The%20Business%20and%20Human%20Rights%20review%20Issue%204.pdf

[79] See: www.gov.uk/government/uploads/system/uploads/attachment_data/file/649906/Transparency_in_Supply_Chains_A_Practical_Guide_2017.pdf

[80] See: www.opendemocracy.net/beyondslavery/patricia-carrier-joseph-bardwell/how-uk-modern-slavery-act-can-find-its-bite

[81] See note 34.

[82] See note 34, p 9.

[83] See: www.ardeainternational.com/tackling-modern-slavery-supply-chains-modern-slavery-act-done-improve-matters/

[84] See: www.legislation.gov.uk/ukpga/2010/23/contents

[85] See: https://business-humanrights.org/en/uk-modern-slavery-Act-registry

[86] See: https://tiscreport.org/

[87] See: www.business-humanrights.org/sites/default/files/documents/FTSE%20100%20Modern%20Slavery%20Act.pdf

[88] See: https://business-humanrights.org/sites/default/files/FTSE%20100%20Report%20Public.pdf

[89] See p 1, at: https://business-humanrights.org/sites/default/files/FTSE%20 100%20Report%20Public.pdf

[90] See: http://corporate-responsibility.org/wp-content/uploads/2017/10/ 171003_Risk-Averse-FINAL-1.pdf

[91] See: http://ergonassociates.net/modern-slavery-reporting-working/

[92] See: http://resources.altiusva.com/modernslavery2017

[93] See Howard and Lebaron, at: www.opendemocracy.net/beyondslavery/ ilc/neil-howard-genevieve-lebaron/making-supply-chains-work-for- workers-2016-international

[94] See note 34, pp 52–5.

[95] See: www.bakermckenzie.com/-/media/files/newsroom/2016/04/ brochure_csb37264_amiller_gsc_1118_v2.pdf?la=en

[96] See note 95, p 22.

[97] See note 93.

[98] See: www.responsiblejewellery.com/

[99] See: www.kimberleyprocess.com/

[100] See p 13, at: www.allenovery.com/SiteCollectionDocuments/The%20 Business%20and%20Human%20Rights%20review%20Issue%204.pdf

[101] See: www.ardeainternational.com/training-education/publications/guide- eu-non-financial-reporting-directive/

[102] See: https://knowthechain.org/wp-content/uploads/2015/10/Know TheChain_InsightsBrief_093015.pdf

[103] Hardly soft law.

[104] See: http://corporate-responsibility.org/wp-content/uploads/2017/ 10/171003_Risk-Averse-FINAL-1.pdf

[105] See: https://business-humanrights.org/sites/default/files/FTSE%20 100%20Report%20Public.pdf

[106] See: www.edie.net/registration/regwall.asp?mid=99427&origin= https%3A%2F%2Fwww%2Eedie%2Enet%2Fnews%2F7%2FReport--UK- jewellers--must-do-more--to-combat-potential-human-rights-abuses%2F &title=Report%3A+UK+jewellers+%27must+do+more%27+to+comb at+potential+human+rights+abuses

[107] See: www.theguardian.com/business/2015/dec/10/sports-direct-share- price-falls-following-guardian-working-practices-revelations

[108] See: www.cips.org/supply-management/news/2017/december/
procurement-critical-to-tackling-slavery-in-jewellery-industry/

[109] See: www.gov.uk/government/uploads/system/uploads/attachment_data/
file/654162/iasc_annual_report_2016_2017_web_new.pdf

[110] See the toolkit at: www.ardeainternational.com/toolkits-guides/modern-
slavery-supply-chains/modern-slavery-toolkit/

[111] See: www.cips.org/Documents/About%20CIPS/Ethics/CIPS_
ModernSlavery_Broch_WEB.pdf

[112] See: http://corporate-responsibility.org/mini-briefings-modern-slavery/

[113] See the gap analysis toolkit for business at: www.ardeainternational.com/
toolkits-guides/modern-slavery-supply-chains/modern-slavery-toolkit/

References

Ardea International (2017) *All that glitters is not gold: Shining a light on the supply chain disclosure in the jewellery sector: Has the Modern Slavery Act had an impact?*, Sussex: Ardea.

Lake, Q., MacAlister, J., Gitdsham, M., Page, N. and Berman, C. (2015) *Corporate approaches to addressing modern slavery in supply chains: A snapshot of current practice*, London: Ethical Trading Initiative and Ashridge Centre for Business and Sustainability.

Le Baron, G. and Ruhmkof, A. (2017) 'Steering CSR though home state regulation: a comparison of the impact of the UK Bribery Act and Modern Slavery Act on global supply chain governance', *Global Policy*, 8(53): 15–28.

Phillips, N. (2016) 'Labour in global production: reflections on Coxian insights in a world of global value chains', *Globalizations*, 13(5): 594–607.

Phillips, N. (2017) 'Power and inequality in the global political economy', *Chatham House*, 93(2): 429–44.

NINE

Migrant illegality, slavery and exploitative work

Hannah Lewis and Louise Waite

Introduction

This chapter considers the position of migrants in the UK who experience severe labour exploitation. It addresses how – or whether – the emerging 'modern slavery complex' can adequately respond to the production and continuation of unfree labour relationships that produce conditions now grouped under the umbrella of 'modern slavery'. We start from the point of understanding severe labour exploitation as emerging within a set of multidimensional processes embedded in the operation of labour markets and economies. This includes employer relationships with employees, migrants' work and migration trajectories, and socio-economic and family status. For migrant workers, the backdrop of hostile immigration policies and politics is an important framer. We have argued elsewhere that the susceptibility of certain migrants at particular times to forced labour can usefully be understood as resulting from multidimensional 'hyper-precarity'. Understanding forced labour as part of a spectrum of exploitation, produced by movement along a continuum from decent work to forced labour, necessitates a recognition of severe exploitation as produced within wider structures, including labour markets, migration governance and global inequalities. If the forms of exploitation being conjured in the overlapping concepts of forced labour, modern slavery, human trafficking, domestic servitude, labour exploitation and sexual exploitation are understood not as an exception, but as integral to wider economic systems, then this demands different sorts of responses than those that focus simply on 'rescuing' and removing individuals from moments of exploitation (Lewis and Waite 2015).

This chapter is principally concerned with migrants' labour exploitation. For the purposes of the arguments presented here, it is possible to view various forms of exploitation through the lens of labour relations – including domestic servitude, sex work and, sometimes, transactional arrangements where these become exploitative (for more on the difficulties of distinguishing transactional labour from exploitation, see Waite and Lewis 2017). When we refer to forced labour, we are drawing on definitions developed by the International Labour Organisation (ILO 2012), which has laid out 11 indicators of forced labour. One distinction between forced labour and human trafficking, as defined in international law and guidance, is that human trafficking is understood to include forms of movement, transportation or harbouring, while forced labour can occur without movement or harbouring elements, particularly in situations where a worker enters a labour situation offered under 'decent work' conditions that later deteriorate. In grouping servitude, sexual exploitation and slavery with labour exploitation, it is still possible to delineate these forms. We accept that there are a variety of ways in which coercion, deception and 'force' operate in these distinctive situations, and in how these types of exploitation have been interpreted in legal cases, but there are also many continuities. It is significant that threats associated with the weak position of migrants (due to their socio-legal status and/or lack of familiarity with UK systems, isolation, and sometimes lack of English language) are common to the forms of coercion frequently seen across different types of exploitation. Some of the questions arising from the emergence of 'modern slavery' as the leading policy term used to refer to various forms of severe exploitation in the UK and beyond are explored later.

Migrants are disproportionately concentrated in lower-end, insecure or precarious jobs in major migrant destination countries of the Global North. Migrant workers are often valued by employers for their flexibility, low cost and hard-working ethic. Employers' exploitation of these characteristics sits on a spectrum of migrant labour exploitation that extends from decent work to forced labour. What are the relationships between migrant labour and exploitation? Can framing the severe labour exploitation experiences of migrants as 'modern slavery' contribute to reducing or even ending forced labour in a country like the UK? This chapter considers migrant labour exploitation by unpacking three elements central to understanding the intersection of immigration and 'modern slavery' in the UK: first, the concentration of migrant workers in certain sectors and low-paid jobs; second, the role of immigration status and 'illegality' in relations of force and coercion, and, third, the failure to consider properly the role of immigration regimes in producing modern slavery.

The next section considers the dominant framing of modern slavery as an abuse perpetrated by an exploiter against a victim, and the criminalised approach that promotes an exploiter–exploited dyad, resulting in 'rescue' as a preferred solution. We then discuss the concentration of migrant workers in lower-end, lower-paid labour sectors. The degradation of work conditions and increase in precarious work provides a context in which forced labour may more easily flourish. The fourth section links this occurrence of insecure work with migrant socio-legal status, arguing that migrants with a precarious immigration status are most at risk of severe exploitation. However, processes that weaken the position of migrant workers generally can also affect those with regular status and rights to work and reside, meaning that they can also be susceptible to exploitation. We end with a discussion of whether the 'modern slavery complex' is relevant to tackling severe migrant labour exploitation. In its current framing, the modern slavery complex has so far appeared almost immune to addressing central questions of how exclusionary immigration policies both produce conditions that promote 'modern slavery' and erode efforts to resolve both individual cases, and the continuing production, of migrant labour exploitation.

Creating binaries out of complexity

The archetypal anecdote of human trafficking used in public campaigns or fund-raising features extreme, obvious and deliberate forms of deception or coercion. To take a recent example from the popular media – in the second episode of the BBC1 drama 'McMafia' (BBC 2018) – a Russian girl is encouraged to visit her friend to help work in their beauty parlour but is met by unknown men at the airport. She is driven to a location where she finds other young women being manhandled into the back of a van. From there, a group are transported. A scene during transportation implies that one is raped by a trafficker in plain view. The audience sees cash change hands as they are passed across a border to a new set of traffickers. They move the women to the basement of a building in a city, where they are picked out by pimps linked to (or part of) international serious organised crime networks, according to their language abilities and physical appearance, for a presumed destination of forced sex work. To contrast this, let us consider a different figure recently promoted in UK anti-slavery campaigns – the male, Romanian Roma migrant being paid below the national minimum wage at the hand car wash down the road in any UK city (Callaghan and Jahangir 2016; O'Neill 2017; Bulman 2018). Possibly, this migrant was already in the UK and, facing barriers to decent work due to a lack of English language or qualifications, found employment options highly limited, relying on personal networks to find any work to survive and ending up in the car wash. Maybe he came to the UK having arranged his travel through an agent offering to place him in work and find accommodation. If the promise of work was for pay that he did receive, even if below the National Minimum Wage, could such a situation be considered slavery or forced labour? How do approaches designed to target, arrest and prosecute evil traffickers affect the situation of the Roma car washer? Is it feasible or useful to group such widely different labour situations under one term of 'modern slavery'?

In the last couple of decades, a global moral consensus has emerged around human trafficking and modern slavery as a problem that demands urgent action. The re-emergence of the anti-trafficking discourse in the late 20th century has been described by Milivojevic and Pickering (2013: 595) as having three key pillars: sex and anti-trafficking as a 'moral crusade'; migration (and paternal control over women's bodies as border crossers); and crime, with depictions of folk devils and ideal victims. The resulting 'human trafficking complex' has generated harsher law-and-order policies, including criminal and economic penalties against traffickers, and the pursuit of successful prosecutions of traffickers. Critics of the dominance of criminalised responses to human trafficking highlight how the separation of particularly deserving 'innocent victims' has simultaneously legitimised the growth of exclusionary migration regimes and the proliferation of border controls: 'behind supposed intervention to "rescue the innocents" lies a neo-colonial and punitive, anti-immigration agenda' (Milivojevic and Pickering, 2013: 595). This argument is equally well suited to describing the transformation of anti-trafficking into a 'modern slavery complex'.

The growing popularity of the terminology 'modern slavery' means that 'in the anti-trafficking rhetoric emanating from national and international policy agencies, as well as NGOs [non-governmental organisations], trafficking is now frequently said to be "modern slavery"' (O'Connell Davidson 2017a: 1). Modern slavery is usurping definitions that have been subjected to more than two decades of policy and legal scrutiny, development, guidance and case law, including 'human trafficking', 'trafficking in human beings', 'trafficking in persons' and 'forced labour'. 'Contemporary slavery' was the more common term around the 2007 bicentenary of the UK slavery abolition law, promoted by commentators such as Kevin Bales. Lord Giddens, speaking in the bicentenary Lords debate on slavery, stated:

> I do not think that slavery exists in the modern world. I do
> not mean that there are not rampant forms of exploitation
> and oppression, which are found in all societies, including
> western countries. I want to make a conceptual point, but
> I hope it is not purely academic, because important policy
> implications flow from it. (*Hansard* HL Deb, 7 July 2007,
> col 746)

A decade later and the language of 'modern slavery' has been wholeheartedly adopted by the UK government. Neo-abolitionist frameworks too often see trafficking as the result of malign aggressors and individual incapacity, isolating more extreme cases from other forms of labour exploitation. Too often, there is a narrow focus on 'punishing enslavers and rescuing victims' in the global modern slavery discourse.

Notwithstanding established legal and policy distinctions in definitions, the terms 'human trafficking' and 'modern slavery' are increasingly used interchangeably among the multitude of statutory actors and NGOs and now drawn into addressing modern slavery in the UK. The merging of human trafficking and forced labour offences within the Modern Slavery Act 2015 (MSA) has cemented this fluidity. Writing a year after the Act came into force, Prime Minister May (2016) described the problem of modern slavery as follows:

> From nail bars and car washes to sheds and rundown
> caravans, people are enduring experiences that are simply
> horrifying to their humanity. Vulnerable people who have
> travelled long distances believing they were heading for
> legitimate jobs are finding they have been duped, forced
> into hard labour, and then locked up and abused. Innocent
> individuals are being tricked into prostitution, often by
> people they thought they could trust. Children are being
> made to pick-pocket on the streets and steal from cash
> machines. Others, like a 7-year-old who was found and
> rescued in Wood Green, are held as domestic slaves, while
> some children are raped, beaten and passed from abuser to
> abuser for profit.

This quote demonstrates how, even at the top of the policy chain, the image of the victim is no longer isolated to 'Natashas', 'a generic term used for girls and young women from the Eastern bloc' who were drugged, beaten, isolated and sold to pimps (Milivojevic and

Pickering 2013: 589). The prominence of cases taken forward under the section 71 forced labour offence (Coroners and Justice Act 2009) and MSA have combined with the growing involvement of police in building crime profiles that encompass exploitation beyond sexual exploitation. This appears to have diversified the image of the archetypal victim. The landmark section 71 forced labour case to date is that of the Connors family, an Irish Traveller family group of five adults convicted after being found guilty of targeting drug- and alcohol-dependent homeless males, mostly born in the UK, to work in their patio and paving businesses. These were paid as little as £5 a day, beaten, housed in squalid caravans and forced to perform demeaning tasks while the Connors family drove high-value cars and enjoyed expensive holidays (Davies 2012). The 2014 UK government campaign 'Closer than you think' (pre-dating the passing of the MSA) outlined that modern slavery includes 'sexual exploitation, criminal exploitation, forced labour and domestic servitude', and used a short information video depicting agricultural workers in a field, a domestic servant in a suburban household and a woman in a flat with a bare bed in a residential area (presumably intended to evoke an informal brothel). This diversity has been extended to 17 types of offence outlined in a recent Home Office Modern Slavery Unit typology grouped around the four meta-types of labour exploitation, domestic servitude, sexual exploitation and criminal exploitation (Cooper et al 2017).

However, the responses promoted by the MSA still profile traffickers as folk devils: the Act 'has delivered tough new penalties to put slave masters behind bars where they belong' and a new government task force on modern slavery to 'battle this cruel exploitation' will 'uncover criminal gangs' through international collaboration to share intelligence flows (May 2016). May (2016) evokes a picture of human trafficking as a phenomenon masterminded by serious organised criminals:

> A cross-jurisdiction crime – just like the trafficking of drugs, it is run by criminal groups that evade prosecution because law enforcement face the obvious challenges brought about by criminals networking across borders either physically or via the internet. That's why we need world leaders to challenge their respective law enforcement to join forces with others and come down hard on the organised crime groups and free victims of modern day slavery.

The construction of traffickers as exceptionally evil criminals is at odds with the conceptual development of ideas of continuums and spectrums of forced labour/modern slavery/human trafficking. One of the features of unfree labour is that workers may enter decent work that then deteriorates, and this may have little direct relationship with movement across borders. One major contribution made by Bloch and McKay (2016) on undocumented migrants is to provide a voice to 'ethnic enclave employers', who are more likely to employ migrant workers without requisite paperwork. They found that the employers in their study had themselves been 'pushed' into entrepreneurship due to limited opportunities for advancement in the migrant labour market. They operate under tight margins, where savings on wages are one of the few areas of flexibility allowing them to keep businesses afloat. Consider also the statistic from the National Agency for Prohibition of Trafficking in Persons in Nigeria that 40% of convicted traffickers are women (O'Toole 2018). Migrants who have their mobility blocked need to find livelihoods along transit routes in migration journeys, as outlined in the following:

> Tessa, 32, twice tried traveling to Europe but stopped short, first after she found out she would be forced into prostitution and again after her guide stranded her just before crossing the desert to Libya. Jobless again in Benin City, she applied for a 'travel agent' listing. She took girls to northern Nigeria, where she handed them off to another smuggler. (O'Toole 2018)

Indeed, a study dedicated to a network analysis of smuggling operating on the Horn of Africa–Libya–Northern Europe route found that smugglers are localised – dominated in effect by solo, independent traders – not orchestrated by a hierarchy of transnational serious organised crime gangs (Campana 2018). This is not to excuse or justify labour exploitation, particularly severe forms that involve abuse, deception, confinement and violence. However, it points to the need to also diversify the understanding of 'exploiters'. There are no doubt examples of international human trafficking involving the movement of people in a coordinated way by criminal networks with the intention of profiting from end-point exploitation. However, this stereotypical image of human trafficking is merely part of the picture of exploitation grouped together as 'modern slavery'.

It is probable that many people experiencing severe labour exploitation are not deliberately directed into such work via organised criminal networks, and that the labour situations in which they find themselves may become exploitative due to employers trying to cut corners, rather than being part of organised crime groups. The binaries of free–unfree, perpetrator–victim, free worker–slave and exploiter–exploited are simplistic dichotomies – perhaps useful tools, at times, for people grappling with complex issues. However, the concern is that the reliance on dichotomies conceals social, economic and political causes and effects, thereby misrepresenting the problem and leading to ineffective or even counterproductive responses.

This provides an important framework for what follows in showing how the circulation of the aforementioned binaries in policy and public discourse can oversimplify complex situations. A key problem with the modern slavery complex is the way in which it tends to present slavery-like relationships as an exception. Aside from ignoring long-running arguments in labour studies about how unfree labour is incorporated in, not separate from, global economies (eg Corrigan 1977; Phillips 2013), this has significant consequences for the prioritisation of responses. The persistent valorisation of certain types of victims frames them as '"exceptions" rather than "products" of the globalisation of neoliberal politics' (Andrijesavic and Mai 2016: 2) and often leads to 'rescue' as a preferred solution (see the final section). One of the pervasive characteristics of neoliberal globalisation is the erosion of working conditions, the growth of precarious work in lower-paid labour sectors and the consequent facilitation of conditions of forced labour. We now turn to this area.

Migrants, low-wage labour and exploitation

The concentration of migrants in lower-end, insecure or precarious jobs in major migrant Global North destination countries is an important context for reconsidering effective responses to severe labour exploitation in the UK labour market. Migrant workers have supported the low-wage economy in global cities for generations, but it has been suggested that this dependency has grown in recent years (Burnett and Whyte 2010; McLaughlin and Hennebry 2010). In global cities like New York and London, international migrants underpin both the top and bottom ends of the labour market. However, explaining increased demand for migrant labour as part of a labour market segmentation creating a migrant division of labour (Wills et al 2010) in certain sectors and jobs does not fully substantiate why migrants are prominent in low-paid, insecure work, especially when many are highly skilled and well educated.

Part of the explanation may be related to how newly arrived migrants are typically constructed as being harder working and more reliant and malleable than other workers (MacKenzie and Forde 2009). The greater competition for jobs that this creates leads to a downward pressure on wages and shapes these bottom-end sectors as highly segregated according to particular gendered and racial scripts (McDowell 2008). Despite high levels of educational attainment and qualifications, migrants in the UK tend to be underemployed in jobs that do not correspond with their education and skills (Rienzo 2017). While some migrants enter through highly skilled streams with job offers in higher-paid professions, more foreign-born than UK-born workers are concentrated in two of the lowest-paid occupations. Elementary occupations (eg cleaners and kitchen and catering assistants) had 10.3% UK-born and 16.4% foreign-born male workers in 2015, while processing (transport drivers and food, drink and tobacco process operators) had 9.7% UK-born and 13.6% foreign-born male workers in 2015 (Rienzo 2017). There are similarly unequal distributions among female migrant workers, with more foreign-born females in processing and elementary occupations.

These figures emphasise how reliance on migrant labour is greater in certain occupations and parts of the labour market. A Migrant Advisory Committee (MAC 2014) report concluded that the period 1997–2013 saw an increase of 1.1 million migrant workers in low-skilled jobs; non-European Union (EU) migrants accounted for most of the increase in migrant employment in caring, leisure and other service occupations, whereas A8 and A2[1] migrants accounted for the majority of the increase in process, plant and machine operatives. These sectors are often considered part of the precarious labour market, marked by higher numbers of migrant workers and characterised by the prevalence of zero-hours contracts and casualised and subcontracted conditions of employment (Jayaweera and Anderson 2008; Wintour 2013). Coupled with this are the stark figures on the stagnation of wage levels that have become prominent in discussions of economic outcomes after the Brexit vote, even drawing the Conservative government into discussions about mainstreaming the 'living wage'.

Immigration systems operate as a 'mould', encouraging migrants into and therefore shaping particular areas of the labour market in ways that do not neatly reflect the idea that migrant flows operate like a 'tap' to furnish the employment needs of employers (Anderson 2010). The relationship between supply and demand that shapes immigration controls and the migrant employment experience in destination countries is far more complex than is revealed in counts of labour demand numbers in certain sectors. The simple notion that migrants 'fit' into 'gaps' in the labour market not filled by local workers is only part of the picture. By contributing to the economy, and offering labour at certain skill and value levels, migrant workers make certain businesses viable (Ruhs and Vargas-Silva 2017). Yet, in lubricating the wheels of the economy, migrant workers in low-paid sectors are also often at the coalface of precarity and exploitation. Despite being in employment, such workers remain 'at risk of continuing poverty and injustice resulting from an imbalance of power in the employer–worker relationship' (TUC 2008: 12). These power imbalances contribute to the precarious conditions of migrant workers and, in certain cases, can embody elements of forced labour. In the context of our concern with the emerging 'modern slavery complex' (explored earlier), it is timely to ask whether this prism is helpful, or not, for advancing our understanding of migrants' forced labour. To this end, we now turn to how such exploitation intersects with 'illegality' and coercion in some migrants' lives.

Migrant labour exploitation, 'illegality' and coercion

The previous section established that the reality for many migrants in the UK is working in lower-paid sectors where short-term contracts and payment at or sometimes below the National Minimum Wage is commonplace. The overall degradation of work conditions and increase in precarious work, as seen with the rise of zero-hours contracts, affects millions of workers in the UK.[2] For some migrants, however, holding insecure immigration status can combine with low-paid work in poor conditions to make severe labour exploitation more likely. This differentiates the position of insecure migrants from that of the wider global 'precariat' (Standing 2011), leaving them at risk of disadvantageous power relationships with employers. The resulting weakened bargaining positions can therefore lead some migrants to be more susceptible to severe exploitation. Multiple factors can overlap, stretching back to pre-migration contexts in terms of social, economic and work background, meaning that subsequent migration trajectory, status and labour entry or conditions in the destination country put certain migrant groups at risk, including: trafficked persons; diplomatic domestic workers; migrant domestic workers; irregular migrants; refused asylum-seekers; spouse visa-holders; European accession country nationals (A8 and A2, including Roma); and students (Dwyer et al 2011). Each of these groups have restrictions placed on their labour market entry and access to welfare that may be more likely to create avenues into more exploitative forms of work, but also operate as tools of coercion used by exploitative employers to impose conditions of forced labour (Dwyer et al 2011). Precarious socio-legal status puts migrants in a 'position of vulnerability' that can be exploited by unscrupulous employers. Indeed, in their guidance document on indicators of forced labour, the ILO (2012) specifically mentions denunciation to immigration authorities as a type of threat or intimidation used by employers.

Although migrants with insecure immigration status are clearly in a weaker legal position, the insecurity produced by the threat of losing status and consequent deportation can negatively affect labour relations and produce conditions for exploitation, even for those with rights to work and reside. In Canada, for example, Fudge (2013) argues that the limits and restrictions placed on domestic workers, agricultural workers and low-skilled programme workers tie behaviour in work to the ability to stay or return, giving power to the employer over workers and discouraging them from complaining. Similarly, in the UK, although there is a specific visa for migrant domestic workers, the 2010 Conservative–Liberal Democrat Coalition government revoked the right to change employer in April 2012, identified by Kalayaan (a migrant domestic worker support organisation) as directly leading to a rise in cases of severe labour exploitation or modern slavery, and closing down possibilities for workers to resist or reject exploitation by changing employer (see Chapter Six).

Even workers who have come to the UK under conditions of free movement within the EU and who are ostensibly in a relatively strong socio-legal position in relation to non-EU migrants are affected. Workers from A8 and A2 countries that joined the EU in 2004 and 2007, respectively, were subject to 'transitional arrangements' requiring them to register with the Workers Registration Scheme (WRS, for those from A8 countries, until 30 April 2011) or Accession Worker Card (AWC, for A2 nationals, until the end of 2013). These arrangements required the completion of 12 months of continuous work to be eligible for social security. This meant that workers who switched employers, who were on short-term contracts, whose employers did not complete the necessary paperwork or who became unemployed could not access welfare, creating a sense of being 'illegal' (Dwyer et al 2011). Even broad statistical measures show that workers from A8 states are lower-waged than other migrants, whereas the wages of migrants overall are converging with UK-born workers (Rienzo 2017). Furthermore, the requirement to hand over identity documents to employers for WRS/AWC processing left workers vulnerable. The general confusion created by the complexity of rights under 'transitional arrangements' worked to the advantage of unscrupulous employers and agents or fixers arranging work, and left workers unsure of their position and therefore unwilling to challenge poor conditions, particularly if their accommodation was tied to employment (Scullion et al 2014; see also Netto and Craig 2017).

It must be acknowledged, therefore, that labour exploitation is experienced by migrants with rights to reside and work in the UK. Nevertheless, those 'undocumented' or in some way 'irregular', without permission to work and reside, are most at risk of entering and remaining in situations of severe labour exploitation. In general, as Bloch and McKay (2016: 15) observe, 'it is undocumented migrants who are the most disadvantaged and the least able to secure either human rights or employment rights'. Their study of 55 undocumented workers and 24 migrant 'ethnic enclave' employers found that word of mouth was the most significant form of recruitment and finding work. While they found that social and family connections were vital for initially navigating UK systems and finding work on arrival, they also operated as a trap, constraining workers in certain, limited types of work. They found that the workers they spoke to, despite a couple of exceptions, were only able to progress to slightly higher pay and responsibility before hitting a glass ceiling through which they could not progress without regularising their legal status. This demonstrates how the lack of opportunities for movement outwards into other sectors or occupations, or upwards into positions with higher pay and status, contributes to continuation in exploitative work and a closing down of space or desire to negotiate conditions.

Immigration regimes combine with neoliberal labour markets and low levels of employment regulation to produce migrant illegality through a complex hierarchy of legal statuses. 'Illegality' is not one condition, however. Anderson and Ruhs (2010: 195) usefully note the distinctions between different types of illegality and point out the common practice of 'semi-compliance' in the employment of migrants; these are situations whereby legally resident migrants are employed but their work is in violation of certain employment restrictions attached to their immigration status. This, they argue, 'allows employers and migrants to maximize economic benefits from employment while minimizing the threat of state sanctions for violations of immigration law' (Anderson and Ruhs 2010: 195). Although such semi-compliant employment may be 'chosen' by some migrant workers, such choices must be placed in likely contexts of 'no real or acceptable alternative', coupled with emerging hyper-precarious labour-scapes imbued with damaging and potentially exploitative sets of relationships. There are several features to note in a closer consideration of how insecure legal status relates to labour exploitation.

First, we outlined the connection of low-paid migrant workers with exploitation, but to this must be added the relationship between migrant workers (especially those who are undocumented) and informal sectors of the economy (Reyneri 2001). Informal sectors are less regulated and thus have the ability to shield unscrupulous employers more effectively, leading to exploitative practices. Second, those working without authorisation may experience threats of denunciation to the authorities by employers, and this leverage is often used by employers to impose poor or worsening conditions of employment. The sense of powerlessness surrounding 'illegality' and the fear of detection also routinely operates to discourage workers from pursuing negotiation or redress. Such experiences are particularly damaging for migrant workers under certain immigration and employment conditions, such as those explored in Chapter Six on migrant domestic workers and 'tied visas'. Third, the existence of 'third-party exploitation' is a known phenomenon among undocumented migrants in particular (Lewis et al 2014b). This is where exploitation falls not within the traditionally understood employer–worker relationship, but rather outside this, the typical example being migrants – with or without the right to remain – using another person's bank account to access work (many employers/ agencies will only pay workers through a bank transaction), which makes them vulnerable to losing control over their wages (Burnett and Whyte 2010). Fourth, the landscape for certain categories of migrants has been made tangibly worse in recent years as a deliberate result of everyday bordering practices being rolled out as part of the Conservative government's suite of policies directed, in particular, towards 'illegal' migrants. The Immigration Acts of 2014 and 2016 hold up the creation of a *'hostile environment'* as their explicit goal.[3] The new measures in the Immigration Acts target vulnerable migrants in four realms: 'illegal' working (with associated increased risks of criminalisation of deemed migrant 'offenders'); housing; financial resources (banking); and health care. There is great concern that these policies and the creation of 'discomfort' for irregular migrants have played, and will continue to play, important roles as *facilitators* of exploitative labouring conditions and widespread discrimination (FLEX 2016; Lewis et al 2017; O'Connell Davidson 2017b; House of Commons Home Affairs Committee 2018).

Although not exhaustive, these four faces of the relationship of illegality with exploitation are indicative of current politically regressive climes for many migrant workers. Manufactured 'illegality' has been shown in this section to be multifaceted. As De Genova (2002: 438) has argued, the disciplinary operation of the state apparatus for the everyday production of migrant 'illegality' was never simply intended to achieve the putative goal of deportation, as it is 'deportability, and not deportation *per se*, that has historically rendered undocumented migrant labor a distinctly disposable commodity'. As we found in previous work (Lewis et al 2014b), and echoed by others (Andersson 2014), insecure workers do not universally experience employer threats of denunciation; rather, their lives are imbued with the fear of detection and criminalisation or deportation, which serves to discipline workers not to challenge severely exploitative labour relations.

This section has highlighted aspects of migrants' socio-legal status as a key element of understanding the intersection of migrant labour and severe exploitation, and one that differentiates international migrants from the wider population of precarious workers. Despite the significance of (weak) socio-legal status as a contributing factor, multiple factors contribute to entry into, continuation in or preclusion of exit from forced labour. The lens of hyper-precarity is intended to emphasise how susceptibility to exploitation emerges within a picture of overlapping insecurities at particular points in individual migrants' livelihood journeys. Weakened socio-legal status within highly restrictive immigration regimes is compounded by neoliberal, deregulated labour markets and migrants' trajectories, social position and familial pressures (the hyper-precarious nexus is explained in more detail in Woolfson and Likic-Brboric 2008; Lewis et al 2014a, 2014b; Lewis and Waite 2015). Insecurities contributing to engagement in severely exploitative work at a particular time for any one individual are layered and multidimensional. As Varia (2014) summarises: 'Forced labour and human trafficking are complex and entrenched, and there is no one magic programme that, if funded, would fix the problems. Instead, a holistic approach is needed to address many facets of prevention and response'. Seeing forced labour as an outcome of weak labour rights combined with hostile immigration policies points to a different set of necessary actions to reduce modern slavery than those suggested in the overwhelming focus on prosecuting errant 'traffickers' promoted in the dominant criminalised modern slavery complex.

Migrant illegality or labour exploitation? Troubling identification, questioning solutions

We want to make three key final points. The first regards the 'identification' of 'victims': privileging only the most exploited individuals as 'modern slaves' deserving of protection detracts from addressing wider structural processes of employer behaviour, structural racism and the widespread deterioration of migrants' rights. It is imperative to ask: who gets to be included as a victim and offered support, and who is excluded? The second, linked, point is about the *outcomes* for those individuals who are selected for support. The 'help' on offer through identifying possible 'victims of trafficking' has the potential to, at best, not improve the situation of an individual migrant and, at worst, negatively affect their outcomes in terms of human rights protections. The third key argument we make, alongside others (Sharapov 2015; Andrijasevic and Mai, 2016; O'Connell Davidson, 2017a; LeBaron et al 2018), is that not only does the modern slavery complex exclude many people from its purview, but 'support' systems may accentuate negative outcomes for individuals. Further, the current energy, funding and political attention given to anti-slavery as an endeavour actually produce stricter immigration controls that are, in turn, producing modern slavery processes. We take each of these three points in turn.

First, on narratives of exceptionalism, as Andrijasevic and Mai (2016: 5) say, the pervasive trafficking narrative and victim figure exclude those who do not fit the narrow definition of the ideal victim and also 'mark the boundary between citizens and non-citizens'. Furthermore, there is a strong sense that 'trafficking' is used interchangeably with 'modern slavery', such that trafficking becomes *all* of modern slavery. This 'trafficking as modern slavery' discourse is useful for politicians who have no interest in extending the rights of migrants or workers more generally, and whose self-casting as 'modern day abolitionists' is an expedient sleight of hand to shroud broader anti-immigrant policies (Chuang 2015). As O'Connell Davidson (2017a: 7) poignantly notes: '[M]igrant workers who are exploited or deceived, but have not been bodily shackled, or locked into their squalid accommodation, or raped or beaten or threatened with death, can be ignored in the design and implementation of anti-trafficking policy'. The emerging policy landscape, then, is one that sharply delineates trafficking from migration. When extreme trafficking is packaged together with modern slavery, as is often the case in policy and public discourse, we are left with a narrative that gains and mobilises broad support by separating the innocent trafficking/modern slavery victim from the devious 'illegal' migrant.

Second, it is important to probe what the outcomes are for those trafficked/enslaved individuals who are 'saved' and 'rescued'. However, taking a step back from the 'rescuing' phase first, since the passing of the MSA, a huge amount of energy has been poured into 'awareness-raising' in this realm. A Modern Slavery Helpline was launched in 2016 and is one of the referral routes for the reporting of possible cases of modern slavery to the police by myriad public servants (including the police, local authorities and the Border Force, as required under section 52 of the MSA) and socially engaged individuals trained by anti-trafficking NGOs and initiatives. Across 2017, in particular, much activity revolved around creating resources to help individuals to 'spot the signs' of trafficking/modern slavery. Multiple variations of 'spotting the signs' guidance by professional associations began to circulate, including from the Institute of Health Visiting and the Royal College of Nursing and Community Care. The figurative elephant in the room of the well-intentioned efforts to address modern slavery, however, is: who comes under the gaze of the citizen-spotter,[4] and what happens *next* to those identified?

Identification and referral into the National Referral Mechanism (NRM) (the UK's identification and support system for 'potential victims' of modern slavery) (see Chapter Four) brings a relatively low rate of success (a positive 'conclusive grounds' decision), and an even lower chance of being given leave to remain if a non-European Economic Area (EEA) national.[5] For many, therefore, the NRM is not much of an opportunity to rebuild life if likely refusal means being pushed further into the shadows and at risk of re-trafficking/re-exploitation and/or into potentially more damaging conditions for those deported as part of the process (Plambech 2014; see also the discussion of reasons for migrant domestic workers to avoid referral into the NRM in Chapter Six). Even the minority of individuals who *do* enter the NRM after experiencing trafficking/modern slavery are likely to find themselves at a 'cliff edge' of support withdrawal after the 45 days of statutory provision has ended (if a negative conclusive grounds decision is received, the individual has two days to leave the safe house; if positive, they have two weeks). Two recent damning reports of failures to protect victims of trafficking/modern slavery have come from the Human Trafficking Foundation (2015, 2016), who found that a quarter of victims disappeared even *after* being 'rescued'. It is therefore incumbent to ask whether current efforts at 'rescuing' can realistically improve outcomes for individual migrants given inadequate levels of victim protection in the UK and in the absence of any substantive efforts to address systematic and widespread forms of exploitation of migrants in neoliberal, globalised economies.

This point links to our third and closing argument: that migrant workers' rights are being broadly eroded, but, in particular, in low-paid sectors where the spectre of exploitation is never far away. In focusing on narratives of exceptionalism (see earlier), the trafficking/modern slavery complex excludes many from its view and often damages even those 'rescued'. However, the 'noise' emanating from an ever-more crowded campaigning/awareness-raising field is also distracting attention from abilities to challenge the prevailing status quo of the global neoliberal economic order that is contributing to the *causes* of modern slavery, most particularly through stricter immigration policies and border restrictions (LeBaron et al 2018). The moral panics around sexual slavery (and modern slavery more generally) result in *more* stringent anti-immigration measures that actually serve to widen the spaces of exploitation risk for migrants. We have written elsewhere (Lewis et al 2017) on the current toxic climate in the UK towards certain categories of migrants and the 'hostile environment' that is actually facilitating an environment in which extreme exploitation can flourish. The outcome is quite contradictory with government claims that it wishes to rid the UK of the 'scourge of modern slavery' (May 2014). We are therefore concerned that much of the activity of the modern slavery complex around campaigning and awareness-raising, in particular, is creating little more than 'noise' and the absence of substantive efforts to address the causal mechanisms producing modern slavery. Awareness-raising 'successes' may yet be a troubling pyrrhic victory for campaigners and policymakers alike. The more amorphous actions of states in generating – deliberately or as an unintended consequence – reliance on cheap migrant labour to help deliver cheap goods and services in a globally competitive market, facilitated by labour market deregulation and the lack of enforcement of basic work rights, is, admittedly, much harder to pin down and draw into the lens and spheres of influence that the modern slavery agenda has created.

The issues discussed here raise questions about the efficacy of 'modern slavery' as an effective framework for ending the severe labour exploitation of migrants in the UK. The questions of how and why employers sometimes engage in exploitative practices and how certain migrants become susceptible to entering or remaining in forced labour are complex and multidimensional. We argue that the processes that result in forced labour, including the extent to which workers feel able or willing to resist or negotiate exploitative conditions, are enmeshed in a web of global, national and local labour and immigration policies and social structures. It may therefore be somewhat surprising that the prevailing tendency in policy, criminal, legal, campaigning and service support representations of modern slavery is to offer a depiction of simplistic evil–good and perpetrator–victim binaries. The terms used to refer to severe exploitation shape what is understood about how modern slavery emerges, and therefore what are considered appropriate, viable and sufficient policy responses. A migrants' rights approach needs to be central if the struggle to tackle modern slavery is to be successful in addressing systematic forms of severe exploitation of migrants in general, and particularly of those intentionally weakened through experiences of becoming 'illegalised'.

Notes

1 New European accession countries that joined the EU in 2004 (A8 – Czech Republic, Estonia, Hungary, Latvia, Lithuania, Poland, Slovakia and Slovenia) and 2007 (A2 – Bulgaria and Romania).

2 Office for National Statistics (ONS 2017) figures show that there were 1.4 million contracts classified as 'zero hours' (those that did not guarantee a minimum number of hours). The equivalent figure for 2016 was 1.7 million, but both figures represent 5% of all employment contracts. It must further be noted that the 2017 figures are not necessarily an indication that insecure work is becoming less of a problem as agency work, short-hours contracts and self-employment have all grown substantially in recent years, increasing the number of people in 'atypical' work.

3 As stated as intent by then Home Secretary Theresa May in 2013 (Travis 2013). The 'hostile environment' around immigration has recently (April 2018) been somewhat rebranded by the incoming Home Secretary Sajid Javid in the light of the so-called 'Windrush scandal' (whereby members of the Windrush generation from the late 1940s onwards, as well as their children, have been wrongly targeted by the government's immigration policies to deter 'illegal' immigrants). Javid suggests that immigration practice will become a 'compliant environment' rather than a hostile one. Many commentators remain sceptical of this terminological shift, however, and are concerned that removing the word 'hostile' will not override its original purpose to legitimise general hostility to all migrants regardless of status at all levels of the Home Office. The promotion of hostility as a central policy goal has emboldened punitive policies and an overwhelming anti-migrant culture in the Home Office and beyond, which a shift in language and highly limited U-turns (National Health Service data-sharing with the Home Office and immigration bank checks) will struggle to overcome.

4 A salutary note of alarm in relation to concern about mobilised 'citizen-spotters' has recently come from Cantwell-Corn (2017), who reports Home Office data showing that immigration officers have used racial

profiling techniques to stop and question over 19,000 British citizens over the past five years.

5   In 2012, 80% of EU/EEA referrals received positive trafficking identification decisions against only 20% of third-country (non-EEA) nationals (ATMG, 2013). In 2016, 3,804 people were referred into the NRM, of which 20% received a negative 'reasonable grounds' decision and 16% a positive 'reasonable grounds' decision followed by a negative 'conclusive grounds' decision. So, in 2016, only 24% of those referred received both positive reasonable and conclusive grounds decisions; 39% received positive reasonable grounds and were awaiting a conclusive grounds decision (NCA, 2017). In 2015, of 3,266 potential victims referred to the NRM, 20% were EEA nationals and 74% were non-EEA nationals (Newton, 2017). The House of Commons Work and Pensions Committee (2017) inquiry into the status of 'victims of modern slavery' heard 'contradictory evidence about the interaction between the NRM and immigration status' from the Home Office, described contrarily as 'entirely separate' and 'fiendishly complicated' (House of Commons 2017). In 2015, 379 – 36% of 'confirmed victims' – claimed asylum, and of those, 279 (21%) were granted. In addition, 71 non-EEA 'victims' were granted discretionary leave and seven were granted humanitarian protection (House of Commons 2017).

References

Anderson, B. (2010) 'Migration, immigration controls and the fashioning of precarious workers', *Work, Employment & Society*, 24(2): 300–17.

Anderson, B. and Ruhs, M. (2010) 'Semi-compliance and illegality in migrant labour markets: an analysis of migrants, employers and the state in the UK', *Population, Space and Place*, 16(3): 195–211.

Andersson, R. (2014) *Illegality, inc. Clandestine migration and the business of bordering Europe*, Oakland, CA: University of California Press.

Andrijasevic, R. and Mai, N. (2016) 'Editorial: trafficking (in) representations: understanding the recurring appeal of victimhood and slavery in neoliberal times', *Anti-trafficking Review*, 7: 1–10. Available at: www.antitraffickingreview.org

ATMG (Anti-Trafficking Monitoring Group) (2013) *Hidden in plain sight. Three years on: Updated analysis of UK measures to protect trafficked persons*, The Anti-Trafficking Monitoring Group, London: Anti-Slavery International. Available at: www.antislavery.org/wp-content/uploads/2017/01/hidden_in_plain_sight_executive_summary.pdf

BBC (British Broadcasting Corporation) (2018) *McMafia*, TV programme, BBC1, series 1, episode 2, 2 January.

Bloch, A. and McKay, S. (2016) *Living on the margins. Undocumented migrants in a global city*, Bristol: The Policy Press.

Bulman, M. (2018) 'Widespread use of cheap car washes and nail bars is fuelling modern slavery, warns National Crime Agency', *The Independent*, 5 January. Available at: www.independent.co.uk/news/uk/home-news/cheap-goods-services-modern-slavery-nca-clothes-nail-parlours-food-national-crime-agency-a8143756.html?platform=hootsuite

Burnett, J. and Whyte, D. (2010) *The wages of fear: Risk, safety and undocumented work*, Leeds: PAFRAS and the University of Liverpool.

Callaghan, D. and Jahangir, R. (2016) 'Tesco car wash workers got half of minimum wage', BBC News, 2 October. Available at: www.bbc.co.uk/news/uk-england-37499241

Campana, P. (2018) 'Out of Africa: the organization of migrant smuggling across the Mediterranean', *European Journal of Criminology*, first published online, 21 January. Available at: https://doi.org/10.1177/1477370817749179

Cantwell-Corn, A. (2017) 'Brits most "stopped and checked" for immigration crimes they can't commit', *The Bristol Cable*, 9 October. Available at: https://thebristolcable.org/2017/10/brits-stopped-checked-immigration-crimes-cant-commit/

Chuang, J. (2015) 'The challenges and perils of reframing trafficking as "modern-day slavery"', *Anti-Trafficking Review*, 5: 146–9. Available at: www.antitraffickingreview.org

Cooper, C., Hesketh, O., Ellis, N. and Fair, A. (2017) *A typology of modern slavery offences*, Research Report 93, October, London: The Home Office.

Corrigan, F. (1977) 'Feudal relics or capitalist monuments? Notes on the sociology of unfree labour', *Sociology*, 11(3): 435–63.

Davies, C. (2012) 'Traveller family jailed over forced labour', *The Guardian*, 19 December. Available at: www.theguardian.com/uk/2012/dec/19/traveller-family-jailed-forced-labour

De Genova, N.P. (2002) 'Migrant "illegality" and deportability in everyday life', *Annual Review of Anthropology*, 31: 419–47.

Dwyer, P., Lewis, H., Scullion, L. and Waite, L. (2011) *Forced labour and UK immigration policy: Status matters?*, York: Joseph Rowntree Foundation.

FLEX (Focus on Labour Exploitation) (2016) 'FLEX briefing: Immigration Bill part one – January 2016'. Available at: www.labourexploitation.org/sites/default/files/publications/ FLEXImmBillBriefFINAL.pdf

Fudge, J. (2013) *Precarious migrant status and precarious employment: The paradox of international rights for migrant workers*, Centre of Excellence for Research on Immigration and Diversity Working Paper No. 11-15, Vancouver, BC: Metropolis British Columbia.

Hansard (2007) HL Deb, 7 July. Available at: https://publications. parliament.uk/pa/ld200506/ldhansrd/vo050707/text/50707-05. htm.

House of Commons (2017) *Victims of modern slavery*. Available at: https://publications.parliament.uk/pa/cm201617/cmselect/ cmworpen/803/803.pdf. Accessed July 2018.

House of Commons Home Affairs Committee (2018) 'Immigration policy: basis for building consensus'. Available at: https://publications. parliament.uk/pa/cm201719/cmselect/cmhaff/500/500.pdf

House of Commons Work and Pensions Committee (2017) 'Victims of modern slavery', Twelfth report of session 2016-17. Available at: https://publications.parliament.uk/pa/cm201617/cmselect/ cmworpen/803/803.pdf

Human Trafficking Foundation (2015) 'Life beyond the safe house'. Available at: https://static1.squarespace.com/static/ 599abfb4e6f2e19ff048494f/t/599eeb28914e6b9ddcceace2/ 1503587117886/Web_Life+Beyond+the+Safe+House.pdf

Human Trafficking Foundation (2016) 'Day 46: is there life after the safe house for survivors of modern slavery?'. Available at: https://static1.squarespace.com/static/599abfb4e6f2e19ff048494f/ t/599eeb28914e6b9ddcceace2/1503587117886/Web_ Life+Beyond+the+Safe+House.pdf

ILO (International Labour Organisation) (2012) *ILO indicators of forced labour*, Geneva: ILO.

Jayaweera, H. and Anderson, B. (2008) *Migrant workers and vulnerable employment: A review of existing data*, report for TUC Commission on Vulnerable Employment, Oxford: COMPAS.

LeBaron, G., Howard, N., Thibos, C. and Kyritsis, P. (2018) 'Confronting the root causes of forced labour: restrictive mobility regimes', Open Democracy, 10 January. Available at: www. opendemocracy.net/beyondslavery/genevieve-lebaron-neil-howard-cameron-thibos-penelope-kyritsis/confronting-root-caus-4

Lewis, H. and Waite, L. (2015) 'Asylum, immigration restrictions and exploitation: hyperprecarity as a lens for understanding and tackling forced labour', *Anti-Trafficking Review*, 5: 49–67. Available at: www.antitraffickingreview.org

Lewis, H., Dwyer, P., Hodkinson, S. and Waite, L. (2014a) 'Hyper-precarious lives? Migrants, work and forced labour in the Global North', *Progress in Human Geography*, 39(5): 580–600.

Lewis, H., Dwyer, P., Hodkinson, S. and Waite, L. (2014b) *Precarious lives: Forced labour, exploitation and asylum*, Bristol: The Policy Press.

Lewis, H., Waite, L. and Hodkinson, S. (2017) '"Hostile" UK immigration policy and asylum seekers' susceptibility to forced labour', in F. Vecchio and A. Gerard (eds) *Entrapping asylum seekers: Social, legal and economic precariousness*, Basingstoke: Palgrave Macmillan.

MAC (Migrant Advisory Committee) (2014) 'Report on growth of migrants in low-skilled work'. Available at: www.gov.uk/government/uploads/system/uploads/attachment_data/file/333083/MAC-Migrants_in_low-skilled_work__Full_report_2014.pdf

Mackenzie, R. and Forde, C. (2009) 'The rhetoric of the "good worker" versus the realities of employers' use and the experiences of migrant workers', *Work, Employment & Society*, 23: 142–59.

May, T. (2014) 'Modern Slavery Bill'. Available at: www.gov.uk/government/news/modern-slavery-bill-published (accessed 29 January 2018).

May, T. (2016) 'Defeating modern slavery', 16 July. Available at: www.gov.uk/government/speeches/defeating-modern-slavery-theresa-may-article (accessed 11 January 2018).

McDowell, L. (2008) 'Thinking through work: complex inequalities, constructions of difference and trans-national migrants', *Progress in Human Geography*, 32: 491–507.

McLaughlin, J. and Hennebry, J. (2010) 'Pathways to precarity: structural vulnerabilities and lived consequences for migrant farmworkers in Canada', in L. Goldring and P. Landolt (eds) *Producing and negotiating non-citizenship: Precarious legal status in Canada*, Toronto: University of Toronto Press.

Milivojevic, S. and Pickering, S. (2013) 'Trafficking in people, 20 years on: sex, migration and crime in the global anti-trafficking discourse and the rise of the global trafficking complex', *Current Issues Criminal Justice*, 25: 585–604.

NCA (National Crime Agency) (2017). *National referral mechanism statistics – end of year summary 2016*. Available from www.nationalcrimeagency. gov.uk/publications/national-referral-mechanism-statistics/2016-nrm-statistics/788-national-referral-mechanism-statistics-end-of-year-summary-2016/file. Accessed July 2018.

Netto, G. and Craig, G. (eds) (2017) 'Migration and differential labour market participation', *Social Policy and Society* (Special Issue).

Newton, S. (2017) 'Letter from Sarah Newton MP to the Chair. Evidence to the Victims of Modern Slavery inquiry', 17 February. Available at: www.parliament.uk/documents/commons-committees/work-and-pensions/Letter-from-Sarah-Newton-MP-to-Chair-re-modern-slavery-session-17-2-2017.pdf

O'Connell Davidson, J. (2017a) 'Editorial: the presence of the past: lessons of history for anti-trafficking work', *Anti-Trafficking Review*, 9: 1–12. Available at: www.antitraffickingreview.org

O'Connell Davidson, J. (2017b) 'Bank account checks and modern slavery', *The Guardian*, 27 September. Available at: www.theguardian. com/uk-news/2017/sep/24/bank-account-checks-and-modern-slavery

O'Neill, S. (2017) 'Car-wash worker kept as modern slave electrocuted as he showered', *The Times*, 19 January. Available at: www.thetimes. co.uk/article/car-wash-worker-kept-as-modern-slave-electrocuted-as-he-showered-z037kp0r9

O'Toole, M. (2018) 'Nigerians return from slavery in Libya to thriving sex industry back home', *The Seattle Times*, 23 January. Available at: www.seattletimes.com/nation-world/nigerians-return-from-slavery-in-libya-to-thriving-sex-trafficking-industry-back-home/ (accessed 25 January 2018).

ONS (Office for National Statistics) (2017) 'Contracts that do not guarantee a minimum number of hours: September 2017'. Available at: https://www.ons.gov.uk/employmentandlabourmarket/peopleinwork/earningsandworkinghours/articles/contractsthat donotguaranteeaminimumnumberofhours/september2017. Accessed July 2018.

Phillips, N. (2013) 'Unfree labour and adverse incorporation in the global economy: comparative perspectives on Brazil and India', *Economy and Society*, 42: 171–96.

Plambech, S. (2014) 'Between "victims" and "criminals": rescue, deportation, and everyday violence among Nigerian migrants', *Social Politics*, 23(3): 382–402.

Reyneri, E. (2001) *Migrants' involvement in the underground economy in Mediterranean countries of the European Union*, Geneva: International Labour Organisation.

Rienzo, C. (2017) 'Outcomes of migrants in the UK labour market', Migration Observatory Briefing. Available at: www.migrationobservatory.ox.ac.uk/resources/briefings/characteristics-and-outcomes-of-migrants-in-the-uk-labour-market/ (accessed 5 December 2017).

Ruhs, M. and Vargas Silva, C. (2017) 'The labour market effects of immigration', Migration Observatory Briefing. Available at: www.migrationobservatory.ox.ac.uk/resources/briefings/the-labour-market-effects-of-immigration/ (accessed 5 December 2017).

Scullion, L., Lewis, H., Dwyer, P. and Waite, L. (2014) 'Exploring the link between forced labor and immigration status in the UK', in K.K. Hoang and R. Parreñas (eds) *Human trafficking reconsidered: Rethinking the problem, envisioning new solutions*, New York, NY: IDebate Press.

Sharapov, K. (2015) 'Traffickers and *their* victims', *Critical Sociology*, 43(1): 91–111.

Standing, G. (2011) *The precariat: The new dangerous class*, London and New York, NY: Bloomsbury Academic.

Travis, A. (2013) 'Immigration Bill: Theresa May defends plans to create "hostile environment"', *The Guardian*, 10 October.

TUC (Trades Union Congress) (2008) *Hard work, hidden lives. The full report of the Commission on Vulnerable Employment*, London: Trades Union Congress.

Varia, N. (2014) 'Debate: prevention and victim compensation', *Anti Trafficking Review*, 3.

Waite, L. and Lewis, H. (2017) 'Precarious irregular migrants and their sharing economies: a spectrum of transactional laboring experiences', *Annals of the American Association of Geographers*, 107(4): 964–78.

Wills, J., Datta, K., Evans, Y., Herbert, J., May, J. and McIlwaine, C. (2010) *Global cities at work: New migrant divisions of labour*, London: Pluto Press.

Wintour, P. (2013) 'Zero-hours contracts could be subject to new legislation', *The Guardian*, 5 August. Available at: www.theguardian.com/uk-news/2013/aug/05/zero-hours-contracts-legislation-cable

Woolfson, C. and Likic-Brboric, B. (2008) 'Migrants and the unequal burdening of "toxic" risk: towards a new global governance regime', *Debatt'e*, 16(3): 291–308.

TEN

The UK's approach to tackling modern slavery in a European context

Klara Skrivankova

Introduction

This chapter discusses a transnational response to trafficking in human beings, with reference mainly to some key media stories and legal cases that have been influential in understandings and legal definitions of forced labour/modern slavery. In doing so, it places the UK response to date firmly within a European context.[1]

Modern slavery, particularly one of its forms – trafficking in human beings – is often described as transnational organised crime. 'Modern slavery' is also a term most commonly used in the UK to describe a number of situations, including trafficking in human beings and forced labour. However, the term that is most commonly used internationally, and in Europe in particular, is 'trafficking in human beings'.

These terms are often used interchangeably, and they have also been defined in international law, although there is no one single definition of the meaning of 'modern slavery'. Complex international legal definitions can simply be described as follows:

- Human trafficking is a process of bringing (often across international borders) a person into a situation of exploitation, which includes at a minimum forced labour and sexual exploitation[2]; and
- Forced labour is a situation in which a person is required to undertake work or services involuntarily under a menace of penalty.[3]

While it is debatable to what extent those who engage in and organise the exploitation of others are, indeed, operating sophisticated mafia-like structures or are mere collectives of opportunistic individuals, its international nature is, however, indisputable. In the UK and across the whole of the European Union (EU), more victims are trafficked into countries of which they are not nationals than those who get trafficked within their own country. Similarly, we often consume goods and services produced by foreign labour trafficked and exploited in the UK or produced by forced labour somewhere else around the world, in what are often long and complex global supply chains. The case in Box 10.1 illustrates an example of situations that are not uncommon in Europe – cases of trafficking for forced labour into the food production sector.

Box 10.1: Fear, hunger and dirt: Lithuanian migrants on their life as chicken catchers (extract from Felicity Lawrence, 10 August 2015, *The Guardian*)

Laurynas Kelpsa was just 19 when he saw an advertisement for jobs in England on the internet in 2011. Opportunities in his home town in Lithuania were limited and the advert promised good wages of £250–£350 a week with accommodation, so he called the mobile phone number given and spoke to a bus company owner called Saulius. A couple of days later he was on his way across Europe, heading for Kent, nervous but excited, unsure of the details of the work.

He was dropped outside what looked like an ordinary suburban house in Old Tovil Road, Maidstone. Walking through the door, 'I was shocked', he recalled. There were several men to each room, some sleeping on mattresses on the floor, in a dirty and overcrowded house.

A traumatic period of 12 months working for DJ Houghton Catching Services, was about to begin.

Kelpsa and two of his fellow migrant workers have spoken exclusively to the *Guardian* about their experiences. They said they were the victims of violence, described the process of being debt-bonded on arrival, spoke of their accommodation being riddled with bedbugs and of becoming so hungry that they ate raw eggs.

Laurynas Kelpsa did not use the word 'modern slavery' in his description of his situation (see Box 10.1), but that is what it was. He and his colleagues laboured under the threat of violence in a situation of debt bondage, with dreadful living and working conditions – three indicators that, when taken together, are conclusive of forced labour. He was recruited through deception and subjected to exploitation through the means of coercion – which are key elements of trafficking for the purposes of forced labour as defined in international law. This case could be referred to as a 'textbook' example of modern slavery.

The situation that Kelpsa described to *The Guardian* is not an uncommon one in the UK. The UK government estimated a few years ago that there are between 10,000 and 13,000 people in slavery in the UK at any one time. The National Crime Agency estimates the figure to be considerably higher; however, the number of potential victims identified every year is much lower. In 2017, only 5,145 potential victims were identified in the UK, most of them from five countries: Albania, Vietnam, Nigeria, China and Romania (NCA 2017).

In the EU, the situation is not too dissimilar. Eurostat, the statistical agency of the EU, published a report on trafficking in human beings collated from information provided by the national statistical agencies of the member states. Based on those data, the report concluded that 'the top five countries of citizenship within the EU, in terms of absolute numbers of registered victims, were Romania, Bulgaria, the Netherlands, Hungary and Poland. For non-EU citizens, the top five countries were Nigeria, Brazil, China, Vietnam and Russia' (Eurostat 2015).

The available data show that within Europe (and in the UK), migrants, including EU nationals, are particularly vulnerable to slavery.[4] This is also confirmed by a separate *Guardian* investigation that uncovered the extensive enslavement of Romanian migrants in Italian agriculture (Todno and Kelly 2017), of African migrants enslaved in Spanish agriculture (Lawrence 2011) and of Asian workers enslaved in Irish fisheries (Lawrence 2015). All of them were working at some point in the food production supply chains that supplied major well-known supermarkets across the EU.

In some cases, the exploitation of migrants is planned and prepared by criminal gangs in their country of origin working in collusion with other criminals in the country of destination. However, more often, it is likely to be the mere vulnerability of being a migrant – with the lack of a fixed address, little money, poor documentation, limited access to services and uncertain immigration status – that renders people vulnerable to the exploitation that occurs once they have arrived in a foreign country.

However, modern slavery is not simply caused by the actions of criminals; understanding it merely as a matter of crime would be too narrow a perspective. It is important to understand more broadly that the way in which we govern our societies is creating situations of vulnerability that render individuals vulnerable to modern slavery. The policies of some nations towards the human rights protections of workers suggests that some governments have calculated that they can obtain competitive advantage by allowing exploitative labour systems, including forced labour and slavery, to evolve. Similarly, some businesses choose to ignore or tolerate modern slavery in their supply chains to draw competitive advantage.

The situational vulnerability of migrants (United Nations Office on Drugs and Crime 2012) stems from the lack of social support networks in the countries where they seek work, their frequent ignorance of their rights, the lack of understanding of systems and language barriers in those countries. These are the most common factors that render them vulnerable to exploitation – factors that are often driven by demand for cheap services and goods.

As can be seen from the previous examples, even EU citizens with rights guaranteed by EU law are vulnerable to exploitation in another EU country. Non-EU citizens who do not have such well-established rights are even more vulnerable. This is because it is often not just migrants who are ignorant of their rights, but the agencies of state who lack the knowledge about their responsibilities and legal obligations towards migrants who are likely victims of trafficking.

The author of this chapter dealt with one case where a migrant approached two police stations in two different cities of the UK to complain that he suspected that he had been trafficked for forced labour. On both occasions, in contravention of their positive obligations to investigate such crimes, the migrant was told that this was an immigration matter and not a police one.

While this particular case occurred before the introduction of the UK Modern Slavery Act (MSA) in 2015, this type of experience continues, and cases like these are not, in reality, just isolated incidents. Similar scenarios are still commonly discussed among anti-slavery professionals in 2018.

The international nature of trafficking in human beings requires a transnational response, a response that should come in a number of forms. This chapter will focus on three of these:

- first, there is a need for law enforcement cooperation to deal with the criminal aspects of trafficking in both countries of origin and countries of destination;
- second, there is a need for developing international understanding of trafficking to ensure that national and international aspects of the

rule of law itself are fit for purpose where it relates to international norms and standards; and

- third, there is a need for extra-territorial legislation to deal with slavery and forced labour carried out by citizens, including corporate citizens, in third countries.

Law enforcement cooperation in Europe

The EU has a range of instruments available to law enforcement agencies within the EU that provide police forces with both the tools and the powers to investigate organised crime, including modern slavery cases, both effectively and efficiently. These are constructed to help police forces and criminal justice agencies to use the differences in legal systems and criminal procedural law to achieve the best possible outcomes. Working in parallel and in coordination in multiple jurisdictions is essential if any significant disruption of transnational criminal activity is to be achieved. The possibility of collaborative work of this kind may well be impaired by Brexit unless specific arrangements can be protected during and after the transition of the UK out of the EU. The case included in Box 10.2 from Europol (2017) illustrates the significance of international policing cooperation and the use of EU policing tools to disrupt the operation of trafficking networks.

Box 10.2: Human trafficking ring dismantled by Romania and the UK with Europol support (Europol, 2017)

Europol has supported a major international operation on human trafficking led by Romania and carried out jointly with law enforcement agencies from Belgium, the Czech Republic, Germany, Switzerland and the United Kingdom. The operation aimed at disrupting a highly organised crime group active in trafficking young women for the purpose of sexual exploitation and money laundering.

On 19 June 2017, police officers from Piteşti Brigade for Combating Organised Crime and prosecutors from D.I.I.C.O.T. [Directorate for Investigating Organised Crime and Terrorism] – Piteşti Territorial Service searched 71 houses in Romania, which led to the detention of 35 suspects.

Significant amounts of cash in different currencies were seized (EUR 151,910, RON 170,483, CHF 30,100, USD 720, SEK 3,800), which demonstrates the mobility and international reach of this criminal network. In addition, 500 grams of gold, 34 luxury watches (with an estimated value of EUR 210,000), 8 luxury cars (worth around EUR 200,000), 8 properties (estimated at EUR 1.2 mil) and other assets (a grinder, 3 machetes, 1 compressed air gun and 4 carbine cartridges) were also seized, alongside other items that will be further examined as evidence (24 laptops, 92 smartphones, 9 tablets and 2 hard-drives).

Simultaneously, NCA [National Crime Agency] officers, with support from Northumbria Police and Home Office Immigration Enforcement, executed search warrants at addresses in the UK. Three suspects were detained and 10 potential victims were safeguarded as part of the operation. Officers seized thousands of pounds in cash from the various properties, as well as one round of ammunition and some pepper spray.

Further police actions were carried out in Belgium and Switzerland in support of the main operation.

Making extensive use of special investigative techniques, the competent authorities were able to detect this well-organised crime group and to put an end to their illicit and very profitable activity, as demonstrated by the value of the assets seized and bank transfers traced down (some EUR 5 mil).

Europol actively supported this investigation by providing operational and analytical support and contributed to the smooth exchange of information among the countries concerned. Several operational meetings were held at Europol and human trafficking specialists equipped with a mobile office were deployed to Romania and the UK, from where they supported the action day by cross-checking intelligence.

Eurojust provided logistical and financial support to the joint investigation team (JIT) on the basis of the agreement that was signed between Belgium, Romania and the UK. In addition, Eurojust received and facilitated the execution of requests for cooperation submitted within this investigation from countries not party to the JIT.

The case outlined in Box 10.2 is typical of many cases combating this sort of transnational trafficking. EU member states often rely on European tools for cooperation, most notably, through Europol (the EU Police Agency), which has human trafficking as one of its priority crime areas, and Eurojust (the EU's Judicial Cooperation Unit), which plays a key role in supporting EU efforts to tackle human trafficking, most crucially, through facilitating and funding joint investigation teams (JITs), as mentioned in the case in Box 10.2.

A JIT consists of judicial and police authorities from at least two member states (and can include also a non-member), who collaboratively conduct a special cross-border criminal investigation for a limited period. JITs have the added value of enabling law enforcement authorities to gather and exchange information and evidence, in real time, without having to rely on the usual slow methods of *mutual legal assistance*.

Of the 148 JITs facilitated by Eurojust in 2016, 40 (27%) were related to human trafficking.[5] In 2016, the UK received the most funding of all EU member states to establish JITs – 32 in total (ATMG 2017: 10). As the Anti-Trafficking Monitoring Group (ATMG 2017: 10) reported:

> In evidence to the European Union Committee [of the UK Parliament] in 2013, Kier Starmer QC, the-then Director of Public Prosecutions stated that the benefits of JITs included:
> - speedier cross-border coordination,
> - enabling the deployment of UK law enforcement authorities to other Member States,
> - providing all participating Member States with direct access to the same evidence, as well as the increased admissibility of this evidence, which was commonly challenged before the courts under the previous bilateral agreements.

Furthermore, the value of Eurojust is not limited to JITs. The institution can provide a wide range of other support that is required to resolve casework issues in human trafficking cases, particularly where there is a requirement for enquiries and evidence from other jurisdictions. It also: provides support for European Arrest Warrants and extradition; assists in live links for witnesses to give evidence; advises on offences and legal systems in other jurisdictions – particularly helpful for Slavery and Trafficking Prevention Orders (STPOs) (which were created in the MSA and parallel legislation in Northern Ireland and Scotland) on sentencing; and provides ready access to prosecutors from every EU member state to enable successful prosecutions (ATMG 2017).

The value of Europol is not, however, limited to technical assistance enabling practical collaboration between the police forces and judicial authorities of member states. Europol provides analytical support and can act as a repository of intelligence-building pictures of trends and threats. It operates a number of analytical projects that can deploy resources to:

- analyse information and intelligence to obtain as much structured and concrete information as possible for law enforcement authorities;
- facilitate operational meetings between partners involved in cases;
- provide expertise and training to law enforcement authorities to support cases and share knowledge;
- deploy Europol mobile offices to the field for operations, giving live access to Europol's secure information exchange network and databases; and
- provide support for judicial cooperation and for the tackling of other related criminal activities uncovered in the course of investigations, such as money laundering (United Nations Office on Drugs and Crime 2012).

One analytical project, entitled Phoenix, has been set up to look at human trafficking across Europe in response to the increasing number of trafficking cases reported to Europol. The Europol website states that the project deals with different forms of exploitation, with current priority areas linked to sexual and labour exploitation, forced criminality and begging, forced marriages, child trafficking, and human organ trafficking.

These mechanisms of European judicial and law enforcement cooperation allow closer collaboration between the police forces and other criminal justice actors in EU member states in order to dismantle trafficking networks and bring traffickers to justice. They were established in recognition of a need for collaboration in criminal justice matters not just in an ad hoc manner, but through a coordinated approach and institutional infrastructure that fosters the collaboration.

The rule of law and policy coherence

The basic principles of the rule of law are that it should not be administered arbitrarily; it should be applied consistently by actors of the state and everyone within its jurisdiction should have recourse to the protection under the law. This principle should also be upheld with regards to policymaking designed to assist states in ensuring compliance with basic human rights requirements, including that of freedom from slavery and forced labour (enshrined in Article 4 of the European Convention on Human Rights). However, in practice, we often find that while anti-trafficking (and anti-slavery) laws and policies are designed in compliance with Article 4 in principle, other polices and laws are commonly found to undermine their impact.

The conflict between immigration and anti-trafficking law and policy has been perhaps the most apparent one. In 2003, Anti-Slavery International published *The migration–trafficking nexus* (ASI 2003), a report that identified the particular vulnerabilities to trafficking that migrants face because of systematic failures of destination countries to protect their human rights. There have been significant changes in law and policy across Europe since then, including the Council of Europe Convention on Action against Trafficking in Human Beings (CoE 2005) and the EU Anti-Trafficking Directive (EU 2011), which have compelled states that are members of the Council of Europe and the EU to develop more robust approaches to address human trafficking. However, despite the development of what appear to be comprehensive legal and policy frameworks, there remain shortcomings in European anti-slavery law and policy – and implementation.

For example, there may be gaps in law enforcement arrangements arising from financial cuts to policing as a consequence of recent financial crises or insufficiencies in labour inspectorates. Or, there may be unintended consequences of other laws or regulations; in the UK, for example, the effective tying of the Overseas Domestic Worker visa to specific employers provides a de facto licence for trafficking for domestic servitude (see Chapter Six).

Most EU countries also operate systems of tied visas for certain categories of migrant labour, which creates an imbalance of power between an employer and a foreign worker. Additionally, in the UK, the Immigration Act 2016, by introducing the offence of 'illegal work', threatens to criminalise many who have been trafficked for forced labour.

The tensions between policies, in particular, immigration policies and anti-trafficking policies, have always been present. However, these tensions have increased further in recent years as a consequence of the so-called global migration crisis. This has resulted in a confused use of terminology, describing the operations of smugglers in the Mediterranean as trafficking and therefore justifying anti-immigrant measures as measures to 'prevent' people from being trafficked. In other words, the shortcomings may arise not only from shortages of resources, but also from ill-conceived policies, or policies that are insular rather than truly appreciating and reflecting the international dimension of modern slavery.

The European institutions of the rule of international law are important in guiding states towards much more effective anti-slavery policy frameworks. Article 4 of the European Convention on Human Rights, which is administered by the European Court of Human Rights (ECtHR), recognises slavery as a human rights abuse and has, in the past decade, provided guidance for states on implementing the provision. Cases presented to the ECtHR on this subject include ones against Greece (see Box 10.3), France, Cyprus and Russia, and the UK. All of these cases pointed out deficiencies in the policies and laws of the respective states and required corrective actions. They have also provided useful guidance and benchmarks for other states to measure their legislative and policy readiness against.

A 2012 case (*CN v the United Kingdom*[6]) concerned allegations of domestic servitude by a Ugandan woman who complained that she had been forced into working as a live-in carer in the previous decade. The ECtHR held that there had been a violation of the Convention, finding that the legislative provisions in force in the UK at the relevant time had been 'inadequate to afford practical and effective protection against treatment contrary to Article 4 [prohibiting slavery and forced labour]'. This case is an example of failures of the rule of law allowing CN not to be afforded recourse to the protection under the law that she should have received.

In the time between the case being lodged in the ECtHR and the court's ruling, the UK Parliament introduced, in 2009, a provision outlawing forced and compulsory labour in section 71 of the Coroners and Justice Act in order to avoid a similar judgment that was passed by the ECtHR in *Siliadin v France*[7] in 2005. In this case, the ECtHR ruled that states have a positive obligation to address criminalised acts enshrined in Article 4 of the European Convention.

The most recent case considered by the ECtHR, *Chowdhury & Others v Greece*[8] (see Box 10.3) not only illustrates another failure of a state to act with due regard to its positive obligations, but also, more importantly, highlights the implication that poor policymaking can have in practice. The victims in this case were mistreated by both the perpetrators and subsequently by the state because they were migrants and their immigration status was precarious. Precarity of immigration status is often a barrier to accessing justice for migrant workers who find themselves in a situation of forced labour but are unable to enforce their rights because of their irregular status.

Box 10.3: Landmark European victory for exploited migrant workers (Zubier Yazdani)

On 30 March 2017 the European Court of Human Rights handed down its landmark decision in *Chowdhury & Others v Greece*, Appl. No. 21884/15.

The court held that Greece violated Article 4 of the European Convention of Human Rights (CoE 2005) prohibiting forced labour, in that it failed to protect a group of Bangladeshi migrant workers from trafficking and ordered compensation of over €500,000 to be paid. The judgment underlined signatory States' obligations to prevent and investigate trafficking, protect victims and punish traffickers.

The case of the shootings at migrant workers [see Smith 2014a] who went on strike demanding their wages at the strawberry farms in Manolada, a small agricultural town in the Peloponnese, has become notorious and demonstrated the stark lack of protection migrant workers in the agricultural industry in Southern Europe receive.

The incident which took place in April 2013 caused shock and outrage both in Greece and throughout Europe. This was compounded by the Greek court's decision of 30 July 2014 to acquit those involved [see Smith 2014b] in the incident of the charges of trafficking in human beings.

The Greek court declined properly to examine the charge of human trafficking, which formed the basis of an application to appeal to the public prosecutor on 21 October 2014. The request was dismissed, thereby ending the domestic legal proceedings and leaving the victims without any recognition of their status as victims of trafficking.

The judgments of the ECtHR on slavery have advanced the protections of people at risk of slavery across Europe. They have deepened our collective understanding of the manifestations of modern slavery and how it should be combated, compelling unaware or unwilling governments to act to uphold their responsibilities to protect human rights.

Each mature state should welcome this level of scrutiny – a core principle of the rule of law (the oversight of international law over the way national law is administered). However, this also helps to improve action against trafficking by assisting states in identifying where their systems might have failed or fallen short, and by recommending improvements.

Extraterritorial jurisdiction

Creating extraterritorial jurisdiction is a further key prerequisite of successfully countering human trafficking. EU law expects that member states will take this approach – para 6 of the recital of the EU Trafficking Directive (EU 2011), for example, reads that:

> In order to ensure effective prosecution of international criminal groups whose centre of activity is in a Member State and which carry out trafficking in human beings in third countries, jurisdiction should be established over the offence of trafficking in human beings where the offender is a national of that Member State, and the offence is committed outside the territory of that Member State.

Similarly, jurisdiction could also be established where the offender is a habitual resident of a member state, the victim is a national or a habitual resident of a member state, or the offence is committed for the benefit of a legal person established in the territory of a member state, and the offence is committed outside the territory of that member state. The Council of Europe Convention against trafficking takes a similar position in Article 31.

Many European states have adopted the extraterritorial application of trafficking and modern slavery offences. For example, trafficking offences in the MSA have extraterritorial application. However, for the extraterritorial legislation to be effective, it needs to be applied for acts committed by both individuals and legal entities (eg businesses). Article 5 of the EU Anti-Trafficking Directive sets out the liability of legal persons for the crime of trafficking. The first clause of the article states:

> Member States shall take the necessary measures to ensure that legal persons can be held liable for the offences referred to in Articles 2 and 3 committed for their benefit by any person, acting either individually or as part of an organ of the legal person, who has a leading position within the legal person, based on:

(a) a power of representation of the legal person;
(b) an authority to take decisions on behalf of the legal person; or
(c) an authority to exercise control within the legal person.

The intention of this provision cannot be met without recourse to extraterritorial law. This reality comes into sharp focus when 'legal persons' such as corporations and businesses with international supply chains are considered (for a full discussion of supply chains, see Chapter Nine). In some cases, businesses may seek to reduce costs by knowingly establishing supply from businesses based overseas that employ enslaved labour, for example, from some of the manufacturing sectors of South and South-East Asia about which there are extensive reports of human rights abuses. Without extraterritorial law to hold legally liable 'legal persons', both businesses and individual business executives, for this sort of behaviour, exploitation and abuses overseas may be committed with impunity.

The need for extraterritorial law is reflected in Principle 2 of the United Nations (UN) Guiding Principles on Business and Human Rights (UNGPs), which state that: 'States should set out clearly the expectation that all business enterprises domiciled in their territory and/or jurisdiction respect human rights throughout their operations'. In the commentary on this principle, the UNGPs go on to note that:

> There are strong policy reasons for home states to set out clearly the expectation that businesses respect human rights abroad, especially where the State itself is involved in or supports those businesses. The reasons include ensuring predictability for business enterprises by providing coherent and consistent messages, and preserving the State's own reputation.[9]

Since 2010, there have been a number of notable initiatives in relation to this approach against human trafficking and modern slavery. These include:

- The California Transparency in Supply Chains Act 2010. This requires all businesses trading in California and with a turnover of greater than USD60 million to report on how they were combating slavery.
- In 2015 in the UK, with a similar measure, as part of the various MSAs (for a discussion of the three UK Acts and the differences between them, see Chapter Five). This requires all commercial

organisations trading in the UK and with a turnover of greater than £36 million to publish an annual statement on what they are doing to eliminate slavery from their supply chains. This, incidentally, also covers large charities such as Oxfam, although not, as yet, public sector organisations.

- The 2017 French law on human rights due diligence for multinational businesses, introduced in response to the Rana Plaza disaster in Bangladesh.
- The German Sustainable Textiles Initiative.
- The Dutch Industry Covenants signed in 2016 for the textile sector and the banking sector.
- The endorsement by Dutch business, including Nestle Nederland and Heineken, of the imposition by the Dutch government of a legal duty of care on all companies to prevent the supply of products created by child labour to the Dutch market.
- Debates also continue at the international level, including a debate about a possible new International Labour Organisation (ILO) Convention focused on decent work in global supply chains and a possible new binding UN treaty on business and human rights.

Businesses are increasingly coming out in favour of mandatory supply chains disclosure. The UK law, in particular, was a direct result of lobbying of the British government by UK businesses involved in the Ethical Trade Initiative and the British Retail Consortium, as well as by a number of key non-governmental organisations (NGOs) and individuals.

These businesses recognised that their efforts towards ethical practices were undermined by competitors who were able to undercut them with impunity by adopting exploitative labour practices, including slavery.[10] These businesses therefore wished for increased regulation in order to 'level the playing field' somewhat by compelling unethical competitors to be more transparent about their practices. This has led to the introduction of the transparency in supply chains provision in section 54 of the UK MSA. The provision requires any commercial organisation to annually and publicly disclose the steps that it has taken to identify and address risks of modern slavery in their supply chains and own operations. It is expected that more than 20,000 businesses operating in the UK will be required to report under the provisions. While the provision is light touch in legal and enforcement terms, it has led to fairly considerable change in the level of scrutiny by stakeholders – not just from civil society, but increasingly from investors and business partners.

However, of course, as the UNGPs recognise, and earlier sections of this chapter demonstrate, human rights standards in business supply chains are not merely the result of business policies, no matter how ethical or unethical a particular company may be. They are also a result of law and government policy and practice. Where standards of rule of law and human rights protections are poor, then the opportunities to exploit workers increase.

Failures in rule of law and human rights protections are not always, of course, a result of oversight or omission by governments. Sometimes, they are a result of deliberate intent: consistently to refuse to protect a group being discriminated against, for example; or to refuse to appoint sufficient judges, police or labour inspectors to uphold the law and protect the rights of citizens and migrants alike; or corruption among official bodies such as the police. This means that slavery enters into international supply chains and systems of trade, tilting the playing field in a manner that can only ever be addressed by diplomacy and trade negotiations. This, in turn, requires market weight to address. No individual EU member state could ever alone hope to sway India, for example, away from its acquiescence in caste-based discrimination, as well as its poor record in establishing a robust response to slavery practices within its borders. A collective engagement by the EU over issues of trade could more realistically seek to achieve the basic human rights standards and worker protections that are fundamental to the ideals of a Social Europe at the heart of any trade deals that are sought. This, again, at the time of writing, is a major concern in relation to Brexit negotiations.

Conclusion

Modern slavery continues to thrive largely due to the lack of state responses that would recognise and address the problem in its complexity and ensure that anti-trafficking (anti-slavery) measures are mainstreamed across key policy areas. Modern slavery is a matter not just for the criminal justice system, but for many other areas of government, including the labour market, social affairs, trade and aid, and it impacts on areas such as health, housing, social assistance and education.

Too strong a focus on criminal justice measures fails to deal with the situations that render individuals vulnerable to exploitation in the first place. Consequently, policing and prosecuting those responsible, if, indeed, they are brought to justice, has very little impact on addressing the underlying causes and contributing factors, in particular, those that are linked to contradictory and conflicting policies.

The significance of partnership and collaboration for effective anti-slavery responses is also often underestimated. Countering modern slavery should not be conceived of as a competition among states, where one is a leader and others are consigned to the place of followers. The claim of the UK government that it is a world leader in addressing modern slavery is not only demonstrably false or, at best, very partial, but also besides the point. It is a matter not for competition, but for learning from each other as to what constitutes best practice. Governments can only be effective in tackling the issue if they can establish strong frameworks for collaboration and partnership – not just among themselves, but with others, including civil society and businesses. Traffickers are able to operate so effectively across borders and are able to overcome possible bureaucratic obstacles by skilfully navigating the gaps and differences in policies and laws of different countries because they are working together towards a common goal (which, in their case, is significant profits from criminal activity) in an effective manner.

International collaboration and partnership is of utmost importance for the UK as the majority of modern slavery situations related to the UK have an international dimension, either because the victims are foreigners or because a product sold in the UK has been made by forced labour abroad. European institutions, such as the EU and the Council of Europe, recognised the need for international collaboration on trafficking not just in principle, but also in law. EU legislation and policy, as well as the Council of Europe Convention, have been designed to foster this collaboration through a common understanding of what constitutes trafficking in human beings and providing tools, especially criminal justice provisions, to make judicial collaboration between individual states easier and speedier. Being part of a regional response is essential for the UK's anti-slavery policing capability. The UK needs to take into account the requirements and assessments by European bodies to benchmark its performance on combating modern slavery against other European countries, but, more importantly, to continue to utilise those measures to work with others to combat this human rights abuse across destinations.

Notes

[1] The impact of Brexit on anti-slavery work within the UK is discussed elsewhere in this book, but see also: www.edf.org.uk/anti-trafficking-monitoring-group-briefing-brexit-modern-slavery/

2   The full definition can be found in the European Union (EU) Trafficking Directive 2011/36, the Council of Europe Convention on Action against Trafficking in Human Beings, and the United Nations (UN) Palermo Protocol.

3   The full definition can be found in the International Labour Organisation (ILO) Forced Labour Convention No 29.

4   The term 'slavery' is used throughout the chapter as an overarching term that covers trafficking in human beings as well as forced labour.

5   Europol, 'Crime areas trends'. Available at: www.europol.europa.eu/crime-areas-trends/europol-analysis-projects (accessed 28 January 2018).

6   *CN v the United Kingdom*, 2012, https://ec.europa.eu/anti-trafficking/legislation-and-case-law-case-law/cn-v-united-kingdom_en

7   *Siliadin v France*, 2005, https://ec.europa.eu/anti-trafficking/legislation-and-case-law-case-law/siliadin-v-france-application-no-7331601_en

8   *Chowdhury & Others v Greece*, 2017, https://ec.europa.eu/anti-trafficking/case-law/chowdury-and-others-v-greece-0_en

9   See: www.ungpreporting.org/resources/the-ungps/

10 Although, as we argue in the Editorial Introduction, there may also have been more strongly commercial reasons, such as arguments about loss of market share, which motivated some companies to support this innovation.

References

ASI (Anti-Slavery International) (2003) *The migration–trafficking nexus*, London: Anti-Slavery International. Available at: www.antislavery.org/wp-content/uploads/2017/01/the_migration_trafficking_nexus_2003.pdf (accessed 28 January 2018).

ATMG (Anti-Trafficking Monitoring Group) (2017) *Brexit and the UK's fight against modern slavery*, London: Anti-Trafficking Monitoring Group.

CoE (Council of Europe) (2005) 'Convention on Action against Trafficking in Human Beings'. Available at: www.echr.coe.int/Documents/Convention_ENG.pdf (accessed 28 January 2018).

EU (European Union) (2011) *Directive 2011/36/EU of the European Parliament and of the Council of 5 April 2011 on preventing and combating trafficking in human beings and protecting its victims, and replacing Council Framework Decision 2002/629/JHA*, Brussels: European Union.

Europol (2017) 'Human trafficking ring dismantled by Romania and the UK with Europol support. Press release', 22 June. Available at: www.europol.europa.eu/newsroom/news/human-trafficking-ring-taken-down-spanish-and-bulgarian-authorities (accessed 28 January 2018).

Eurostat (2015) *Report on trafficking in human beings*, Brussels: European Union. Available at: https://ec.europa.eu/anti-trafficking/sites/antitrafficking/files/eurostat_report_on_trafficking_in_human_beings_-_2015_edition.pdf (accessed 28 January 2018).

Lawrence, F. (2011) 'Spain's salad growers are modern-day slaves, say charities', *The Guardian*, 7 February. Available at: www.theguardian.com/business/2011/feb/07/spain-salad-growers-slaves-charities (accessed 28 January 2018).

Lawrence, F. (2015) 'Revealed: Trafficked migrant workers abused in Irish fishing industry', *The Guardian*, 5 November. Available at: www.theguardian.com/global-development/2015/nov/02/revealed-trafficked-migrant-workers-abused-in-irish-fishing-industry (accessed 28 January 2018).

NCA (National Crime Agency) (2017) *National Referral Mechanism annual summary 2017*, London: National Crime Agency. Available at: www.nationalcrimeagency.gov.uk/news/1315-national-referral-mechanism-annual-summary-2017 (accessed 28 January 2018).

Smith, H. (2014a) 'Greece's migrant fruit pickers: "They kept firing. There was blood everywhere"', *The Guardian*, 1 September. Available at: www.theguardian.com/world/2014/sep/01/greece-migrant-fruit-pickers-shot-they-kept-firing (accessed 28 January 2018).

Smith, H. (2014b) 'Greek court acquits farmers who shot 28 Bangladeshi strawberry pickers', *The Guardian*, 31 July. Available at: www.theguardian.com/world/2014/jul/31/greek-court-acquits-farmers-shot-strawberry-pickers

Todno, L. and Kelly, A. (2017) '"Terrible conditions": police uncover abuse and exploitation on farms in Sicily', *The Guardian*, 31 October. Available at: www.theguardian.com/global-development/2017/oct/31/terrible-conditions-police-uncover-abuse-and-exploitation-on-farms-in-sicily (accessed 28 January 2018).

United Nations Office on Drugs and Crime (2012) 'Guidance note on abuse of a position of vulnerability', p 2. Available at: www.unodc.org/documents/human-trafficking/2012/UNODC_2012_Guidance_Note_-_Abuse_of_a_Position_of_Vulnerability_E.pdf (accessed 28 January 2018).

Index

Note: Page numbers for tables appear in italics.

Printed in Great Britain
by Amazon